A Film Theorist's Companion

FIRST EDITION

LINUS LAU

LONG BEACH CITY COLLEGE

 cognella® | ACADEMIC PUBLISHING

Bassim Hamadeh, CEO and Publisher
Kassie Graves, Director of Acquisitions
Jamie Giganti, Senior Managing Editor
Jess Estrella, Senior Graphic Designer
Bob Farrell, Senior Field Acquisitions Editor
Gem Rabanera, Project Editor
Elizabeth Rowe, Licensing Coordinator
Rachel Singer, Associate Editor
Kat Ragudos, Interior Designer

Cover image copyright © Depositphotos/razoomgames.

Printed in the United States of America

ISBN: 978-1-5165-0239-4 (pbk) / 978-1-5165-0240-0 br)

cognella® | ACADEMIC PUBLISHING

CONTENTS

PART 03: THE WAY WE DECIDE

INTRODUCTION

This new compendium of critical media studies is at once a simple reader for the contemporary film student and a focused look at what critical film theorists consider important today.

Much has been surmised about films being cultural artifacts, a means of studying not just cinema itself but our fellow man. Films are a deeply rich resource of psychoanalytic data that we can and must revisit by way of learning and re-learning who we are. Much has also been adduced about films as pillars of our cognitive processes. These monuments that we leave behind us are key reminders of who we once were: how we once felt. how we once observed. how we once made decisions as a nation and as a culture. A passing film enthusiast could tell you that movies reflect not the values and fervor of the time period depicted but rather the time period from when those movies were made.

The overwhelming means with which we have to create media is at the same time as staggering as it is fascinating. Grassroots reporters have the ability to distribute news faster than official news outlets. Computer junkies write puns and create animated gifs and memes faster than a staff writer can pen a script on a comedy show. High-quality images, stored on the most concealed and convenient modes of documentation, can be wielded and shared without all the procedure and ceremony perhaps needed a decade ago.

We are all inherently filmmakers, whether by passion or occupation, separated simply by our access to specific creative tools. A keen and rather necessary observation one could make is that film is a celebration of shared perspective—the shared perspective between film watcher and filmmaker, audience and showman. And however difficult it may be to see, this relationship dynamic is an unbalanced one: our willful acceptance of restraint caters to the comfort of being entertained, at the same time rendering us mute against those who would inveigle passage to our actions and voices.

Film study would be underserved were it simply a blue ribbon. a certificate of achievement. retroactive publicity aimed at the unconvinced, pandering to the voice of the privileged. Nor would film study be properly positioned relegated to the realm of past tense, imprisoned in a filigreed yet sarcophagal cinematic archive. Film study is, more inclusively, the fascination behind the process of absorbing and encoding human experiences.

It is not just the technology to which we have this incredible access. The tremendous accessibility we have to a worldwide community of film fans, to the respected voice of our artistic community, to the illuminating discourse teeming from the mouths of patrons once they leave the theater, enriches our experience of movie spectatorship. One could probably posit that the overwhelming amount of media we have at our fingertips pales only in comparison to the amount of material being written about our media.

Amateur film criticism proliferates as quickly as gossip. There was once a time in my own life, when opening night tickets were harder to come by than a spoiler. But as incessant as this need is for the premature review—as easy as it is to pass negative, haphazard judgment on art forms beyond one's understanding—however simple the grammar of film criticism may be to grasp, it is comforting to know that our artistic culture still demands opinions of and dialogue with our most respectable, most thoughtful, and most informed members.

This tome is for readers who are interested in film studies but perhaps feel they lack the necessary tools with which to decipher film and—more sensibly—challenge it. Much in the analects of film critique either hone in on a myopic area of the craft or serve the reader with an overwhelming obstruction of material. This collection of carefully selected readings is a student's companion to contemporary media criticism. It is by no means biblical restoration of established textbooks, but rather a supplemental piece to extant literature. It perhaps hopes to elucidate and embolden the least experienced critic or newly hatched filmmaker. Seasoned readers might be so enlightened to discover a hidden gem.

While presumptuous it may be to say, it is a film professor's wish to impress upon his or her students a rich language, the friendly voice of a curator guide, an accompaniment to fandom. Let us move forward into the proud and bright future of our cinematic culture and contribute to the lexicon our critical thought and conscientious critique, to remind the powerful that we're still here.

To broach the sociological impact films have on viewers is to begin a dialogue with the film-makers themselves. A college film studies course comprised of film majors and non-film majors alike might be the best "first step" in learning about movies. Watching films with a large audience and engaging with the cultural resonances each film brings is to really participate in what a film-viewing experience is all about. Experience with value begets purpose and when the viewer understands the purpose of viewing an event—be it a play, short film, or feature—mere participation is to be on board for the full journey. That is, even spectatorship for the sake of entertainment is engagement. Our experiences watching film build upon themselves. And with each subsequent film we watch, every film we truly *read*, our understanding of who we are as members of film culture expands. That understanding is awareness of our dormant power—the ability to speak *back* to the filmmakers through our discretionary attendance, our fervent criticism, and our meaningful investment.

Strangely enough, one might argue that the more distance one feels from the "business" of making films—the closer one finds himself or herself to being the consumer of media—the more power one wields in *dictating* a film's cultural significance. When my own students watch films with me in my film survey classes, especially when watching films of historical distance, some of the common questions we broach in class discussion are—*What cultural significance does this film have? Does this film still speak to you today? If you were the filmmaker, what would you do differently?* The articles contained in this first section attempt to address some of these questions.

THE WAY WE FEEL

The following readings represent a broad range of sociological perspectives, ranging from Tina Olsin Lent's thoughtful analysis of on-screen love relationships in *Love and Friendship: The Redefinition of Gender Relations in Screwball Comedy,* to Philippa Gates' fascinating breakdown of film noir in *The Maritorious Melodrama: Film Noir with a Female Detective.* These newly published studies truly reveal to a contemporary scholar that there is always something new to discover about early films. It is also important to note that of these myriad perspectives, several stand-out, political ideas also emerge: a challenge to an accepted perspective on feminist scholarship in Jane Gaines' *White Privilege and Looking Relations* argues that the existing narrative of "sexist" cinema—wherein male spectatorship serves primarily as a suppressor of on-screen femininity—excludes the perspective of non-heterosexual viewers. Moreover, extant rhetoric concerning feminist filmmakers may have inadvertently universalized feminist film critique such that it includes only the perspectives of white women. Marilyn Fabe's critique in *Feminism and Film Form* addresses how it is not just feminist films that imbue different gazes and values, but how *female* directors employ very specific approaches to filmmaking outright, an observation that sadly requires a cultural microscope so to speak—what with our predominant (and which someone might argue perverse) scopophilia being voiced only by male viewers. Students will also find enjoyment out of reading the play-by-play breakdowns of familiar films in the articles of Cecilia Sayad and Karen A. Ritzenhoff.

At the end of each of these three sections, there are some discussion questions meant to supplement the student's self-reflection.

TINA OLSIN LENT

ROMANTIC LOVE AND FRIENDSHIP: THE REDEFINITION OF GENDER RELATIONS IN SCREWBALL COMEDY

In the early 1930s, several popular Hollywood films depicted the relationship between men and women in a fresh, new way that focused on their enjoyment of each others' company, their shared sense of fun and companionship and the complementary nature of their partnership. Preeminent among such films was Frank Capra's *It Happened One Night* (1934), the archetype of the screwball comedy genre.[1] The screwball comedy adapted the new ideal love relationship, referred to by a contemporary writer as "love-companionship," to the realm of middle-class experience and to a variety of middle-class characters.[2] By repeatedly showing the redefined relations between the genders, the screwball comedy made this style of love its central focus, and thereby represented the theme's most in-depth exposition on the Hollywood screen.

Film was only one of several popular media that participated in the thoroughgoing exploration and reconceptualization of the ideal love relationship between men and women. During the 1930s, similar discussions appeared in commercial fiction, popular nonfiction (specifically college texts, marriage manuals and advice literature) and mass market periodicals.[3] Most of the popular media considered women to be their primary audience; female taste not only dictated the content of most periodicals, but also shaped the film and best-seller market.[4]

The widespread discourse on love that permeated the popular media signified a contemporary concern (especially among women) about the institution of marriage, which experts and the public alike perceived as being in crisis.[5] This view rested, in part, on contemporary statistical evidence: during the 1920s the divorce rate had increased to approximately one in seven. Between 1929 and 1932, the marriage rate in the United States declined abruptly, reaching a record low in 1932.[6] Liberal reformers in the late 1920s and early 1930s sought to reappraise and redefine the institution of marriage. Their writings verified to the reading public that the older Victorian model of marriage had lost social credibility.[7] Margaret Sanger, Ernest Groves, Ben Lindsey and others predicated the new marriage on a revised model of male/female relationships, based on love and companionship. These changes came on the heels of a cultural revision of the ideology of femininity that repudiated the nineteenth-century cult of domesticity, and superseded it with the "New Woman" of the 1920s.[8] The widespread discourse on love and marriage in film and popular literature helped to disseminate, naturalize and sanction the newer male/female relationships during a time when Depression conditions caused Americans to focus greater attention on marriage. Marriage became more desirable during the 1930s due to its postponement. By the end of the decade, the marriage rate exceeded any previous year on record. The family became the locus of social interaction, emotional support and entertainment, due to declining financial resources.[9]

In the 1930s, screwball comedy specifically addressed love and marriage. The films' plots characteristically involved a sexual confrontation between an initially antagonistic couple whose ideological differences heightened their animosity. Their courtship entailed the verbal and physical sparring referred to as the battle of the sexes, and their recognition of mutual love and decision to marry (or remarry) ultimately reconciled the sexual and ideological tensions.[10] Class conflict frequently motivated the ideological clashes in the early examples of the genre; one of the romantic pair was often identified as being middle or working class. By interjecting their class perspective into the life and circumstances of the other, upper-class half of the pair, they exacerbated the sexual tension, but eventually humanized the wealthy partner.[11] Conflicts in class ideology gave way in many later (post-1937) screwball comedies to other ideological disputes (city/country, home/work, reason/intuition). However, the genre always retained its focus on the comedic situations arising from the dual tensions of sexual and ideological conflict between its romantic leads. By multiplying the couple's fundamental disagreements, screwball comedy intensified the normal concern of romantic comedy (whether a couple will marry) by decreasing the probability that they would overcome their significant and numerous differences.[12]

The *style* of male/female interaction was a central concern of screwball comedy. Many critics and historians have offered interpretations of which audience interests, needs and desires screwball comedies addressed. Some writers have asserted that the characters' eccentric behavior and "lunacy" provided models for sanity and survival in a crazy and overly conventional world.[13] Other writers have maintained that screwball comedy constructed a model for reconciling the socioeconomic disparities that threatened national unity.[14]

To read the screwball comedy as an exegesis on a new style of love is not to contradict these other readings. Rather, such an interpretation will situate these films within the historical context of the Depression years, and link screwball comedy with ideas prevalent in other forms of popular media. The lack of contextualization of specific films in their historical milieu has resulted in many film historians and critics making oversimplifications.[15] In 1975, Robert Sklar wrote that critics and historians could arrive at a "considerably more accurate idea" of the messages a work of art communicated if they were placed within the "broader framework of imaginative communication" in the culture to see how they relate to the "recurring themes, images, characters, situations and resolutions that make up the conventions of artists and entertainment workers in many media."[16] This idea has received greater theoretical grounding and articulation in the work of the new social historians and feminist historians, who have shifted their attention away from the public sphere of politics and policy to study the private sphere of daily life. Working from such materials as the mass market writings of sociologists and psychologists, advice literature, popular periodicals, general-interest and women's magazines, commercial fiction and advertisements, a historian can reconstruct a period's recurrent themes, images and rhetoric. Reading films in relation to other mass media firmly grounds them in their contemporary culture, suggesting the meanings they carried for their audiences.[17]

Screwball comedies focused on the primary intimate relationship most Americans would engage in during their lives, love and marriage, and provided an ideal model for successfully achieving this union based upon contemporary social thought. Departing from the traditional filmic depiction of love and marriage, screwball comedy built upon three major sources: a redefined image of woman, a redefined view of marriage and a redefined idea of cinematic comedy.[18]

The "New Woman," or the flapper, evolved from cinematic and literary sources of the 1920s, presenting a redefined image of the modern woman. This cultural revision of femininity, conducted primarily through the mass media, incorporated some of the features of radical female dissent, but altered them to conform to the needs of the hegemonic culture. The "sexual revolution" of the 1920s commercialized the more politically radical sexual revolution among the working class and the Greenwich Village bohemians in the previous decade. The political and economic critique of the *status quo* implicit in the prewar movements were lost, as the dominant culture used the popular media to sell the sexual revolution and its complementary cult of consumption to the middle class in the 1920s.[19] The flapper challenged earlier codes of feminine behavior through her consumption of such commodities as short and revealing clothing, silk stockings for everyday wear, cosmetics, cigarettes, perfume, jewelry, sweets, hairstyling and popular public entertainment (such as movies, dancing and amusement parks),[20] but broke with the feminist ideas of political and economic equality.[21]

The flapper's consumer-based "revolution" masked her continued and more profound conformity to the dominant ideology of women's subordination, economic dependency and powerlessness, and her acceptance of her primary role as wife and mother. The movies depicted the flapper's new manners and morals as integrally tied into a larger quest for self-fulfillment, a desire satisfied through the new " 'fun' morality and a consumer life-style."[22] The eminent psychologist G. Stanley Hall suggested, in the *Atlantic Monthly* in 1922, that the high school flapper imitated her favorite movie actress, and that films had fashioned her tastes and style, if not her very code of honor.[23] Robert S. Lynd and Helen Merrell Lynd's influential 1925 study of Muncie, Indiana, indicated the effect of movies on behavior (for example, on the use of clothing for social recognition) as well as on social mores.[24] Both contemporary sources indicated that the flapper was, above all, a consumer. The focus on consumption and behavioral freedom in the popular culture of the 1920s sidetracked the larger issue of women's real freedom through economic equality, hopes dashed with the failure of the Equal Rights Amendment in 1926.[25] Although the rubric of "the flapper" subsumed many different aspects of modern female behavior, and although the flapper image declined under Depression conditions, the female protagonists of screwball comedy were the repositories for some of her characteristics.[26]

In three significant areas, the screwball women protagonists perpetuated the attributes of the flapper: her personality and behavior, her participation in the paid labor force, and her more egalitarian relationship with men. Although they lacked the flapper's overt sexuality, the screwball heroines shared her vitality, physical freedom, spontaneity and vivaciousness.[27] Margaret Thorp commented in 1939 that the more natural, down-to-earth looks of the "screwball heroines" made them easier to identify with; discussing the change in the concept of "glamour" in Hollywood, she wrote:

> The glamorous star today is as natural as possible. She does not pluck her eyebrows and paint in new ones; she develops the natural line. She does not tint her hair to exotic hues. She does not try to be a fairy-tale princess, but an average American girl raised to the nth power. "Vivid" is the adjective she works for hardest.[28]

In the women's magazines of the 1930s, both advertisements for beauty products and feature articles on makeup and hairstyle frequently used Hollywood stars as the epitome of the new, more natural style. Advertising copy featured words like "natural seductiveness," "nature's colorings," "vitality and buoyant grace," "radiance," "animation and vitality," to sell such diverse produces as face rouge, Max Factor make-up, health shoes and canned pineapple.[29] Max Factor ads featured Claudette Colbert and Joan Crawford, and Lux soap ads depicted Barbara Stanwyck and Mae West (the text accompanying Stanwyck tells the reader that nine out of ten Hollywood stars use Lux).[30] Even a General Mills brochure on bread commented that "motion picture stars take no chances with their diet; to insure the energy essential to glowing beauty and vitality, they include bread in every meal."[31]

In terms of her outward behavior, the movie and literary flapper enjoyed new personal freedom in manners and morals; she could work, smoke, drink, dance, dispense with constricting undergarments, and engage in "petting."[32] As a working woman, however, the only employment opportunities available to the flapper were pink-collar jobs whose low wages and limited promotions provided neither a living wage nor the possibility of economic independence; the dominant ideology had already predetermined that she defined her ultimate goal as a homemaker, wife and mother—not a wage earner.[33] The flapper did not challenge the social conventions of premarital chastity, matrimony and economic dependence.[34] Despite their freedom and assertiveness, the female protagonists of screwball comedy also conformed to contemporary expectations that a woman's ultimate goal was marriage, and that a married woman's place was in the home.[35]

A second characteristic of the flapper that the screwball heroine adopted was her participation in the paid labor force. The working-class movie flapper helped to legitimize the single woman's role in the work force (which had been increasing since the beginning of the twentieth century), and leading women in screwball comedies were frequently assertive "working girls."[36] Their premarital careers and jobs included newspaper reporters (*Mr. Deeds Goes to Town, His Girl Friday, Meet John Doe, Woman of the Year*); writers (*Easy Living, Theodora Goes Wild*); secretaries (*You Can't Take It With You, Mr. Smith Goes to Washington*); department store clerks (*Bachelor Mother*); and a factory worker (*Nothing Sacred*). Although married women were increasingly working, the ideology of the period, expressed in the films and popular literature of the 1920s, never fully supported their presence in the work force.[37] Despite these economic realities, public rhetoric strongly supported women's traditional role as homemaker.[38] The government and unions strongly opposed working wives out of fear of their displacing or competing with the supposedly more needy male breadwinners. Ironically, the gender-segregated work force, which prevented women from competing with men in the higher-paying, more depressed manufacturing sector of the economy, provided them with increased employment opportunities in the lower- paying, growth sectors of clerical and service work, where men did not want jobs.

The screwball comedy, as well as the popular literature of the 1930s, supported the ideology of domesticity that maintained that women could work while single, but should not pursue a career that superseded marriage and motherhood as their life goal. The majority of the screwball comedies with working heroines (with the possible exceptions of *His Girl Friday* and *Woman of the Year*) implied that they would "return" to the home after marriage.[39] Similar images of women and marriage emerged from *The Saturday Evening Post*, the largest-circulation magazine in the world in the 1930s, and the representative of American middle-class culture. The ideal *Post* story heroine of the early Depression years was "witty, athletic, self-possessed, urbane" and appeared as a "competent secretary, aggressive business woman, ambitious college graduate, adventurous aviator" as well as a successful author, show business star and athlete.[40] The majority of female characters fell into one of three traditional categories: the silly, irrational childish woman; the beautiful, vain parasitic woman; and the wholesome, supportive girl-next-door.[41] The stories' overriding message was that women were to subordinate their career ambitions to those of their husbands, and that the successful career women were single, preferably widowed. Severe censure was meted out to working married women, who ignored their maternal responsibilities and damaged their husband's egos.[42] As in screwball comedies, these widely popular magazine stories underwrote women's more liberalized manners and morals, while subscribing to the dominant ideology of female domesticity.

Thirdly, the screwball heroine adopted the flapper's more egalitarian relationship with men. Popular magazines depicted the high school and college coed flapper as one who treated men as "partners" and "pals," roles that carried an aura of adventure, innovation and equality with men.[43] Describing the flapper in 1922, G. Stanley Hall wrote, "In school, she treats her male classmates almost as if sex differences did not exist. Toward him she may sometimes even seem almost aggressive. She goes to shows and walks with him evenings, and in school corridors may pat him familiarly on the back, hold him by the lapel and elbow him in a familiar and even 'de-haut-en-bas' way."[44] This type of relationship characterized many screwball comedies, where the leading romantic pair became partners in an enterprise (eluding detectives in *It Happened One Night*, tricking the newspaper and the public in *Nothing Sacred*, finding the intercostal clavicle in *Bringing Up Baby*, saving Earl Williams in *His Girl Friday*) and had fun as they shared the adventure. The image of the pal also appeared in contemporary advertisements. An ad for Woodbury's creams showed a woman and man on a bobsled (she driving, he steering), enjoying a "glorious sport" but one that roughened hands.[45] An ad for Frostilla lotion made the message even clearer: " 'Men want so much!' They expect their girls to be good pals—and good lookers! They want us to romp with them by day—and romance at night. They don't consider that wind and weather roughen our hands—but they do expect us to give them smooth hands to hold."[46]

Although the flapper viewed herself as a man's pal, her relationship with men was generally more sexualized, and thus more prone to overt tension and animosity than that of the screwball female protagonist. When the flapper was the protagonist in a film (as in *It*), she was usually more three-dimensional than the male characters with whom she interacted. She viewed men with a mixture of cynicism, distrust and disgust, seeing them as weak and easily manipulated; men were her ticket to economic security.[47] Responding to Production Code restrictions, screwball comedy downplayed the female lead's physical sexuality to the point of ignoring (or sublimating) it.[48] At the same time, the films strongly delineated the male lead and a playful companionship became their major focus. Here, the male represented an entertaining friend. Whereas the films featuring the flapper depicted gender inequality (she had strength of character, while he had social and economic power), the screwball comedy depicted greater gender equality.[49]

The redefinition of marriage in the 1920s was a second source for the altered image of gender relations in screwball comedy. Sociologists, psychologists, psychiatrists, jurists and physicians, writing in marriage manuals, college texts and in the popular literature of advice columns and mass-circulation magazines, attempted to shift the primary focus of marital happiness from the family to the romantic-sexual union between the husband and wife.[50] Marriage became less a social and economic institution based upon spiritual love and more a sexual and emotional union based upon sexual attraction.[51] The aims of the ideal contemporary marriage were romantic satisfaction achieved through sexual gratification and friendship—a "love-companionship."[52] Liberal reformers Ernest Groves and Margaret Sanger, among other writers, saw mutual sexual attraction and desire as the "virtual foundation and essence of love" and the primary basis for marriage.[53] The quality of friendship, companionship or fellowship also featured prominently in writings on marriage. Marriage was an "adventure in fellowship." Its "vitality and permanency" required a "common basis of interest, a cooperative give and take, a continuing delight in association."[54] Courtship "must be adventurous, daring, exciting, romantic. The great danger ... is not that it be too recklessly romantic, but that it be too tamely accepted, too anemic, too lifeless."[55]

The screwball comedies were, above all, stories of courtship, where friendship developed along with love. The rapid pace and comedic nature of the physical movements and verbal exchanges served as courting rituals. These films depicted the energy and vitality generated by strong sexual attraction and a desire for personal happiness through fun. In Capra's *It Happened One Night* (1934), the alliance between Ellie Andrews (Claudette Colbert) and Peter Warne (Clark Gable) originally rested on mutual convenience and sexual attraction, feelings cemented into love (and marriage) by the fun and companionship which developed as they shared the adventure of traveling from Miami to New York. In Hawks's *Bringing Up Baby* (1938), Susan Vance's (Katharine Hepburn) attraction for David Huxley (Cary Grant) led to mutual love (and we assume marriage) as a result of their sharing adventures and fun. In Cukor's *Holiday* (1938), the relationship between Johnny Case (Cary Grant) and Linda Seton (Katharine Hepburn) originated as friendship and developed into love, as their anarchic personalities found their complement in the other's rebellion against the conventional and stultified atmosphere of the Seton mansion. In Hawks's *His Girl Friday* (1940), Walter Burns (Cary Grant) and Hildy Johnson (Rosalind Russell) had previously been married. She was about to remarry, to become a "real woman" with a home and children. Walter combined his sexual charms and energy with a journalistic crusade, creating a shared adventure that rekindled their love and led to their remarriage.

The screwball comedy also illustrated the value of play as a means of establishing the companionship so essential to contemporary love. A fundamental aspect of the youth culture of the 1920s was its pursuit of fun through activities like dating, dancing, sports and other forms of mass entertainment. The "fun morality" advocated fun as a new obligation, and defined too little fun as something to be feared; one could not have enough fun, and it even became part of work.[56] *Bringing Up Baby* developed the idea of play as a metaphor for Susan's vitality, spontaneity and sexuality, qualities noticeably absent in David. From the beginning, David misunderstood the nature of play, seeing the golf game with Mr. Peabody as an extension of work, while Susan understood that it was "only a game." Later on, as she and David pursued George to find the missing bone, Susan commented, "Isn't this fun, just like a game." Immediately prior to the final embrace and declaration of mutual love, David admits that the day they spent together was the best he ever had, signifying his conversion to her worldview. *Holiday* went even further in advocating the benefits of play. Here play itself became the language by which the authentic lovers discovered their affinity. Suggested by its title, the concept of play permeated the film, surfacing in Johnny's exuberant entrance into Nick and Susan's apartment where he wrestled with them, then exited, doing a cartwheel, in the juxtaposition of the formal rooms in the Seton mansion (comfortably occupied by Mr. Seton and Julia) with the playroom (inhabited by Linda), in Johnny and Linda's pursuit of amusement through toys and acrobatics, and in Johnny's understanding that amassing money was not the ultimate goal of life, but the means to an end that he wanted to discover. In McCarey's *The Awful Truth* (1937), both Jerry Warriner (Cary Grant) and Lucy Warriner (Irene Dunne) actively and enthusiastically played with the dog, Mr. Smith, when their marital strife disrupted their ability to play together. The protagonists C. K. Dexter Haven (Cary Grant) and Tracy Lord Haven (Katharine Hepburn) in Cukor's *The Philadelphia Story* (1940) had shared fun and play aboard the sailboat *True Love* (and other activities like swimming and hunting) which provided the common language and experiential base uniting them despite their divorce. In Wellman's *Nothing Sacred* (1937), Wally Cook (Fredric March) and Hazel Flagg (Carole Lombard) played together on a sailboat, while in Capra's *You Can't Take It With You* (1938), the transforming power of play beneficially affected not only the lovers, but everyone else.

The screwball comedy also used role-playing to show how the companionable relationship emerged from separate, often hostile, identities. By playing fictional characters, the screwball characters freed themselves of their original personalities, expectations and value systems. Experimenting with other identities allows them to grow together. In *It Happened One Night*, Peter and Ellie played a married, working-class couple, while Hildy in *His Girl Friday* played

Bruce's fianceé, the traditional, middle-class version of nurturing and respectable femininity. In *Nothing Sacred*, Hazel Flagg impersonated a strong and heroic dying woman, while David in *Bringing Up Baby* (whose identity had already been stripped of its professional signifiers when he donned a negligee, then hunting clothes and sandals) impersonated a big-game hunter, Mr. Bone, and a gangster, Jerry the Nipper ("a regular Don Swan").[57] In *The Philadelphia Story*, the entire Lord family put on an affected and obnoxious upper-class act for the benefit of the *Spy* reporters Mike and Liz. In *The Awful Truth*, both Lucy and Jerry Warriner put on elaborate acts to embarrass the other: Jerry feigned sincerity when waxing eloquently to Dan about his desires to live in Oklahoma, and to Dan's mother about how pure and above suspicion Lucy was. Lucy enacted the role of Lola Warriner, Jerry's "sister," to embarrass him in front of his wealthy new girlfriend and her family.

Several women's magazines from 1934 (the date of *It Happened One Night*) carried stories dealing with the positive values of companionable love between active, enterprising women and men. In "The American Thing" (*Women's Home Companion*), a thirty-five-year-old single woman saved her family business and her town's economy. She found a lover-companion-husband in the lawyer who was going to foreclose on her house. His mind was changed by the fun of the endeavor to salvage the old way of life.[58] In "Marriage is Like That" (*McCalls*), the young wife feared she was losing her husband's affections to a widow at the office. After trying a new wave and facial, a new dress and his favorite dinner, to no avail, she regained his love by their companionable interest in their pet dog, who the widow found totally objectionable.[59] In "I'll Give You a Ring Some Day" (*McCalls*), a female dance teacher (again in her thirties) married a man who at first awakened a feeling of comradeship in her, due to their mutual interests and experiences. He was a temporary teacher whose music class was next door to her dance class.[60] Gaiety and vibrancy were codes for the desirable quality of fun in romance: a cover description of a serialized novel, *Modern Merry-Go-Round*, read, "A New Novel of Young Moderns in a Modern World ... He brought gayety [*sic*] to love and, in some inexplicable way, drama."[61]

Not only were romantic love and friendship the basis for a love relationship; contemporary sources also defined the sexes as complements of one another. Due to the complementary nature of their physical and psychological characteristics, men and women were incomplete without each other. When their interests did not fuse, the complementary nature of the genders provoked the clashes described as sexual antagonism.[62] The battle of the sexes became a convention of the screwball comedy. In *It Happened One Night*, the mutual antagonism between Ellie and Peter stemmed from both sexual attraction and ideological conflict. Their clearly delineated socioeconomic differences compounded the tension arising from their erotic desire. By the end of the film, their shared experiences and interests allowed them to discover their complementary natures.

In *Bringing Up Baby*, perhaps more than any other screwball comedy, the romantic couple represented polar opposites, and their final pairing signified the perfect complementariness of the male/female relationship.[63] The conflict in this film, as in *It Happened One Night*, was also sexual and ideological, although here the ideological clash was between the intellect and emotion, reason and feeling, work and fun, confinement and freedom, rigidity and spontaneity. Hawks's *His Girl Friday* was a remake of Milestone's *The Front Page* (1931), which had focused on the companionable relationship of two male journalists and the conflict between them due to one's desire to leave the newspaper business to marry and settle down. The narrative's central opposition was between the spheres of work and domesticity, between the world of men and the world of women. Hawks's transformation of the male Hilde Johnson into a female compounded the ideological conflict between Johnson and Walter Burns, adding sexual conflict through the device of their recent divorce. The divorced couples in *The Philadelphia Story* and *The Awful Truth* also possess sexual knowledge from their earlier marriage. In the former film, the differences between Tracy and Dexter rested on his knowledge of her sexual coolness, her emotional remoteness and her disdain for human frailty (particularly emotional weakness). Tracy experiences a sexual awakening and an emotional "thaw," leading to their remarriage. In *The Awful Truth*, the couple was already perfectly matched but needed to experience their incompatibility with others (Dan Leeson and Barbara Vance) to realize their complementariness.

Dorothy Parker's short stories from the 1930s also depicted various male/female relationships during courtship and marriage, and revealed the complementary qualities that signified a well-matched pair. For Parker, the linguistic form of the argument became the mode of engagement for the battle of the sexes.[64] In "The Sexes," she depicted a courtship entirely through a bickering conversation dealing overtly with lack of communication and jealousy. Like the feuding couples of screwball comedy, the argument entailed their intense interaction with and concentration on each other and ended with harmony.[65] In "Here We Are," a couple departing on their honeymoon progressed from stilted conversation to full-scale bickering (complete with the man's continual, accidental and embarrassed references to sex), as they adjusted to being alone together.[66]

Building upon the contemporary ideology that love required a male/female friendship based on fun, and that play melded the complementary aspects of their natures into a harmonious whole, a contemporary marriage required a union that took more than a license or certificate to forge. Many screwball comedies dismissed older ideas of marriage, to advocate the newer ideas of a love-companionship between two complementary opposites. *It Happened One Night* explored the contrast between a legal marriage and a real one, in the triangular relationship of Ellie, her husband King Wesley, and Peter. Although they both come from wealthy, leisured backgrounds, Ellie and Wesley's marriage was nominal; they had experienced neither a sexual nor companionable union, and their marriage represented the older legalistic definition of the institution. Ellie's legal marriage was as bogus as the series of pretend marriages she and Peter enacted during their journey (for the benefit of a traveling salesman on the bus, various auto court owners and her father's detectives). Her legal marriage was actually more fraudulent, because as Ellie and Peter played married lovers, they built the necessary foundations (familiarity, friendship and nurturance) for an authentic marriage. By the journey's end, Ellie declared her love for Peter, and at the film's end, they entered into an authentic marriage.

Marriage was also the central motif in *Bringing Up Baby*, and the film had recurrent references to it.[67] When David and his fiancée, Miss Swallow, discussed their upcoming marriage, she primly informed him they would have no honeymoon and no children, because his work came first. David's forthcoming marriage spurred Susan's virtual abduction of him to Connecticut, and it formed a continual refrain of his lament while there. In contrast to Miss Swallow's image of the brontosaurus-skeleton-as-child, Susan provided David with a live Baby (the leopard).[68] The audience learned of Susan's intentions to marry David early in the film, and by the end he finally recognized that the fun they had had together revealed the falseness (and sterility) of his previous relationship. The film clearly contrasted the formal, lifeless, work-oriented relationship between David and Miss Swallow with the unconventional, fun-filled adventures of David and Susan. Although David and Miss Swallow have more in common intellectually, the film championed David and Susan's relationship, based on shared experiences of fun and play.

Marriage was also the central motif in the films that featured divorced couples. *His Girl Friday* opened with Hildy's announced intentions to marry her fiancé Bruce (Ralph Bellamy), and ended with her planned remarriage to Walter. In between, contrasts were made between two different types of men (Bruce had good manners, was honest and sincere—qualities notably absent in Walter) and different types of marriage. Bruce offers a home, children and a mother-in-law, contrasted with a first honeymoon with Walter in a collapsed coal mine and a second one following up a story in Albany, which was, after all, on the way to Niagara Falls. As in the earlier examples, the film advocated the nontraditional marriage choices that incorporated fun, adventure and excitement. Just as *It Happened One Night* contrasted Ellie's legal marriage to King Wesley with her authentic relationship with Peter, *His Girl Friday* maintained that, although legally divorced, Hildy and Walter were still a couple. Similarly, the concept of what constituted a "real" marriage was the central concern of *The Awful Truth* and *The Philadelphia Story*, both of which began with couples separating, and ended with their reconciliation. Divorce as a legal institution did not sever the complex affectional ties between Lucy and Jerry Warriner nor between Dexter and Tracy Haven. Their separations appeared fraudulent when juxtaposed with the superficiality of their new relationships, the hopeless mismatches of Lucy and Dan (Ralph Bellamy) and Tracy and George Kittredge (John Howard). Their reconciliations seemed a natural outgrowth of their obvious complementary characteristics.

Dorothy Parker also dealt with the contrast between the traditional view of marital harmony and the contemporary perception of a "real" partnership in her story "Too Bad." Framed by the conversation of two women discussing the divorce of a mutual friend, Mrs. Weldon, whose marriage had seemed the one happy and congenial one, the story's central section depicted the actual relationship between Mr. and Mrs. Weldon. Although they laughed and talked easily in the company of others, they could not carry on even polite conversation when alone. Mrs. Weldon wondered, "What did married people talk about, anyway, when they were alone together? She had seen married couples ... at the theater or in trains, talking together as animatedly as if they were just acquaintances. She always watched them, marvelingly, wondering what on earth they found to say."[69] Although the women discussing the Weldons concluded that they got along so beautifully that they must have been crazy to get a divorce, the disparity between what seemed an ideal marriage and what the marriage actually entailed was apparent.

Screwball comedy redefined film comedy in the 1930s and the conventions of this new genre were the third major source for the modification of the portrayal of gender relations on the Hollywood screen. Not only was there an equal teaming of a male and female star in screwball comedy, but for the first time the romantic leads were also the comic leads.[70] Screwball comedy combined the sophisticated, fast-paced dialogue of the romantic comedy with the zany action, comic violence and kinetic energy of slapstick comedy. The underlying premise of slapstick comedy was the "miraculous survival of the human in a world in which man is treated as a machine" and which depended upon collision as its dominant force.[71] In contrast to slapstick comedy, which relied upon a central actor (usually male) whose identity developed from film to film, who was misogynistic in vision and was innocent of sex, the screwball comedy divided the central figure into a male and female, was more egalitarian in its vision, and featured sexual antagonism as the motivating force.[72] The romantic leads often had eccentric qualities, and their unconventional behavior was both a form of social criticism and anarchic individualism. Although screwball comedy and the sophisticated romantic comedy of the early 1930s both demonstrated the limits of conventional morality, they differed in the physicality of the assault on society perpetrated by the romantic leads.[73] A contemporary film historian, Lewis Jacobs, who referred to the screwball comedies as "daffy" comedies and the activities of the heroine as "screwball," commented that in these films the "genteel tradition is 'knocked for a loop': the heroes and heroines are neither ladylike nor gentlemanly. They hit each other, throw each other down, mock each other, play with each other"[74] Another contemporary, Margaret Thorp, wrote that, "Today a star scarcely qualifies for the higher spheres unless she has been slugged by her leading man, rolled on the floor, kicked downstairs, cracked over the head with a frying pan, dumped into a pond, or butted by a goat."[75] The screwball antics also functioned as a substitute for expressions of overt sexuality. As such, they showed the influence of the prohibitions and restrictions imposed by the Production Code, as well as the ideology of the companionate marriage.[76] Allusions to sexuality replaced the overt, explicit physical sexuality depicted in earlier films, and double entendre, allusion, humor, symbol and metaphor abounded in screwball comedy. Many screwball comedies, in fact, ended without the lovers even kissing on screen.[77] The most famous sexual image in *It Happened One Night* was the blanket (referred to as the "Walls of Jericho" during the course of the film) hung between Ellie and Peter's beds in the auto courts, and which fell, to the sound of a toy trumpet, after Ellie and Peter married. During their first night together, Peter undressed in front of Ellie (performing a virtual striptease as he removed everything except his trousers), while giving her a lecture on how men remove their clothes. Ellie, undressing on her side of the blanket, inadvertently made the blanket move suggestively and then hung her undergarments on it. A traveling salesman named Shapely ("Shapely's the name and that's how I like them"), a lifted skirt as a hitchhiking ploy, and a hungry Ellie daintily munching on a carrot were other sexual referents.[78] Sexual innuendo ran rampant throughout *Bringing Up Baby*, from David's reference to the intercostal clavicle as his bone ("My bone. It's rare, it's precious!") to his explanation for dressing in Susan's negligee ("I've gone gay all of a sudden!"). Hildy and Walter, in *His Girl Friday*, already had a rich sexual-companionable relationship. Walter's attraction to Hildy was clear through his many antics to regain her affection both during and after their divorce. During the actual proceedings he had hired an airplane to skywrite, "Hildy, don't be hasty, remember my dimple … Walter." She told him that stunt delayed their divorce for twenty minutes while the judge went out to watch, and he responded, "Well I still have the dimple, and in the same place," implying it was not the one in his chin.

Aside from obvious sexual innuendo, screwball antics drew attention to both the sexual and companionable aspects of the developing romantic relationship, as the films seemed to have imposed a taboo on the clichés of romance.[79] The extreme physicality allowed the characters to touch intimately, but humorously, offering alternative outlets for repressed sexual energy.[80] Furthermore, the screwball antics paired the would-be lovers to show their physical harmony and compatibility, as in the parallel movements of David and Susan (tearing each others' evening clothes, falling down a hillside, submerging in a stream, and swaying on either side of the brontosaurus skeleton).[81] The harmony of Hildy and Walter's movements showed that these two characters were perfectly complementary. They carried on a rapid, bickering dialogue as they circled his desk in one scene, and traversed the pressroom in a later one. They were so familiar with each others' actions that Walter insulted her while simultaneously ducking to avoid the purse he knew she would throw at him and chiding her for loosing her aim. These antics intensified the fun and excitement the characters experienced together, and these feelings further heightened sexual awareness. The screwball antics reinforced the characters' growing friendship because, like the rapid dialogue that accompanied these actions, they focused the couple's attention on each other, and created familiarity. In *Nothing Sacred*, Wally and Hazel kissed behind some crates on the pier after he saved her from "suicide," but their most intimate physical moment came when they engaged in a fistfight to help her simulate the symptoms of pneumonia, after which they sat in parallel positions, each with a swollen jaw. In *Holiday*, the screwball antics, particularly the acrobatic tricks, performed by Johnny and Linda became the signifiers of their feelings for each other. Although such physical comedy characterized all the films in this genre, none has the sheer energy of *Bringing Up Baby*. The romantic couple's pranks and pratfalls dominated this film from the moment David and Susan met. The characters continually fell down, ran around, tore clothes, dug holes in the ground, smashed and stole cars, threw stones, chased animals all over the countryside, and sang "I Can't Give You Anything But Love, Baby."

The rapid-paced, constant dialogue of the screwball comedy also functioned as both sexual and companionable interaction, and provided an aural counterpoint to the physical action. The mode of verbal exchange was bickering; the argument, verbal wrangling, was the characteristic sound of screwball comedy, as if this high-spirited, intellectual repartee was a new symbolic language of love.[82] Talking together was being together, and their use of language forged the bond between them.[83] What was important to the lovers was not merely what they said or did, but the fact of saying or doing it together.[84] The screwball banter clearly differed from the nagging argument of a "traditional" marriage by its speed and its context of fun and adventure rather than domesticity. In *It Happened One Night*, Ellie and Peter staged a marital argument to elude discovery by her father's detectives. The tone, content and context of their quarrel convinces the detectives that they were a working-class married couple. From the moment of their first encounter in *Bringing Up Baby*, David and Susan engaged in fast, bickering conversation which not only contrasted with David's usual mode of communication with Miss Swallow, but became a gauge of his basic incompatibility with her when she could no longer understand the meaning of his discourse. The dialogue between Johnny and Linda in *Holiday* was faster and more playful than between Johnny and his fiancée, Julia. Julia's inability to engage in playful discourse with Johnny (or with his friends Nick and Susan) signified the deep ideological gap between them that could not be bridged. Hildy and Walter also engaged in rapid, bantering dialogue from the beginning of *His Girl Friday*, another sign that they, rather than Hildy and Bruce, belonged together. The image of the ideal male/female relationship that emerged from these and other screwball comedies is one that emphasized multiple levels of interaction and satisfaction: the couple was sexually attracted to each other, had fun together, shared adventures, and developed a singular mode of discourse—all of which resulted in the completion of each person by the complementary characteristics of the other.

Contemporary analysts of real-life gender relationships in the 1930s depicted a picture closer to Dorothy Parker's Weldons than to Walter Burns and Hildy Johnson or Dexter and Tracy Haven. In *Middletown in Transition*, the Lynds described the world of the two genders in 1935 as complementary and reciprocal, but as something akin to separate subcultures.[85] Although there was more change and choice open to women to enlarge their social roles, married women clearly saw themselves in a secondary role; high school girls, on the other hand, seemed to be showing more independence by their desire to work after leaving school, rather than immediately marrying and having families.[86] Adolescent behavior had changed the most since the earlier study in 1925, and the Lynds attributed some of the changes to the movies, the newer and more potent agent of cultural dissemination.[87]

The lessons taught by the movies were vivid reinforcements of those learned from other channels of the popular culture and meant different things to different viewers. While the younger, less tradition-bound audience had the values of their developing youth culture validated and substantiated, the older audience saw their values and beliefs, particularly those supporting the Victorian ideology of love and marriage, challenged. While movies, especially screwball comedies, provided an escape and a fantasy for contemporary viewers, it was an escape to a world that did not seem so remote and unattainable. Although that world may have been inhabited by heiresses with wealth and leisure (*It Happened One Night, My Man Godfrey, Holiday, The Philadelphia Story, Bringing Up Baby*) or working women suddenly transported into a realm of excitement, prominence and wealth (*Easy Living, Nothing Sacred*), the women in the movies had the same objective as the middle- and working-class female inhabitants of Muncie, Indiana: to find an emotionally satisfying, sexually exciting, physically compatible, fun-filled love-companionship was the goal of the female characters featured in the screwball comedy, as well as of the women who went to movies, read *The Saturday Evening Post* and women's magazines, consumed popular literature, and followed the advice of Dorothy Dix and other writers of advice literature. Through its discourse on the ideal relationship, the screwball comedy created a heightened awareness of the new expectations for love and marriage. While not a blueprint for actual gender relationships, the screwball comedy was part of the new liberal ideology that redefined gender relations and focused on the sexual and companionable components of intimacy.[88] Along with the other popular media, these films helped to sanction and naturalize these beliefs so that they attained social dominance during the 1930s.

ENDNOTES

1. Other examples of films that addressed the new relationship between men and women were the Fred Astaire-Ginger Rogers series of musicals (beginning in 1933) and *The Thin Man* series of detective stories (beginning in 1934). Both featured costarring couples, whose verbal repartee and active physical relationships (involving dancing and detecting) showed that love included fun and friendship, as well as romance. The recurrent pairing of the same stars in both the Astaire-Rogers musicals and *The Thin Man* series, however, the more elite realms in which they lived, and the more specialized expertise they exhibited, restricted the impact of their message regarding the possibilities of redefined gender relations for those middle-class, nondancing, nonsleuthing Americans.
2. The term "love-companionship" was used by Ernest R. Groves, *Marriage* (New York: Holt, 1933), p. 6.
3. According to the Lynds' 1925 study of Muncie, Indiana, periodicals (including *The Saturday Evening Post, American Magazine, Ladies' Home Journal, McCalls,* and *Women's Home Companion*) operated more powerfully than books to shape the practices, manners and outlook of a city; they also mentioned that the "most potent single agency of diffusion from without shaping the habits of thought in Middletown in regard to marriage" was the advice columnist Dorothy Dix. Robert S. Lynd and Helen Merrell Lynd, *Middletown: A Study in American Culture* (New York: Harcourt, Brace and World, 1929), pp. 239 and 116 (note 10).
4. Lynd and Lynd, *Middletown* 239; Margaret Ferrand Thorp, *America at the Movies* (New Haven: Yale University Press, 1939), p. 5; the female spectator and consumer is also discussed by Miriam Hansen, *Babel and Babylon: Spectatorship in American Silent Film* (Cambridge: Harvard University Press, 1991), pp. 114–25, 245–68.
5. Steven Seidman, *Romantic Longings: Love in America, 1830–1980* (New York: Routledge, 1991), p. 71.
6. Seidman, pp. 71–72; he adds that, according to contemporary sources, for marriages entered into from 1922–1926, the chance of divorce climbed to one in five or one in six; Lynd and Lynd, *Middletown*, p. 149; Peter Gabriel Filene, *Him/Her Self: Sex Roles in Modern America* (New York: NAL, 1974), p. 164.

7. Seidman, p. 73.

8. For a discussion of the larger cultural context in which these changes occurred, see Seidman, pp. 66–74.

9. Filene, p. 164; Nancy Woloch, *Women and the American Experience* (New York: Knopf, 1984), p. 443.

10. Frank Capra, *The Name Above the Title: An Autobiography* (New York: Macmillan, 1971), p. 164, acknowledged *The Taming of the Shrew* (the prototypic battle of the sexes) as the model for *It Happened One Night*.

11. Thomas Schatz, *Hollywood Genres: Formulas, Filmmaking, and the Studio System* (New York: Random House, 1981), p. 150.

12. Stanley Cavell, *Pursuits of Happiness: The Hollywood Comedy of Remarriage* (Cambridge: Harvard University Press, 1981), p. 85. He discusses the concerns of comedy in his introductory chapter.

13. Lewis Jacobs, *The Rise of the American Film: A Critical History* (New York: Harcourt, 1939) p. 535; Ted Sennett, *Lunatics and Lovers: A Tribute to the Giddy and Glittering Era of the Screen's 'Screwball' and Romantic Comedies* (New Rochelle, NY: Arlington House, 1973), p. 14.

14. Andrew Bergman, *We're in the Money: Depression America and Its Films* (New York: Harper, 1971), pp. 132–148; Schatz, pp. 150–185. Robert Sklar, *Movie-Made America: A Cultural History of American Movies* (New York: Vintage, 1975), pp. 187–188; Karyn Kay, " 'Part-Time Work of a Domestic Slave,' or Putting the Screws to Screwball Comedy," *Women and the Cinema: A Critical Anthology*, eds. Karyn Kay and Gerald Peary (New York: Dutton, 1977), p. 319; Jim Leach, "The Screwball Comedy," *Film Genre: Theory and Criticism*, ed. Barry K. Grant (Metuchen, NJ: Scarecrow Press, 1977), p. 77; and Andrew Sarris, "The Sex Comedy without Sex," *American Film* 3:5 (1978), p. 11. For typical contemporary film reviews of *It Happened One Night*, see: *The Literary Digest* 117 (March 10, 1934), p. 38; *Nation* 138 (March 14, 1934), p. 314; *New Republic* 78 (May 9, 1934), p. 364.

15. Sklar discusses this methodological pitfall in a more generalized analysis in Robert Sklar, "The Imagination of Stability: The Depression Films of Frank Capra," *Frank Capra: The Man and His Films*, eds. John Raeburn and Richard Glatzer (Ann Arbor: University of Michigan Press, 1975), p. 125.

16. Sklar "Imagination," p. 125.

17. Obvious and direct links between screwball comedy and popular periodical fiction exist. The magazine story "Night Bus," was the basis for *It Happened One Night*, and the Hagar Wilde story, "Bringing Up Baby," originally appeared in *Collier's* (April 10, 1937). Also see Note 67.

18. Cavell (p. 16) posits that the screwball comedy required the creation of a new woman and that this phase of cinema history is bound up with a phase in the history of the consciousness of women.

19. Linda Gordon, *Women's Body, Women's Right: A Social History of Birth Control in America* (New York: Grossman, 1976), p. 190.

20. Paula S. Fass, *The Damned and the Beautiful: American Youth in the 1920's* (Oxford: Oxford University Press, 1977), pp. 21–22; G. Stanley Hall, "Flapper Americana Novissima," *Atlantic Monthly* 129 (1922), pp. 774–775.

21. Fass, p. 23.

22. Lary May, *Screening Out the Past: The Birth of Mass Culture and the Motion Picture Industry* (Chicago: University of Chicago Press, 1980), p. 203.

23. Hall, p. 775; Fass (pp.119–123) develops the rise of the youth culture of the 1920s as originating as a college phenomenon that "trickled down" to the high schools later in the decade.

24. Lynd and Lynd, *Middletown*, pp. 160–161 and 267–268.

25. In spite of Charlotte Perkins Gilman's radical statements that economic independence was the crucial ingredient in women's freedom, women were still unable to attain this freedom in the 1920s because of the structural biases and inequalities of the labor market. See Charlotte Perkins Gilman, *Women in Economics: A Study of the Economic Relation between Women and Men as a Force in Social Evolution* (Boston: Small, Maynard, 1899); and Alice Kessler-Harris, *Out to Work: A History of Wage-Earning Women in the United States* (New York: Oxford University Press, 1982), pp. 217–49.

26. Mary P. Ryan, "The Projection of a New Womanhood: The Movie Moderns in the 1920s," *Our American Sisters: Women in American Life and Thought*, eds. Jean E. Friedman and William G. Slade (Boston: Allyn and Bacon, 1976), p. 381; Woloch, p. 458. Molly Haskell, *From Reverence to Rape: The Treatment of Women in the Movies* (New York: Penguin, 1974), p. 45, notes the time lag in movies, and that it was not until the early 1930s that the revolutionary spirit of the 1920s, at least in the questioning of marriage and conventional morality, took hold. Elsie Clews Parsons "Changes in Sex Relations," *Our Changing Morality: A Symposium,* ed. Freda Kirchwey (New York: Boni, 1924), p. 41, also notes that the movies are a "great ... vehicle of traditional manners and morals."

27. Ryan, pp. 368–370. The correspondence of the Production Code and the origins of screwball comedy has been treated by Sarris and Haskell, and results in a more oblique treatment of the sexual dimension of love in these comedies, which will be discussed later in this essay.

28. Thorp, pp. 5, 70–71.

29. Angelus Rouge Incarnat, Max Factor Makeup, Vitality Health Shoes, Canned Pineapple: *McCalls* (March 1934), pp. 140, 135, 141, 38.

30. Max Factor advertisements: *McCalls* (March 1934), p. 135 and (April 1934), p. 142; Lux soap advertisements: *McCalls* (March 1934), back cover and (May 1934), p. 37.

31. General Mills, *Vitality Demands Energy*, 1934, cited in Jane and Michael Stern, *Square Meals* (New York: Knopf, 1984), p. 11.

32. Fass, pp. 262–70; Seidman, p. 71. Fass pp. (264, 268) points out that petting was an elaborate code of "eroticism with very clear limits of permissible expression" which was "distinctly marriage-oriented."

33. Kessler-Harris, pp. 217–49; see quote from Fass in Note 32.

34. William Chafe, *The American Woman: Her Changing Social, Economic, and Political Roles, 1920–1970* (New York: Oxford University Press, 1972), p. 100; Marjorie Rosen, *Popcorn Venus: Women, Movies, and the American Dream* (New York: Coward, McCann & Geoghegan, 1973), pp. 104, 144; Susan Ware, *Holding their Own: American Women in the 1930s* (Boston: Twayne, 1982), p. 187; Haskell, p. 82.

35. June Sochen, "Mildred Pierce and Women in Film," *American Quarterly* 30 (Spring 1978), p. 12; (Susan) Elizabeth Dalton, "Women at Work: Warners in the 1930s," in *Women and the Cinema: A Critical Anthology*, eds. Karyn Kay and Gerald Peary (New York: Dutton, 1977), p. 267. Neither the 1920s films featuring the flapper, nor the 1930s films featuring the screwball heroine, were intended as feminist statements. What is surprising is not, as many contemporary feminist film critics state, that Hollywood films supported the traditional, male-biased *status quo*, but that, in spite of this bias and the basic conservatism of the film industry, women were depicted as freer and subject to less societal restrictions. For writers who critique these films for their incorporation of male biases, as opposed to being truly liberated statements, see Dalton and Kay. Ware (p. 187) implies that the marriage is tacked on at the end, and speculates whether the audience could see the independent woman beyond the conventional ending. She infers that the endings are not integral parts of the narratives.

36. Ryan, p. 375; Woloch, p. 458. Wealthy, leisured heroines appear in *It Happened One Night, Bringing Up Baby, My Man Godfrey, The Awful Truth, The Philadelphia Story* and *Holiday*.

37. For the economic role of women during the Depression, see Kessler-Harris, pp. 250–272; Ruth Milkman, "Women's Work and the Economic Crises," *A Heritage of Her Own: Toward a New Social History of American Women*, eds. Nancy F. Cott and Elizabeth H. Pleck (New York: Simon & Schuster, 1979), pp. 507–541; Lois Scarf, *To Work and To Wed: Female Employment, Feminism, and the Great Depression* (Westport CT: Greenwood Press, 1980), pp. 43–65, 86–109.

38. A study of popular women's magazine fiction in the 1920s and 1930s upholds this view: successful marriage was a "constantly reiterated theme" that was magnified in contrast to women's publicly changing role, while women with successful careers suffered for that success in the realms of love and affectional relationships. Patricke Johns-Heine and Hans H. Gerth "Values in Mass Periodical Fiction, 1921–1940," *Mass Culture: The Popular Arts in America*, eds. Bernard Rosenberg and David Manning White (New York: The Free Press, 1957), p. 229.

39. Babe Bennett, the newspaper reporter in *Mr. Deeds Goes to Town,* quit her job before she (in her "real" persona) and Deeds reconciled at the end of the film; in most of the films the incompatibility of work and home is made through inference. Only in the two films where the woman's **career** is equated in importance with the man's (*His Girl Friday* and *Woman of the Year*), and where the conflict between the realms of work and home are incorporated into the larger ideological conflict between the leading couple, is the return of the woman to the female sphere left in question.

40. Maureen Honey, "Images of Women in 'The Saturday Evening Post' 1931–1936," *Journal of Popular Culture* 10 (1976), pp. 353.

41. Honey, pp. 353–355.

42. Honey, pp. 355–356.

43. Woloch, pp. 402–403.

44. Hall, p. 776.

45. *Woman's Home Companion* (January 1934), p. 73.

46. *McCalls* (February 1934), p. 95.

47. Ryan, p. 378.
48. The idea of zany physical (screwball) activities as substitutes for, or sublimations of, female sexuality due to Code restrictions is dealt with by Sarris (pp. 11–13) and Haskell (p. 125).
49. Cavell coined the term "comedy of equality" to refer specifically to the screwball comedies concerned with the issue of remarriage; this is to differentiate them from Old Comedy where the woman is dominant, and from New Comedy where the man is dominant. Haskell (p. 130) also refers to these films as battles of equals, as does Sarris (p. 11).
50. Woloch, pp. 407–408. Examples of marriage manuals and college texts include: *Our Changing Morality: A Symposium*, ed. Freda Kirchwey (New York: Boni, 1924), particularly Ludwig Lewisohn's "Love and Marriage," p. 200; Margaret Sanger, *Happiness in Marriage* (New York: Brentano's, 1926); Judge Ben B. Lindsay and Wainwright Evans, *The Companionate Marriage* (New York: Boni & Liveright, 1927); advice columns dealing with marriage were written for the daily papers by Dorothy Dix, as cited by Lynd, *Middletown*, p. 116 (note 10) and James McGovern, "The American Woman's Pre-World War I Freedom in Manners and Morals," *Our American Sisters,* pp. 345–365.
51. Sanger, p. 20; Parsons, p. 40; Lewisohn, p. 200; Floyd Dell, "Can Men and Women Be Friends?" in *Our Changing Morality: A Symposium*, p. 184; Lindsey, p. 263.
52. Groves, p. 6. This accompanied a redefinition of women's sexuality. Also see Gordon, pp. 186–245; Seidman, pp. 73–77.
53. Seidman, pp. 73, 79.
54. Groves, p. 36.
55. Sanger, pp. 47–48.
56. Martha Wolfenstein, "The Emergence of Fun Morality," *Mass Leisure*, eds. Eric Larrabee and Rolf Meyerson (Glencoe, Illinois: The Free Press, 1958), pp. 93–94.
57. Babington (p. 13) wrote, "Impersonation … becomes in these films almost a necessary sign of the heroine's refusal to play overdefined roles." This is also true of the male characters; in *Bringing Up Baby* David Huxley's fiancée Miss Swallow had even warned him not to forget who he was as he departed for the ill-fated golf game with Mr. Peabody. Bruce Babington & Peter William Evans, *Affairs to Remember: The Hollywood Comedy of the Sexes* (Manchester: Manchester University Press, 1989).
58. Francis Sill Wickware, "The American Thing," *Woman's Home Companion* (January 1934), pp. 24–25, 65–66.
59. Brooke Hanlon, "Marriage is Like That," *McCalls* (January 1934), pp. 10–11, 25–26, 28.
60. Mary C. McCall, Jr., "I'll Give You a Ring Someday," *McCalls* (February 1934), pp. 10–11, 94–96, 101.
61. Cover, *McCalls* (February 1934).
62. Groves, p. 13.
63. This idea of complementariness appears in much Howard Hawks criticism, both in relationship to characters within the comedies, and to the dual nature of his work as a whole. See particularly Peter Wollen, *Signs and Meaning in the Cinema* (Bloomington: Indiana University Press, 1972), pp. 74–115. The idea is not related to the screwball genre in general, nor to contemporary ideas about marriage.
64. I will discuss the use of language and argument in screwball comedy later in this essay.
65. Dorothy Parker, "The Sexes," in *Here Lies: The Collected Stories of Dorothy Parker* (New York: Viking, 1939), pp. 11–18.
66. Parker, "Here We Are," *Here Lies*, pp. 51–66.
67. Hagar Wilde, "Bringing Up Baby," *Collier's* (April 10, 1937) reprinted in *Bringing Up Baby*, ed. Gerald Mast (New Brunswick: Rutgers University Press, 1988), pp. 235–248.
68. The absence of children in the screwball comedy is partially accountable by the fact that these are courtship stories, but even in the remarriage variations treated by Cavell, children are missing. This supports the contemporary ideology of love-companionship by downplaying the former procreative rationale for marriage to focus on sexualized love as the meaning and justification for marriage. Seidman, p. 82.
69. Parker "Too Bad," *Here Lies*, p. 92.
70. Sarris, p. 9.
71. Leach, p. 76.
72. Leach, p. 77.
73. Leach, p. 84.
74. Jacobs, pp. 535–536.

75. Thorp, p. 76.

76. See Cavell's chapters on *It Happened One Night* (pp. 73–109) and *Bringing Up Baby* (pp. 113–132); Sarris, pp. 13–14; Haskell, p. 130; Leach, pp. 77–78. The dancing in the Astaire/Rogers films can also be read as a substitute for overt sexuality.

77. For example: *It Happened One Night, My Man Godfrey, Bringing Up Baby, His Girl Friday, Mr. Smith Goes to Washington, Meet John Doe.*

78. All direct quotes are from the films.

79. Babington, p. 28.

80. Haskell, p. 125. It is notable that both partners participate in screwball antics; they are not just the domain of the female character.

81. Babington (p. 9) writes of the mutual swaying around the brontosaurus in final scene in *Bringing Up Baby*, "The scene once more emphasizes their antic harmony and, at the same time, suggests the obvious connotations of rhythmic excitement followed by surrender and climactic fall in the all too familiar patterns and cycles of the act of love itself."

82. Cavell, p. 86.

83. Cavell, p. 88.

84. Cavell, p. 88.

85. Lynd and Lynd, *Middletown in Transition*, p. 176.

86. Lynd and Lynd, *Middletown in Transition*, pp. 178–179.

87. Lynd and Lynd, *Middletown in Transition*, p. 262. There was widespread concern in the early 1930s that the movies were having a profound (and negative) influence on the beliefs and attitudes of young viewers, but contemporary studies provided contradictory evidence of this. While the Lynds believed in the strong influence exerted by the movies, and Forman believed they were a "school of conduct," and influenced behavior and attitudes (particularly regarding sex), others indicated that while actions were imitated, other factors were more important in influencing the conduct and attitudes of children. Foreman, p. 155; Frank K. Shuttleworth and Mark A. May, *The Social Conduct and Attitudes of Movie Fans* (New York: Macmillan, 1933), p. 83.

88. Seidman, p. 73.

PHILIPPA GATES

THE MARITORIOUS MELODRAMA: FILM NOIR WITH A FEMALE DETECTIVE

Feminist critics tend to disagree whether the parachuting of women into traditionally male roles—for example, that of detective—results in a feminist representation.[1] The female detective of the 1930s, however, can be seen to offer a decidedly positive feminist hero in that she defies the stereotype of the "masculine" (i.e., unnatural) woman—especially when one considers the time in which she appeared and representations of female detectives in contemporary film.[2] Despite popular conceptions of classical film, Hollywood did offer progressive representations of working women, ironically in the decade characterized by economic and social upheaval during the Depression. The prolific female detective of 1930s B-films and series is an independent woman who puts her career ahead of the traditional female pursuits of marriage and a family, and who chases a mystery as actively as, and with greater success than, the men who populate the police department or a rival newspaper's staff. However, during World War II and especially its aftermath, the representation of the female detective began to change, and the independent woman came to be depicted as all but the criminal herself.

Philipa Gates, "The Maritorious Melodrama: Film Noir with a Female Detective," *Journal of Film and Video*, vol. 61, no. 3, pp. 24-39. Copyright © 2009 by University Film and Video Association. Reprinted with permission. Provided by ProQuest LLC. All rights reserved.

Critics of film noir have discussed at length the figure of the femme fatale as dangerous femininity, but noir's female investigative protagonists have been ignored.[3] This article focuses on the representation of the female detective in film noir of the 1940s and the shift from the celebration of the independent and career-oriented woman to her demonization. More specifically, it examines how the sex of the investigating protagonist complicates the traditionally male noir detective narrative. The result is a hybridization of generic conventions: the narrative is driven forward as much by the female protagonist's personal desires familiar in many types of melodrama (specifically the woman's film) as by her investigation, which usually drives the narrative of a detective film;[4] however, at the same time, the heroine's independence as a detective poses an undesirable challenge to the masculinity of her husband (or husband-to-be), as with film noir. Just as the maternal melodrama demanded a woman make personal sacrifices to facilitate her daughter's success in the world, so too do these noir films demand the sacrifice on the part of the female protagonist to see the man she loves returned to his "proper" place as head of the household. Thus, I term these films "maritorious melodramas" as opposed to "maternal melodramas" because they see the female protagonist "excessively devoted" to her husband.[5] In the noir films *Phantom Lady* (1944), *Black Angel* (1946), and *Woman on the Run* (1950), the heroine is offered simultaneously as a progressive image of femininity—because she occupies the center of, and drives forward, the investigative narrative—and as a contained one because ultimately she is proven incompetent as a detective and is returned to the prescribed social role of devoted and sacrificing wife.

The female detective was an ideal heroine for the Production Code, as one whose sexuality was literally kept under the wraps of her tailored suit while the focus of the narrative was on her investigation of a crime.[6] Although her popularity and increased presence on screen by the mid-1930s might be related to the stricter enforcement of the Code by 1934, the female detective was a notable figure in the early 1930s as well and was most likely the result of the industry-wide shift to sound at the dawn of the decade. Certainly the fast-talking woman and her penchant to engage in witty banter with male rivals seemed well suited to the "talkies" and saw the detective film in keeping with the themes of the screwball comedy—including the inversion of sex roles. The female detective was a woman operating in the male-dominated world of criminal investigation and, as a woman with authority and power over men, could be regarded as a potential disruption to dominant masculinity—just like the criminal. Kathleen Gregory Klein suggests that the female detective must be put in her "proper" (i.e., secondary) place: "Like the criminal, she is a member of society who does not conform to the status quo. Her presence pushes off-center the whole male/female, public/private, intellect/emotion ... dichotomy" (4).

Although this may be true in the films of the 1940s, the 1930s offered a relatively unproblematic celebration of a "masculinized" woman. The woman detective of the 1930s was most often a girl reporter, the most famous being Torchy Blane. In *Smart Blonde* (1937), Torchy (Glenda Farrell) chases a train on foot: Torchy leaps on board the deck of the caboose as a male action hero would and then simply straightens her coat in order to enter the train car and pass as a "respectable lady." This strong female role on screen was facilitated by the socioeconomic moment—as the reality of the Depression saw more women seeking employment out of necessity—and also the social climate, with a seeming social desire for gender equality. Klein argues that the growing availability of birth control in the 1920s, and more importantly its social acceptance, with popular marriage manuals encouraging its use, helped to redefine marriage (at least for middle-class women), emphasizing the wife's "companionate" rather than maternal role (97). This shift to a "companionate" role was reflected in 1930s films with a new gender equality defining heterosexual relationships. As Philip Hanson notes,

> Approved heterosexual male and female romantic equality becomes the desired ideal. Especially in an economic period when positing an alternative ideal in place of the perceived failed dynamics of the Hoover era was bankable with mass audiences, a new romantic equilibrium materialized on the screen. (132)

This equilibrium resulted in the depiction of the female detective being more interested in catching her man—as in the criminal—than in catching *a* man, as in a husband. The 1930s detective film always concluded with the solution of the mystery but often also a marriage proposal for the heroine from her investigative rival. Although many female detectives did accept the proposal, just as many others did not—especially those who starred in film series. After all, getting married would undoubtedly mean giving up her career (and the end of the series), and the female detective was not always ready to assume her prescribed social role.[7] As Florence Dempsey (also played by Glenda Farrell) in *Mystery of the Wax Museum* (1933) tells her more feminine friend Charlotte (Fay Wray), "You raise the kids; I'll raise the roof!... I would rather die with an athletic heart from shaking cocktails and bankers than expire in a pan of dirty dishwater!"

Carla Kungl notes that, in the heyday of detective fiction during the 1920s and 30s, not to be married signaled the failure of the female detective as a woman (88). Therefore, what is interesting about the Hollywood's female detective is not that she could be a detective *and* attract a man, but that she attracted her man *because* of her masculinity—her outspoken nature, her independence, and her careerist ambition, drive, and success. In other words, she was presented as a positive feminist role model: a woman who could be masculine *and* valued, respected, and desired rather than seen as unnatural (i.e., a lesbian). In this way, the female detective of 1930s Hollywood film defies both the assumptions and stereotypes of the detective tradition and the representation of women on the screen—that women had to be the epitome of glamour and femininity to be regarded as models of womanhood. Although female aggression in the 1920s had been, as Hanson notes, "consistently contained by being enfolded in male authority" (132 n. 39), in the 1930s it was sometimes celebrated but *always allowed*. The female detective was simultaneously masculine and feminine, successful in a man's world and a woman's, and was not punished for her social transgressions.

America's involvement in World War II sparked, however, not only the repolarization of gender roles but also a desire for introspection. This resulted in both the phasing out of the female detective and any comedy from the detective film and the emergence of film noir and its focus on a male protagonist and social critique. The focus of the detective film in the 1930s, in a reflection of British golden age detective fiction, was on the solution to the mystery and the restoration of order to what was regarded as a generally good society; however, film noir, in a reflection of American hardboiled detective fiction, was more concerned with the darker side of human relationships (especially betrayal) and presented a society that was flawed and often corrupt. In Hollywood's darker film noir, the female detective became a rarity, and in the few films in which she appeared, she was most often a housewife trying to clear her husband's name.[8]

NOIR AND MELODRAMA

Phantom Lady (1944), *Black Angel* (1946), and *Woman on the Run* (1950) have all been identified as film noir by critics, the Internet Movie Database, and/or distribution companies that have released these titles as part of noir DVD collections. I will, therefore, not spend time establishing how these films can be regarded as noir but will begin with that assumption and, instead, explore how they are also melodrama. There is something different about the film noir featuring a female protagonist. As Donald Phelps notes, "the best of the Woolrich adaptations—epitomized by Roy William Neill's *Black Angel*—express something virtually alien to *noir* mood and *noir* ethos: a lingering, faintly nostalgic sensitivity, a persistent albeit wistful humanism" (64), leading Phelps to define such films as "cinema *gris*" rather than noir. I would argue that similarly *Phantom Lady* (another Woolrich adaptation) and *Woman on the Run* possess a "nostalgic sensitivity" in keeping with the tradition of melodrama. However, it is not just a female protagonist and a sense of nostalgia or humanism that complicate the identification of these films as noir but also their moments of excess in terms of representation.

Films are identified as belonging to a specific genre based on their emotional effect (e.g., the horror film), content (e.g., the musical), themes (e.g., the social problem film), setting (e.g., the Western), or protagonist (e.g., the gangster film). However, both melodrama and film noir are examples of categories that have been constructed by critics rather than the film industry itself and have resisted a clear delineation as genre. The label *film noir* was applied retrospectively by French critics to describe a body of Hollywood films that appeared during World War II. At the time of their release, these films were sold by studios as detective films, crime melodramas, or thrillers; indeed, many of the films were adaptations of hardboiled stories by American authors such as Woolrich, Dashiell Hammett, and Raymond Chandler. Critics have disagreed over whether film noir is a genre, a style, or a movement but tend to agree that, whatever it is, classic film noir saw its heyday during and immediately after World War II.[9] Film noir arose in a rebellion against the stylization of classical Hollywood film and offered, in contrast, darker narratives, characters, themes, mood, and cinematography. As James Naremore argues, the use of the term *film noir* was not widespread until the 1970s and was a creation of a belated rereading of classical Hollywood by scholars and critics (14)—as was the case with melodrama. Today, the term *melodrama* is most often associated with films featuring heightened emotionality and female protagonists, aimed at an assumed female audience. However, as Ben Singer argues, *melodrama* was initially a term used by the film industry during the silent era to describe films with "action, thrilling sensationalism, and physical violence" (95). Similarly, Steve Neale suggests that in classical Hollywood film, the term was used by studios to describe "war films, adventure films, horror films, and thrillers, genres traditionally thought of as, if anything, 'male'" ("Melo" 69)—rather than the woman's film. The term's association with narratives driven by female desire has been the result of feminist and psychoanalytic critical discourse of the 1980s and 90s that applied the term to classical Hollywood films that, at the time of their release, were labeled—and often dismissed as—woman's films or "weepies."[10]

Critics identify visual style as a key component of film noir. Hollywood directors and cinematographers developed a dark and ominous tone by opting for a *chiaroscuro* visual style—with contrasting light and dark shadows—versus Hollywood's dominant style of high-key lighting. Echoing German Expressionism of the 1910s and 20s, film noir offered a highly stylized visual design that drew attention to itself and suggested an exteriorization (or expression) of a character's internal state of mind. Neale argues that the elements regarded "as exclusive to *noir*" and "its principal hallmarks" are "the visual and aural rhetoric—the use of extreme *chiaroscuro*, discordant sounds and music, and other expressive and 'expressionistic' devices" (*Genre* 169–70); however, I would note that such "visual and aural rhetoric" have also been identified as the hallmarks of melodrama. As Laura Mulvey notes, "the melodrama is characterized by the presence of a protagonist whose symptomatic behavior emerges out of irreconcilable or inexpressible internal contradiction, and this 'unspeakable' affects and overflows on to the *mise en scène*" ("It" 125). The heightened emotionality of noir, however, does tend to result from violence, whereas melodrama's stems more often from pathos; this is most likely why a murder was added to James M. Cain's novel *Mildred Pierce* (1941) in the film noir adaptation of it (1945). Melodrama's visual design includes an emphasis on the symbolic nature of everyday objects as defining social and psychic space: clothing, colors, and household objects become invested with meanings beyond their superficial or obvious ones. Critics have argued that the moments of excess in melodrama puncture the surface realism of the text and can allow for a "reading against the grain" that reveals meanings in opposition to the dominant discourses of capitalism (in the case of a Marxist approach) and patriarchy (in the case of a feminist approach).[11] This reading of the melodramatic text through a psychoanalytic lens treats the text as a hysterical body like that of the patient in psychoanalysis: the surface of the text exhibits symptoms (the moments of excess) that are caused by the contradictions present beneath a surface that cannot contain them (i.e., patriarchal capitalism in opposition to an individual's own desires). Both noir and melodrama offer symbolic images that invite a reading beyond their presence merely as objects befitting their settings: the television that represents how the consumerist trappings of a suburban lifestyle have all but embalmed widow Cary Scott (Jane Wyman) in *All that Heaven Allows* (1955) functions similarly to the image of the "Spade and Archer" sign cast in shadow (and in reverse) on the office floor between the two detectives in *The Maltese Falcon* (1941) that represents the dissolution of their supposed partnership.

As I have discussed elsewhere, the term *melodrama* does not have to be restricted to the discussion of classical Hollywood woman's films but is applicable to male genre films as well—for example, the cop-action film.[12] I would argue that so too can the term be more closely associated with the predominantly male genre of film noir, whereas other critics—for example Steven Gale and Pam Cook—have seen it as an either/or debate. I argue that melodrama and film noir are not so distinct from one other but operate similarly as modes of representation that utilize their visual and aural expression to invite their symbolic interpretation. Unlike the classic realist text in which the mise en scène—including sets, costumes, music, and lighting—is expected to perform merely as the backdrop to the story and characters, the noir or melodramatic text sees its mise en scène highlighted, offering a second level of representation through which to interpret the themes and characters.

The most obvious difference between melodrama and film noir is the sex of the protagonist and that of the film's intended viewer. Although some films identified as noir have a female protagonist at the center of their narrative (for example, *Mildred Pierce* starring Joan Crawford), the vast majority of noir films have male heroes (or anti-heroes). Similarly, although some well-known family melodramas have a male protagonist at their center (for example, *Written on the Wind* [1956] starring Rock Hudson), the majority of melodramas are regarded as "women's films"—films starring, and aimed at, women. Certainly, the main thrust of film noir seems to be a negotiation of the anxieties of postwar masculinity. Ex-servicemen returning from the war faced unemployment, alienation, degradation, disablement, and broken homes. Many of these problems were regarded as the result of increased female independence and changing gender roles. In reality, many women had left the home to take up employment and pursued sexual gratification in the absence of their husbands; in film noir, these women were branded as evil—competing with men in the workplace for jobs, at home as breadwinners, and in bed by challenging their husband's masculinity. In melodrama, on the other hand, men were often the cause of the female protagonist's problems—from authoritarian patriarchs to lovers who wished to quell her independence and force her to assume her socially prescribed role as wife and mother. Christian Viviani argues that the Americanization of melodrama made it relevant for the social realties of the 1930s and resulted in the subgenre of the "maternal melodrama," in which a mother makes sacrifices for her child in order to right her social wrong (96). In general, melodramas center on female sacrifice: for example, *Dark Victory* (1939), which sees Judith Traherne (Bette Davis) punished for her independent nature with a terminal illness but rewarded for her devotion to her doctor with happiness for a brief while as his wife, and *Now, Voyager* (1942), which sees Charlotte Vale (Davis again) sacrifice a relationship with a married man in order to see his daughter (unwanted by her own mother) have a happy childhood.

I would like to suggest that *Phantom Lady, Black Angel,* and *Woman on the Run* are not just noir but also melodrama—in both the conventional sense and my complication of those definitions as outlined above. The visual style of the three films is consistent with that traditionally defined as noir, but all three films have key moments of excess that are more in keeping with conventional notions of melodrama, including the drum solo in *Phantom Lady,* Marty's amnesia in *Black Angel,* and the roller coaster ride in *Woman on the Run.* As Neale explains, most critics argue "that desire in *noir* tends to be marked as dangerous or destructive, and that it tends to be represented from a male point of view" (*Genre* 160). And it is in this way that the three films I explore are different from traditional noir: female desire is seen as salvation and is represented from a female point of view. Rather than the exposure of the hero's love interest as a femme fatale and his rejection of her as is typical of noir. *Phantom Lady* and *Black Angel* begin with a femme fatale's demise and conclude with the creation of a new family order. Noir has also been seen as the site of male crisis,[13] but these films focus instead on a crisis of female identity in terms of what role these heroines will play to save the men they love—from lounge singer to detective, from adulteress to dutiful wife.

Scholars such as Tania Modleski and Diane Waldman suggest that a small group of gothic thrillers centered on a female protagonist, including Alfred Hitchcock's *Rebecca* (1940) and George Cukor's *Gaslight* (1944), can be regarded as film noir; however, Neale argues that the position of these films has "always been ambiguous or marginal, as far as proponents of noir have been concerned" (*Genre* 163). Catherine Ross Nickerson argues that detective fiction in general grew out of the gothic tradition, including Edgar Allan Poe's seminal tales of ratiocination (xiii); however, there is an even closer connection between the gothic and women's detective fiction arising from the tradition of the "female gothic" established by Ann Raddiffe's *The Mysteries of Udolpho* (1794) in which a female protagonist is faced with a secret or mystery. However, the female gothic thrillers of the 1940s tend to feature women in period piece settings and in roles typical of the woman's film, not, as the three films I discuss, in contemporary urban settings and in the traditionally male and noir role of detective.[14]

Phantom Lady, Black Angel, and *Woman on the Run* offer an interesting hybridization of what are regarded as traditionally either noir or melodrama conventions: they offer the female protagonist of the melodrama and a narrative driven by her desires but a protagonist who is simultaneously the problematic independent women of the wartime-era film noir. Like the women of the maternal melodrama who had to sacrifice their own desires to see their children thrive, these female protagonists must make sacrifices in order to reinstate their husbands to their patriarchal position—from criminal to head of the household. It is this excessive devotion to their husbands that invites me to term these films "maritorious melodramas."

THE MARITORIOUS MELODRAMA

Whereas the 1930s had seemed to call for new kinds of gender roles, and Hollywood had answered with gender-bending female detectives, the 1940s seemed to desire the return to traditional polarization of masculinity and femininity: in other words, men had to be re-masculinized and women re-feminized. *Phantom Lady, Black Angel,* and *Woman on the Run* all suggest that the marriages that begin the films have failed because an imbalance in gender power occurred: the wives became too tough or independent and the husbands too "soft"—to use Carol Richman's description of her boss in *Phantom Lady.* In a reflection of this repolarization of gender, the female detective's only outings in film noir are as a wife (or future wife) attempting to clear her husband's name and repair the broken home. Both *Black Angel* and *Phantom Lady* are based on novels by Cornell Woolrich, and as Phelps says of Woolrich's detective heroines, "the women are fired with devotion, defiance, maternal passion" (66). Just as in the maternal melodrama, "the mother's fall from grace was symbolized by a tormented odyssey which marked an opposition to the permanence of the bourgeois household" (Viviani 86), so too is these three film heroines' descent into the seedy underbelly of America marked by a tormented odyssey through the public spaces of the city—the courthouse, the night club, the seedy hotel, and the street—in order to return permanence to the bourgeois household. All three films are noir detective films with an expressive use of *chiaroscuro* visual style and an exploration of the seedier side of America's urban life (New York, Los Angeles, and San Francisco, respectively), but each is also a melodrama with a female protagonist at its center, a narrative driven by her goals and desires, and moments of excess that puncture the surface realism of the text.

Phantom Lady finds Scott Henderson (Alan Curtis) in a bar alone: he was making one last attempt to heal the estrangement between him and his wife with a night out to celebrate their fifth anniversary, but his wife refused to join him. Scott blames his wife for the collapse of their marriage: she was "too spoiled and too beautiful," he explains to the police. Scott is unaware his wife, Marcella, has been, according to his friend jack Marlow (Franchot Tone), "amusing herself" with him. When Marcella admits to Jack that she has no intention of leaving her husband for him, he strangles her in a fit of rage. As Scott explains to Inspector Burgess (Thomas Gomez), Marcella refused to be "his wife" (i.e., his lover) but also refused him a divorce (giving him the freedom to pursue another), giving him motive and making him the prime suspect in her murder.

In a melodramatic manner, Marcella haunts the early part of the film but is never shown in person. While the police question Scott about his wife, her full-length portrait dominates the wall behind them (using the same technique that is identified with Otto Preminger's *Laura* released later that year). When the paramedics carry her out, the camera pans somewhat awkwardly past Scott, mirroring her body's passage through the room. Scott exclaims in horror, "Look what they're doing! Her hair ... along the floor!" but the audience sees nothing but the frozen portrait on the wall behind. Marcella is, ironically, not the "phantom lady" of the film's title; the "phantom lady" is Anne Terry (Fay Helm), the woman with whom Scott spent his anniversary evening but who cannot be found by the police to corroborate his alibi.

The film introduces the heroine, Scott's assistant Carol Richman (Ella Raines), at work listening to his Dictaphone message until the story in the paper about Marcella's murder catches her eye. Scott calls her "Kansas," after her home state and to highlight that she is a small-town girl now living in the big city. Carol is in love with her boss, and when he is convicted of murder and sentenced to death row, she decides to play detective to clear his name. She pursues people in the case who swore

Figure 2.1. In *Phantom Lady* (1944), Carol "Kansas" Richman (Ella Raines) is willing to "humiliate herself" in order to save the man she loves from a death sentence.

they never saw the phantom lady; as Carol suspects, each has been bribed to remain silent. Her search leads her through the underbelly of the city, and although these shady places are typically noir, they are also presented through melodramatic excess. Carol stalks the bartender at work and then on his way home: as they wait alone on the platform for the train, the bartender advances threateningly toward Carol, and his implied desire to push her in front of the train is halted only by the arrival of another passenger. The tension of the scene is released by the loud squeal of the train's wheels on the track as it rushes past them. This is echoed in the following scene when the bartender accidentally steps out in front of a car to escape her interrogation, and the screams of a woman fuse with the screeching of car tires.

Similarly, the film's most notorious scene—the drum solo—is notable because of its excess. In order to get close to drummer Cliff Milburn (Elisha Cook Jr.), Carol presents herself as a cheap

Figure 2.2. This studio still for Black Angel (1946) suggests that Catherine Bennett (June Vincent) loves Martin Blair (Dan Duryea); however, it is her husband to whom she is "excessively devoted."

"dame" and gives him "the eye." He takes her to a basement jam session in which he plays the drums and she dances. Her masquerade of available sexuality is successful at least in his eyes and broken only for a moment when she catches the sight of her own image in a mirror while reapplying her lipstick: she shakes her head in disgust at what she sees. Tension in the scene is built through the frenzied music and atypical cinematography—low and canted angles coupled with tight close-ups—and then released with the drummer's orgasmic crescendo. Carol agrees to go back to Cliff's place, knowing that he expects her to have sex with him. When she plays hard to get, and he spies the police file in her purse, he turns violent and—it is suggested—decides to rape her. He says menacingly, "Wait until I get you!" but she escapes. When Jack (the man responsible for the murder and bribery) turns up after Carol's sudden departure, he says to Cliff, "She was magnificent! She loathed you but she went with you. She would have humiliated herself to make you talk." Her willingness to "humiliate herself" in order to save the man she loves sees Carol rewarded. When Jack warns Carol that she is risking her life pursuing what he calls "a man's job" (i.e., playing detective), Carol retorts, "Do you think I'd care? Do you think I'd want to live?"

The film ties the loss of love to madness, with two possible outcomes: Anne Terry becomes a reclusive hysteric following her fiancé's death, and Jack Marlow becomes a "homicidal paranoiac" when Marcella rejects him. The former represents Carol's possible future if she does not save Scott from death row. Saving him is, in every way, safeguarding her own future as a woman, given that the film suggests that a woman is nothing unless she marries the man she loves. And it would seem that Carol gets her happy ending. Returning to work, Carol finds a proposal from Scott on the Dictaphone: "You know you're having dinner with me tonight, and tomorrow night, and the next night, and then every night." It is on this last phrase that the Dictaphone skips and continues to do so, ending the film with the image of an ecstatic Carol, holding the horn and listening to Scott's disembodied voice repeating "every night ... every night ... every night."

In *Black Angel*, Kirk Bennett (John Phillips) is arrested and later convicted of murdering Mavis Marlowe (Constance Dowling), a singer who is blackmailing him over their affair. Unlike Carol, who is a career woman, Cathy Bennett (June Vincent) is a meek and dutiful housewife, and she stands by her husband even though, as Martin Blair (Dan Duryea) describes it, Kirk "let her down" (i.e., he was unfaithful). She explains to her husband in prison, "Please, Kirk. You're my husband. I'll always stand by you. You know that." Initially, she pursues the other most likely suspect in the case, Mavis's ex-husband Marty, but when it appears that he has a solid alibi, she teams up with him to investigate club owner Marko (Peter Lorre). The missing piece of evidence is the heart-shaped ruby brooch that Kirk swears was on Mavis when he first discovered her body and that was later stolen; without the brooch, there is no evidence of a killer other than Kirk.

Marty and Cathy team up not just as investigative partners but also business partners and gain access to Marko's office and his safe (where Cathy assumes the stolen brooch is hidden) by posing as an entertainment duo: he plays piano while she sings. It is never explained why Cathy's husband strayed and who was to blame, but it is clear that they had become estranged. When Marty asks if she plays the piano, she explains that Kirk used to play while she sang—"At least ... we did when we were first married." One suspects that what attracted Kirk to Mavis was a seductive sexuality and strength of character that Cathy seems, at least initially, to lack. Cathy, however, undergoes a gradual transformation from a meek housewife sporting a checked dress and straw boater to a working woman in a tailored suit and then to a glamorous lounge singer in a black, off-the-shoulder gown. Ironically, it is in the male role of detective that Cathy is re-feminized visually, which attracts Marty, who finds himself falling for his partner. Cathy proves that she does possess a masculine strength of character:

> CATHY: "I was hoping to get closer to that safe."
> MARTY: "That's the *hard* way, isn't it?"
> CATHY: "I have to get into it, Marty ... no matter how."

The "hard way" is to become Marko's lover, and even though Cathy is prepared to "humiliate" herself to save her husband, she is still horrified at the thought of it—and the cinematography expresses that horror. In the midst of an otherwise unremarkable scene in terms of film style, there is a melodramatic medium shot of Cathy teary-eyed, open-mouthed, and swaying with fear that is almost palpable. The moment is made more dramatic when the camera cuts back to an unperturbed Marko taking out a bottle of champagne that he had "been saving for a special occasion" and then cuts back to the odd shot of Cathy, this time trying to force a tearful smile. This moment of visual excess is followed by one of narrative. Because of the quantity of screen time devoted to this avenue of inquiry and the tense climax that arises when Marko catches Cathy at his safe, the audience assumes that Cathy's sacrifice will have been worthwhile—that she will now have the proof to clear her husband. However, this anticipated resolution is frustrated when it is revealed that Marko does not have the brooch and was in police custody at the time of the murder—and therefore is *not* the murderer. Cathy, in despair, attempts to express the ineffable—her realization that her sacrifice has been in vain: "You mean we ... All this time, just wasted."

Black Angel is, as many melodramas are, characterized by the return of the repressed. As Peter Brooks argues, "melodrama refuses repression, or rather, repeatedly strives for moments where repression is broken through, to the physical and verbal staging of the essential" (19). The essential in *Black Angel* is "whodunit?"—who is responsible for Mavis's death? The film—just like the killer, it turns out—attempts to repress the story of the crime, but eventually both recall and reveal the truth. Since he met Cathy, Marty has remained sober; however, her rejection of his love sends him on a bender, like the one he went on the night that Mavis was killed. By returning to the same state in which he committed the murder and through being confronted with the brooch that he and Cathy had been seeking, Marty experiences the return of what he had repressed, and an oral and visual montage reveals Marty's actions on the fateful night. As the doctor at the hospital explains, Marty was suffering from "Korsakoff's psychosis," amnesia brought about by his excessive consumption of alcohol. Although he remembers committing the murder and wishes to confess, Marty finds the doctor at the hospital and the police unwilling to believe him—so he has to escape to tell Cathy the truth. Left alone to wait for the arrival of Captain Flood, Marty begins drinking again. In the film's final moment of excess, Marty hallucinates that he sees Mavis instead of Cathy: Mavis's head and body are superimposed over that of Cathy's, and eerie music accompanies her disembodied form.

Ultimately the film, in keeping with the melodramatic tradition, is about self-sacrifice. Although Cathy gives herself to Marko, the film suggests that this was an admirable even if futile gesture. However, more importantly, Cathy refuses the temptation to fall for her partner, Marty, who—as a nice guy—poses the real threat of replacing Kirk in her affections. Marty professes his love to Cathy: "I knew from the beginning... that you're everything I wanted and everything I'd missed. It has to be you and me, Cathy." The implication is that his marriage to Mavis was less than ideal and that she was not a good wife, a fact supported by her blackmailing of men such as Marko and Kirk. However, Cathy refuses to betray Kirk and tells Marty she can never love another man: "Marty, I can't. There's only been one man. There *can* only be one man ... ever." She is rewarded for her fidelity with Marty's recollection of the truth at the eleventh hour to save Kirk from the gas chamber.

In *Woman on the Run,* it is not the wife, Eleanor Johnson (Ann Sheridan), who is on the run but her husband Frank (Ross Elliott). He has witnessed a murder, and believing that the police cannot protect him from the killer (after all, the victim he saw killed was a witness in police protection), Frank runs. Clear from the start is that Eleanor and Frank's four-year marriage is a disaster. When Inspector Ferris (Robert Keith) asks Frank if he is married, Frank replies "In a way." When Ferris asks Eleanor to describe her husband so that the police can find him, she retorts, "I couldn't. I haven't been able to for a longtime." Ferris is angered by Eleanor's attitude not befitting of a wife, including encouraging her husband to stay on the run.

> FERRIS: "If I had a husband I wanted to get rid of, I'd do exactly what you did."
> ELEANOR: "If he wants to run away, that's his business."
> FERRIS: "And your business too, Mrs. Johnson!"

Indeed, the film suggests that whatever concerns a husband should concern his wife as well: that is her job. Frank's doctor tells her, "But naturally, you must know all about his troubles. I'm only his doctor; you're his wife." But she knows nothing of Frank's life, including that he has

Figure 2.3. In *Woman on the Run* (1950), Eleanor (Ann Sheridan) is sent on an emotional and then a literal roller coaster ride when she tries to find her husband on the run.

a heart condition that has been made more serious because of the stress of their failed marriage.

When Ferris inquires about their relationship, Eleanor replies, "If you want to snoop into the remains of our marriage, that's up to you"; however, the film suggests that it is actually up to her. The mystery that Eleanor as detective must solve is not who shot the witness, but rather who killed the marriage. Frank sends her a riddle in a letter that she must solve: "If you think back, you'll know where to find me." Newspaperman Danny Leggett (Dennis O'Keefe) says to her, "He's asking you to admit that your marriage is a failure and that it's your fault. He's saying that he understands you but that you don't understand him." And he is correct: Eleanor must sift through her memories of the marriage and accept some part of the blame for its going wrong in order to track down her husband and give him his lifesaving heart medication. Eleanor neither kept house nor supported her husband's ambitions. Ferris asks why their kitchen contains no food, and Eleanor replies, "He's not particular, and I'm lazy, so we eat out." Ferris asks her why she didn't get a job if she was so concerned about money, and she replies, "Why should I? That's his responsibility not mine." Ferris hits on the truth when he tells Eleanor, "But I don't think you can find him. I don't think he is running away from us; I think he's running away from you." At the beginning of the film, Eleanor believes that the marriage failed because her husband had let her down by not fulfilling his promise as a successful artist; conversely, through her pursuit of the clues raised in Frank's letter and her resulting investigation of the marriage, Eleanor realizes that she let him down by being too independent. In this film, the repressed that returns is Eleanor's love for her husband and her desire to be a dutiful wife. And for her admission of fault, Eleanor is rewarded with the safe return of her husband.

The melodramatic moments of the film arise from Eleanor's failure in her attempt to subsume male authority and play detective. Despite the fact that Eleanor proves to be successful in figuring out the clues that lead her to her husband's whereabouts, she ultimately fails to keep her husband safe: by trusting Danny, she leads the killer right to his prey. Danny offers them the money to finance Frank's disappearance in exchange for an exclusive story for his paper. The climax of the film is the roller coaster ride that Danny takes Eleanor on, initially to spot Frank in the crowd and evade the police, but subsequently to keep her out of the way so that he can kill Frank. On the first ride, Danny and Eleanor sit together, and the tension builds as they look for Frank from their vantage point. The scene offers a kind of "phantom ride," with the camera mounted on the front of the car to follow their coasting up and down the tracks. This scene is tense, but Eleanor's second ride on the roller coaster alone is far more melodramatic. As Danny pays to have her ride once more, he reminds her that the killer may try to kill Frank again.

The second ride starts then with Eleanor rehearing both Danny's last comment and Ferris's remark from earlier that day—that the killer is the only other person who knows about the attempt made on Frank's life. This realization starts an emotional roller coaster represented through the excess of the cinematography of the literal roller coaster ride. This time the cacophony of noise, laughter, music, and the roar of the roller coaster is increased in volume and discord and is combined with Eleanor's screams for Frank to run away. Instead of a phantom ride offering the view directly ahead of the car, this time the camera looks down through the tracks and over their edge in a series of spiraling, disorienting, and terrifying shots of Frank as a small figure below. Eleanor is yanked from side to side by the motion of the ride, helpless. The most disturbing sound through the entire scene is the mechanical and repetitive laughter of an animatronic figure from an amusement park stall.

Eleanor is finally able to get off the ride, but a series of shots with dramatic canted angles maintains a sense of her anxiety as she dashes through the amusement park trying to find Frank. When she hears a shot fired and sees a body in the water, she—and the audience—assumes it is Frank. Luckily, however, the shot fired was Ferris's and the body Danny's. The film suggests that Eleanor's problem at the beginning of the film was her resistance to submit to male authority— that of her husband and the police; however, her eventual acceptance of both leads to a happy conclusion. Eleanor must relinquish her "uxorodespotic" role and, instead, allow her husband to run their household *and* marriage.[15]

Phantom Lady, Black Angel, and *Woman on the Run* all suggest that a marriage cannot be a successful one if the woman vies for control—either inside or outside the home. That is why *Black Angel* regards Cathy as the superior choice over Mavis for both Kirk and Marty, and why *Phantom Lady* sees the replacement of the original Mrs. Henderson (Marcella) with the new one (Carol) as the key to Scott's happiness. Although marriage and family are presented as the ideal in classical Hollywood film, in film noir they are presented most often as imprisoning or sterile. Sylvia Harvey argues, "The two most common types of women in film noir are the exciting, childless whores, or the boring, potentially childbearing sweethearts" (38). However, in the case of *Woman on the Run* and *Black Angel,* the threat of death for the husband as an assumed criminal and the working as an independent woman as a detective for the wife—in other words, playing roles outside of those socially sanctioned—facilitate a rejuvenation of the failed marriage and the nurturing wife transformed into an exciting lover figure.

As dutiful wives—in other words, a traditionally female role—these women prove themselves successful; however, as detectives—a traditionally male role—they are exposed ultimately as incompetent. Carol does pursue the bartender doggedly, extract information from the drummer, and locate the phantom lady through her hat and milliner; Cathy does discover that both Marty and Marko could have been Mavis's killer; and Eleanor does figure out her husband's riddle and whereabouts. Importantly, many of these discoveries are dependent on specifically female knowledge—that is, of woman's fashion, the seduction of men, and memories of courtship. On the other hand, in each case, these women befriend the real killers (jack, Marty, and Danny, respectively) and risk either their own lives or that of their loved ones without realizing what they have done until it is too late. The message of these films is that women can be either the downfall (i.e., the femme fatale) or the savior (i.e., the wife as detective) of men. Wives who pursue independence outside of marriage, whether in terms of sex or a career, present a challenge to male dominance. Ironically, however, through attempting to help their men, these women *have* to work outside of the home as detectives and sometimes prostitute themselves to other men—and they are never demonized for that, even though the femme fatale always is. Each woman's devotion to the man she loves sees her compensated: in other words, each woman is rewarded with the undivided love of her man—something she did not possess at the beginning of the film. The conclusions of these films are then conservative—if read through the lens of film noir.

If, however, these endings are read through the lens of melodrama, a reading against the grain is made possible. Indeed, the concluding scenes of each film feel contrived, stemming from a desired narrative conclusion of returning women to the home rather than one that logically fits the film that came before it in terms of the actual representation of that narrative. In all three films, the husbands are all but absent, and instead, the relationships that form between their wives and other men (Jack, Marty, and Danny) during the course of the investigation are far more developed, interesting, and exciting. In *Phantom Lady,* the skipping Dictaphone proposal and addition of a happy-go- lucky score do not convince: Scott was oblivious to Carol's affections for him despite her standing by him through the trial, risking her life to find evidence to exonerate him, and confessing to him that she is in love with her boss. Indeed, the final shot of the film is not Carol in Scott's arms but of the Dictaphone horn in hers. Similarly, in *Black Angel,* the final shot of the film is not the reunion of Kirk and his wife but that of Marty and Cathy on the cover of the sheet music for their hit song "Time Will Tell" and Marty's comment that they were "a good team while it lasted." In *Woman on the Run,* the last shot of the film is not of the couple embracing on the midway of the amusement park but of the disturbing animatronic doll as it continues the mechanical cackle that pervaded the roller coaster ride.

Although I have suggested that they share an expressionistic or excessive impulse at the level of representation, film noir and melodrama differ in terms of their ideological motivation. As E. Ann Kaplan suggests,

> It is interesting to compare the *film noir,* with its negative or absent family, with melodrama, a genre in which family and its relations are the focus of ideological rep-resentation. While the family melodrama could be seen to deal with the ideological contradictions within patriarchy in terms of sexuality and patriarchal right within the family, the *film noir* as exemplified by *Double Indemnity* stresses precisely the ordering of sexuality and patriarchal right, the containment of sexual drives with patriarchy as Symbolic Order. Thus there is a sense in which *film noir* could be seen to close off the ideological contradictions of patriarchy that the family melodrama opens up. (18)

Thus, Kaplan sees melodrama as functioning in opposition to noir, opening up the possibility of troubling or subverting the film's concession to dominant discourse. However, the focus on a female protagonist and the employ of other conventions of melodrama allow an alternative reading of these film noir. Tony Williams, reading *Phantom Lady* through a psychoanalytic lens, states,

> At the climax of the film Carol is confined to the office and the offer of monogamy. However, enough remains of the masochistic model in the film to argue that the aesthetic, if *not* dominant, is there as a fissure, a gap in ideology which permits the partial expression of the female voice. It exists as an alternative operation against patriarchal control of the text. Even if subdued at the climax, it is still there, attempting to strain against narrative bounds. (134)

The apparent endings of the three films may seem to fell in line with the ideological concerns of film noir—that is, the return of the women to appropriate gender roles—however, the focus on the female characters as investigators (rather than the man as typical with film noir) and the over-determination of representation (as typical with melodrama) allow for contradictions to resonate past the tacked on endorsement of patriarchal ideology.

In the aftermath of World War II, with broken homes and unemployment rampant, the threat, it would seem, was not women replacing men as detectives (as was the fear in the 1930s detective film), but their replacing them as the head of the household. With the return of men from the war, women had to be returned to their proper place so that men could be returned to theirs—at least that was the general social consensus that Hollywood echoed. Just as the maternal melodrama presented "mother-daughter proximity as dangerous to the daughter's future, and to society" (Whitney 11), so too does the film noir starring a female detective suggest that the wife's appropriation of male power in the marriage is dangerous to the husband's future—and to that of society. Wartime and postwar America needed broken homes mended and gender roles reset to their traditional positions. Whereas the maternal melodrama of the 1930s was "an apologia for total renunciation, total sacrifice, total self-abnegation" (Viviani 96) in a reflection of the impact of the Depression, film noir was similarly a reflection of social attitudes in the 1940s, with its recall of women back into the home. Film noir, with its darker, more introspective and critical tone, offered a vehicle for the narratives of men struggling with the new roles demanded of them in postwar America. The ubiquitous female detective of 1930s film could be outspoken, independent, and career- minded with her triumph as both detective and love interest the result of her successful integration of masculinity into femininity. Conversely, the few female detectives of the 1940s had to relinquish their independence (i.e., masculinity) in order to achieve happiness—the only avenue for which was deemed marriage (i.e., femininity). These female detectives, unlike their 1930s counterparts, however, seemed happy to submit to marital authority, and this is why, in the aftermath of World War II, these women are regarded as meritorious.

ACKNOWLEDGMENTS

The author gratefully acknowledges that financial support for this research was received from a grant partly funded by Wilfrid Laurier University Operating funds and partly by the SSHRC Institutional Grant awarded to WLU. The author would also like to thank Jenny Romero of the Margaret Herrick Library, Heidi Rubenstein of Georgetown University's Special Collections, and Mark Quigley of the UCLA Film and Television Archive for their assistance. Last, thanks to Paul Heyer for introducing me to my first film noir female detective and to Ashley Bell for drawing my attention to even more.

ENDNOTES

1. Brown 52–53; Klein 12 n. 3.
2. For discussion of the contemporary female film detective see Gates, "Manhunting."
3. See essays in Kaplan for discussion of the femme fatale. The opposite of the femme fatale—the nurturing woman—has been the subject of some critical discussions; however, she is a negligible figure in terms of screen time and narrative control. Instead, the nurturing woman is typically a minor character who is there to offer a contrast or alternative to the femme fatale. See Place for further discussion. Although *Mildred Pierce* (1945) does have a female protagonist (Joan Crawford) who drives the narrative forward, Mildred is the suspected murderer and not the detective and is, ultimately, a sacrificial mother.
4. Melodrama is a critical category and a mode of representation that overarches a variety of types of film—including the woman's film, featuring a female protagonist and aimed at a presumably female audience, and the family melodrama, including male protagonists and aimed at an assumed broader audience (Mulvey, "Notes" 76). Having said that, critical attention in film studies has tended to focus on female-centered melodrama because the critics analyzing them have tended to be feminist scholars and theorists.
5. Technically, the term "maritorious" is a manufactured one to offer a parallel for the term "uxorious," meaning "excessive devotion to one's wife." See Grandiloquent Dictionary <www.islandnet.com/~egbird/dict/m.htm>, AskOxford <www.askoxford.com/asktheexperts/faq/aboutwords/uxorious?view=uk>, and World Wide Words <www.worldwidewords.org/weirdwords/ww-mar1.htm>.
6. The Production Code, nicknamed the "Hays Code," was established in 1930 to ensure that "no picture shall be produced which will lower the moral standards of those who see it," as the first general principle of the Code declared. The Code laid out what was or was not considered moral content, and scenes that presented the vicarious treatment of sex and violence and the glorification of lawless and amoral behavior were required to be removed if a film was likely to be granted certification by state and national censor boards. Hollywood adopted this system of self-regulatory censorship in order to prevent the institution of federal censorship.
7. For example, although both spinster sleuths Hildegarde Withers in *Penguin Pool Murder* (1932) and Sarah Keate in *While the Patient Slept* (1935) are proposed to by the police detectives officially in charge of the investigation, both

remained unmarried for all six of their respective films. Similarly, although Torchy Blane and her police detective boyfriend continually aim to get married, Torchy remains unattached for all nine films.

8. Other interesting film noir that offer female detectives are *The Seventh Victim* (1943) and *Shadow of a Doubt* (1943). Both detectives are teenagers, and therefore the plots of these films differ from the ones with which this article is concerned. In *The Seventh Victim,* Mary Gibson (Kim Hunter) investigates the Satanic cult with which her sister is involved. In *Shadow of a Doubt,* "Charlie" Newton (Teresa Wright) investí-gates her suspicion that her uncle is a murderer, and he subsequently attempts to murder her.

9. For a complete discussion of the history of film noir criticism, see Neale (*Genre* ch. 4).

10. See Bratton et al., Doane, and Gledhill.

11. See Doane, Gledhill, and Nowell-Smith.

12. See Gates, "The Man's Film."

13. See Krutnik.

14. Diane Waldman explains, "The plots of films like *Rebecca, Suspicion, Gaslight,* and their lesser- known counterparts like *Undercurrent* and *Sleep My* Love fall under the rubric of the Gothic designation: a young inexperienced woman meets a handsome older man to whom she is alternately attracted and repelled. After a whirlwind courtship (72 hours in Lang's *Secret Beyond the Door,* two weeks is more typical), she marries him. After returning to the ancestral mansion of one of the pair, the heroine experiences a series of bizarre and uncanny incidents, open to ambiguous interpretation, revolving around the question of whether or not the Gothic male really loves her. She begins to suspect that he may be a murderer" (29–30).

15. Uxorodespotic means "tyrannical rule by one's wife." See Babylon <www.babylon.com/definition/uxorodespotic/ English>.

REFERENCES

Bratton, Jacky, Jim Cook, and Christine Gledhill, eds. *Melodrama: Stage, Picture, Screen.* London: BFI Publishing, 1994. Print.

Brooks, Peter. "Melodrama, Body, Revolution." *Melodrama: Stage, Picture, Screen.* Ed. Jacky Bratton, Jim Cook, and Christine Gledhill. London: BFI Publishing, 1994. 11–24. Print.

Brown, Jeffrey A. "Gender and the Action Heroine: Hardbodies and the *Point of No Return.*" *Cinema Journal* 35.3 (1996): 52–71. Print.

Cook, Pam. "Duplicity in *Mildred Pierce.*" *Women in Film Noir.* Ed. E. Ann Kaplan. New ed. London: BFI Publishing, 2001. 69–80. Print.

Doane, Mary Ann. *The Desire to Desire: The Woman's Film of the* 1940s. Bloomington: Indiana UP, 1987. Print.

Gale, Steven H. "*The Maltese Falcon:* Melodrama or Film Noir?" *Literature/Film Quarterly* 24.2 (1996): 145–48. Print.

Gates, Philippa. "Manhunting: The Female Detective in the Contemporary Serial Killer Film." *Post Script: Essays in Film and the Humanities* 24.1 (2004): 42–61. Print.

_____. "The Man's Rim: Woo and the Pleasure of Male Melodrama." *The Journal of Popular Culture* 35.1 (2001): 59–79. Print.

Gledhill, Christine. "The Melodramatic Field: An Investigation." *Home Is Where the Heart Is: Studies in Melodrama and the Woman's Film.* Ed. Christine Gledhill. London: BFI Publishing, 1987. 5–39. Print.

Hanson, Philip. "The Feminine Image in Films of the Great Depression." *The Cambridge Quarterly* 32.2 (2003): 113–41. Print.

Harvey, Sylvia. "Woman's Place: The Absent Family of Film Noir." *Women in Film Noir.* Ed. E. Ann Kaplan. New ed. London: BFI Publishing, 2001. 35–46. Print.

Internet Movie Database (IMDb). Web. 10 May 2008. <http://www.imdb.com>.

Kaplan, E. Ann. "Introduction to 1978 Edition." *Women in Film Noir.* Ed. E. Ann Kaplan. New ed. London: BFI Publishing, 2001. 15–19. Print.

Klein, Kathleen Gregory. *The Woman Detective: Gender and Genre.* 2nd ed. Urbana: U of Illinois P, 1995. Print.

Krutnik, Frank. *In a Lonely Street: Film Noir, Genre, Masculinity.* London, Routledge, 1991. Print.

Kungl, Carla T. *Creating the Fictional Female Detective: The Sleuth Heroines of British Women Writers, 1890–1940.* Jefferson, NC: McFarland & Company, 2006. Print.

Modleski, Tania. *Loving with a Vengeance: Mass-Produced Fantasies for Women.* Hamden, CT: Archon Books, 1982. Print.

Mulvey, Laura. "'It Will Be a Magnificent Obsession': The Melodrama's Role in the Development of Contemporary Film Theory." *Melodrama: Stage, Picture, Screen.* Ed. Jacky Bratton, Jim Cook, and Christine Gledhill. London: BFI Publishing, 1994. 121–33. Print.

_____. "Notes on Sirk and Melodrama." *Home Is Where the Heart Is: Studies in Melodrama and the Woman's Film.* Ed. Christine Gledhill. London: BFI Publishing, 1987. 75–79. Print.

Naremore, James. "American Film Noir: The History of an Idea." *Film Quarterly* 49.2 (1995/1996): 12–28. Print.

Neale, Steve. *Genre and Hollywood.* London: Routledge, 2000. Print.

_____. "Melo Talk: On the Meaning and Use of the Term 'Melodrama' in the American Trade Press." *Velvet Light Trap* 32 (1993): 66–89. Print.

Nickerson, Catherine Ross. *The Web of Iniquity: Early Detective Fictions by American Women.* Durham, NC: Duke University Press, 1998. Print.

Nowell-Smith, Geoffrey. "Minnelli and Melodrama." *Home Is Where the Heart Is: Studies in Melodrama and the Woman's Film.* Ed. Christine Gledhill. London: BFI Publishing, 1987. 70–74. Print.

Phelps, Donald. "Cinema Gris: Woolrich/Neill's *Black Angel.*" *Film Comment* (2000): 64–69. Print.

Place, Janey. "Women in Rim Noir." *Women in Film Noir.* Ed. E. Ann Kaplan. New ed. London: BFI Publishing, 2001. 47–68. Print.

Singer, Ben. "Female Power in the Serial-Queen Melodrama: The Etiology of an Anomaly." *Camera Qbscura* 22 (1990): 91–129. Print.

Viviani, Christian. "Who Is Without Sin? The Maternal Melodrama in American Rim, 1930–39." *Home Is Where the Heart Is: Studies in Melodrama and the Woman's Film.* Ed. Christine Gledhill. London: BFI Publishing, 1987. 83–99. Print.

Waldman, Diane. "'At Last I Can Tell It to Someone!' Feminine Point of View and Subjectivity in the Gothic Romance Film of the 1940s." *Cinema journal* 23.2 (1984): 29–40. Print.

Williams, Tony. *"Phantom Lady,* Cornell Woolrich, and the Masochistic Aesthetic." *Film Noir Reader.* Ed. Alain Silver and lames UrsinL 7th Limelight ed. New York: Limelight Editions, 2003. 129–43. Print.

Whitney, Allison. "Race, Class, and the Pressure to Pass in American Maternal Melodrama: The Case of *Stella Dallas." Journal of Film and Video* 59.1 (2007): 3–18. Print.

SELECTED FILMOGRAPHY

Black Angel. Dir. Roy William Neill. Perf. Dan Duryea, June Vincent, and Peter Lorre. Universal Pictures, 1946. Film.

Phantom Lady. Dir. Robert Siodmak. Perf. Franchot Tone, Ella Raines, and Alan Curtis. Universal Pictures, 1944. Film.

Woman on the Run. Dir. Norman Foster. Perf. Ann Sheridan, Dennis O'Keefe, and Robert Keith. Fidelity Pictures Corp., 1950. Film.

CECILIA SAYAD

THE AUTEUR AS FOOL: BAKHTIN, BARTHES, AND THE SCREEN PERFORMANCES OF WOODY ALLEN AND JEAN-LUC GODARD

Any association between auteurs and fools in the cinema immediately brings to mind the clown-like figures played by Charles Chaplin, Buster Keaton, Jerry Lewis, and Woody Allen, all of whom incarnate similar characters across a vast array of films and in addition direct all or many of the pictures in which they perform. Common to these "fools" is their recurring features and a certain foreignness that posits them as outsiders. In the words of Bakhtin, who theorized about the fool in literature, this figure is endowed with the "right to be 'other,'" "the right not to understand, the right to confuse" (159, 163), thus becoming the mask that the author wears in order to freely question the world, to denaturalize it. This, after all, is the nature of all comedy.

But the fool's inherent marginality goes beyond this figure's subversive attitude, as I argue in this article. The fool's "misplacement" or inappropriateness can be traced back to its origins in the performing arts—to the intermittent quality of the fool's presence in some traditions in popular theater (its role limited to providing comic relief or commentary on the main action) or as the bridge between different numbers in the circus or in variety shows.[1] As thus, the fool often has been perceived as a temporary visitor, as an outsider to the diegesis, existing between the "show" and the audience. Bakhtin's study of the fool in the novel goes even further, claiming that this figure's theatrical genesis (it originates in the public square) positions it as an intruder to the literary genre, thereby bridging also different media (as discussed later). Similarly, I argue that when read through the figure of the fool, the types of authorial self-inscription I analyze in cinematic works constitute the directors as external to the diegesis, crossing, in addition, the boundaries of genre and even the frame. I contrast the ways in which the fools played by Woody Allen and Jean-Luc Godard turn the author's image into the textual manifestation of the problematic connection between their real existence and their screen personas. My goal is to explore how these directors achieve this effect with performances informed by both the fool and, in the works of the American filmmaker, the stand-up comedian. These two figures are somewhat external to the worlds they inhabit and comment on, refusing to fully merge with it. I look into the impact of this refusal on the film-author mixture, questioning whether it produces the chemical precipitation or dissolution of the author component.

The fool's subversive nature carries a self-reflexive element that, though pertaining to all clown-like characters played by famous directors, varies in degree, obtaining different percep-tions of narrative closure and the connections between the filmic and the extra-filmic. But it is particularly in the works by Allen that the fool's foreignness has repercussion in the question of film authorship that I want to discuss. The director promotes a self-reflexive meditation that dialogues with the challenges to the auteur brought about with the structuralist turn in film stud-ies. In fact, I argue that the effects produced by Allen's screen performances make him comparable not so much with the usual suspects of slapstick and screwball comedy, but with none other than

Godard, whose career parallels the theoretical underpinnings of film studies, from auteurism to its total dismissal, culminating with the film collectives of the late 1960s, and also the influence of semiotics, Marxism, feminism, and psychoanalysis. Here, however, the terms of comparison with Allen lie with Godard's appearances in some films of the 1980s—notably as the buffoonish characters of Uncle Jean/Monsieur Godard in *First Name: Carmen* (1983), the Prince/the Idiot in *Soigne ta droite* (1987), and Professor Pluggy/Monsieur Godard in *King Lear* (1987). I argue that these fools embody the director's understanding of his identity as an author.[2]

Whereas Godard's screen presence changes in quality and degree (from cameos to voice-over narration and from appearances as commentator or interviewer to the stylized performances of the 1980s), Allen always incarnates a fictional character. Still, even if the American director is more straightforwardly an actor than Godard, he nonetheless typecasts himself—his image brings to mind his inability to change, even if he plays characters bearing different names and existing in variable backdrops. What then exactly motivates this parallel between filmmakers who, though belonging to the same generation,[3] do not operate in the same mode? First, though Godard's experiments with the medium are far more radical than Allen's self-reflexive narratives, both their forms of self-display produce a tension between a fixed identity and the playful crossing of the boundaries separating the diegetic from the non-diegetic, the fictional from the real, and the film from the extra-filmic. Second, the alien, foreign quality of the characters played by Allen and Godard has both a graphic and a narrative dimension—the former defined by the effects of their emblematic figures and the latter by their position in relation to the diegesis. The two directors share a similar silhouette, defined by a balding and rather disheveled head. Interestingly, they also wear recognizable eyeglasses, which they carry on across diverse roles. Godard's 1986 video interview with Woody Allen, turned into the medium-length *Meetin' WA,* explores this similarity of contours—during the prologue to the interview, a dissolve fuses the outline of Godard's body into a portrait of Allen, in a graphic match that creates a mirroring effect, echoing Godard's desire, revealed in voice-over, to meet his long-missed "friend."[4] These silhouettes, which reappear in many of their respective films, have the branding quality of a logo mark, not unlike that of Hitchcock's cameos, something that adds a non-diegetic dimension to the directors' outlines and in addition opens the films to the outside world.

In Allen's narratives the director's emblematic image merges his public persona with his screen roles. The inadequacy of his eyeglasses in scenarios such as the year 2173 in *Sleeper* (1973), nineteenth-century Russia in *Love and Death* (1975), or medieval England in *Everything You Always Wanted to Know about Sex … But Were Afraid to Ask* (1972) prevents the actor's complete fusion with his characters. Rather than be engulfed by his narratives, Allen's image refuses to be completely absorbed in the filmic text; it chemically precipitates, evoking both the real man and his other pictures. The same holds true for Godard: his eyeglasses, disheveled hair, and cigarette (later replaced by a cigar) attach an emblematic dimension to his screen persona—one that extends to the fools he interprets in his 1980s films.

On the narrative level, the persistence of Allen's visual style attests to his incapacity to be other than the one character he incessantly incarnates: the nervous middle-class Jewish man from Brooklyn with a strong artistic vein and a domineering mother; hopelessly urban; a film and jazz lover; skeptical about religion and psychoanalysis; and fearful of diseases, death, nature, and California. All such traits have their share of biographical truth, however variable. For our purposes, they associate Allen with the parts he has played throughout his career. Although obviously not identical to the real man, Allen's characters function as reminders of his biographical self and, consequently, of Allen as the author of films in which he appears.

Figures 3.1. and 3.2. Godard's silhouette dissolves into Woody Allen's portrait in *Meetin' WA* (1986).

Figures 3.3. and 3.4. Allen's eyeglasses prevent him from completely disappearing into the characters he plays in *Sleeper* (1973) and *Love and Death* (1975).

Figure 3.5. Godard's silhouette in *Carmen* (1983) acquires an emblematic quality.

Likewise, Godard's fools either refer to the director's autobiography or become vehicles for meditations on the medium and on the commerce of cinema. But most importantly, as with his American counterpart, Godard's fools constitute "licensed destroyer[s] of convention and ceremony," as Colin MacCabe pertinently observes (256), traits that do not really contrast with his other, restless, questioning, devil's-advocate-like appearances as Jean-Luc Godard, the auteur, both on- and offscreen. It is as an outsider that the fool becomes the author's mask, constituting what Bakhtin defined as "the mode of existence of a man who is in life, but not of it, life's perpetual spy and reflector" (161). Says Bakhtin, "At last specific forms had been found to reflect private life and make it public" (161). Following along these lines, Godard also refuses to fully merge with the films; in their own ways, the images of Allen and Godard evoke the outside world, often through biographical references. The filmmakers then act as elements of disruption, both on the level of plot and on the level of the viewer's engagement with individual works, for the author's presence establishes the film as artifice. However, in the films of Godard, this presence has greater impact on narrative closure than in those of Allen, as my study shows.

WOODY ALLEN'S BORDER CROSSINGS: THE AUTHOR AS TRESPASSER

The aforementioned emblematic quality of Allen and Godard's silhouettes inevitably brings to mind Hitchcock's cameos. The quick appearances by the British director in his works also produce a momentary alienation; they are a textual reminder of the real human being behind the film, but one who soon withdraws from the frame and allows for the viewer's full submersion in the world of the story. Likewise, the appearances by Woody Allen and Godard brand the films they direct with their signature. In the case of Allen, his body and his physical traits are as constitutive of an authorial mark as his films' recognizable plots, character types, and visual design. The auteur's recurring physical presence impersonates his style—the emblematic body links author and aesthetics. Yet, if in the case of Hitchcock we are only momentarily cued to the auteur existing outside of the film, Allen's presence is a constant reminder of the biographical artist. And whereas Godard's fools are peripheral to the narrative, Allen is for the most part the very star of his movies—which leads me to question whether his image is, like that of Hitchcock, perceived as foreign to the diegesis, producing alienation, or whether, on the contrary, when he plays a character in the story, the author's image is inevitably swallowed by text, reduced to an effect, thereby losing its indexical property.

The latter may be true for other actors-directors—Clint Eastwood, for example, whose performances do not evoke his authorial function. But Allen belongs to a much more self-reflexive universe, appearing in the guise of unreliable narrators, distantiating us from the narrative by means of citations and parody, metalepses, direct address, jokes that evoke events external to the plot, and autobiographical references to his lower-middle-class background, his Jewishness, and his Brooklyn childhood. This combination of alienation and autobiography causes Allen to personify one of the films' elements of disruption. Movies such as *Everything You Always Wanted to Know about Sex … But Were Afraid to Ask, Sleeper, Love and Death, Annie Hall* (1977), *Stardust Memories* (1980), and *Zelig* (1983), to name but a few, let themselves be contaminated by the outside world, opening the films up for dialogue with real-life events.

The medieval fool played by Allen in the first episode of *Everything You Always Wanted to Know about Sex,* for example, simply does not fit into the story world. When seeking a sorcerer's advice on aphrodisiacs, Allen's fool declares his preference for anything he could get "without a prescription," eliciting a comic effect from an anachronism that is typical of both the avant-garde (for example, Alfred Jarry's *Ubu Roi*) and vaudeville acts.[5] By invok-

Figure 3.6. Allen's Fool cannot fit into the story in *Everything You Always Wanted to Know about Sex … But Were Afraid to Ask* (1972).

ing a current dynamics that reminds the spectator of the present and of "real life," Allen temporarily breaks with the fictional illusion, taking us away from the medieval tale. This anachronism configures an estrangement on the level of the plot that does not allow for the consolidation of the diegesis—it constitutes an instance of everyday life's invasion of the domain of fiction. Similar dynamics abound in Allen's filmography and are obviously found in period movies such as *Love and Death,* where in nineteenth-century Russia his character mentions, for example, tips and extras as he confabulates on Napoleon's earnings, or in the time-travel plot of *Sleeper,* where after waking up some 200 years into the future, the protagonist makes references to Greenwich Village and vegetarian restaurants, perceived as just as alienating because they refer the viewer back to the everydayness of present time.

This sense of presentness, in turn, evokes the mode of stand-up comedy. It is this sense of not belonging, which lends an estranged, alien, and foreign quality to Allen's characters, that inspires my analogy with Bakhtin's theories—their otherness lies not only in their anarchic behavior but also in the invocation of the world that originated them, which in the case of Bakhtin's fools is the public square. The rogue, the clown, and the fool, Bakhtin says, "create around themselves their own special little world, their own chronotope" (159). Thus, where in Bakhtin the fool brings the theatricality of the public square into the novel, in Allen it is the stand-up performance that invades the fiction—the acting style that, as we know, is the genesis of the director's career as a comic artist. It follows that Allen's nearly immutable form of self-display and his incessant joke-telling evoke also his stand-up persona, further referring us to the author's biography. After all, for the most part, stand-up comics do not present themselves as fictional figures, appearing instead under their own identity. However performative, and however fictive their stories, such comedians do not usually incarnate characters in the strict sense; whether exaggerating real facts for comic purposes or describing imagined situations, their job is to tell jokes and comment on current events, not to consolidate an altogether fictional world. On the contrary, they tell anecdotes *as if* they had happened in the real world—or at least in the world experienced by their audience—irrespective of how implausible their stories may be.[6]

In his book on stand-up comedy, Oliver Double calls attention to the importance of the present time of the performance, which Tony Allen defines as the "now" agenda, saying that "straight drama shows events from another place and another time, but with stand-up the events happen right here in the venue" (173). Needless to point out, Double is referring to live performance and to the importance of being attuned to the reactions of an audience in a theater. Yet this connection with the real world of the theater (the here and now for the audience) calls for an analogy with the anti-illusionistic dimension of Allen's gags. Many of the comic lines in *Annie Hall,* for example, bring the viewer back to reality. Jokes about the assassination of JFK, Nazis, cultural magazines such as *Commentary,* or Poland (Allen being himself of Polish origin) break with the classical illusion of a self-enclosed fiction, reminding the audience of the here and now of their existence. The clearest example of this dynamics is the Marshall McLuhan scene, where Alvy Singer (Allen's character in *Annie Hall*) turns to the camera to say, "If life were only like this," after literally pulling the intellectual into the scene (and from outside of the narrative) only to support his argument against an arrogant professor pontificating in a movie theater.

For that matter, *Annie Hall* opens with a prologue structured as a stand-up routine—the first line delivered by Allen's hero is a joke about elderly women at a Catskills resort that simply serves the purpose of analogy, furthering no narrative information. Soon Alvy becomes an on-screen, confiding narrator explaining his personal project—to examine his relationship with Annie. Set against a blank wall, the character-narrator's first image isolates him from context—the neutrality of the set places him outside of a specified space. Indeed, this unanchored space evokes another domain of the fool discussed by Bakhtin, namely the entr'acte, the intermission, the interval between two acts in a play.[7] Allen having started as a stand-up comic, such a space also invites identification between author and character. Further linking the director and his protagonist is the recycling of jokes Allen used in his 1960s stand-up routines in Alvy's own numbers and a Woody Allen appearance in *The Dick Cavett Show* standing in for his character in the film[8]—all of which color the fiction with biographical elements, rendering the diegesis vulnerable to the real. In what Nancy Pogel suggests is a postmodern impulse (12), the director also introduces real-life figures amid fictional ones (McLuhan in *Annie Hall*, American intellectuals in *Zelig*) and casts actors according to their past films or personal stories. Paul Simon plays a music producer in *Annie Hall*, Diane Keaton interprets a photographer/singer in the same film (activities she undertook in real life), and Mia Farrow was assigned the various roles of repressed Catholic (*Alice* [1990]), giving mother (*Alice, Hannah and Her Sisters* [1986]), and the daughter of famous and strong women (*Hannah, September* [1987], *Alice*), bringing to mind the actress's own origins (she is of Irish ancestry) and family (Farrow is the mother of fifteen children and the daughter of actress Maureen O'Sullivan). Most significantly in the area of blending of fantasy and reality, *Zelig* portrays a fictional character in documentary style.

The interplay between fiction and real events has incidentally always provided material for Allen's films, which often contemplate the relations between life and art. In *Annie Hall*, Alvy writes a play about his relationship with the title character, and the film was actually seen as a fictional account of Allen's own relationship with Keaton. *Manhattan*'s Isaac is exposed to public scrutiny when his ex-wife publishes an autobiography about their disastrous marriage—prefiguring, as Peter J. Bailey suggests, Farrow's memoir, *What Falls Away*, published after the couple's breakup in real life (Bailey 185). *Stardust Memories* is about a director longing to have his films express the anguish he experiences in life and follows Allen's first dramatic film, *Interiors* (1978). In *Hannah and Her Sisters*, Holly finally launches her writing career with a script based on her sister's privacy. Alice sells autobiographical facts as ideas for television shows. In *September* the character played by Sam Waterston moves between the biographies of his father and his friend's mother. *Deconstructing Harry* (1997) punishes its protagonist (a writer played by Allen) for exposing the intimacy of friends, relatives, and lovers. Finally, David Denby's review of *Husbands and Wives*

(1992) exemplifies how Allen's films are often perceived as autobiography—the critic confesses his embarrassment in the face of what he believed to be Allen's exposure of his relationship with Farrow (60).[9] The very character played by the director in this film writes a novel that ridicules his first encounter with his wife. In the end, the films that focus on the connections between life and art constitute a statement about how Allen's works are perceived—as attest the biographies by John Baxter and Eric Lax,[10] which draw comparisons between Allen's real life and fictional plots, and in a more critical fashion, the study of the director's oeuvre by Bailey, who analyzes those narratives discussing life as material for art.

Still, though in Allen's films self-reflexivity is translated into plot-driven narratives, the characters he plays do not really constitute psychological beings enclosed within the diegesis, but stand-up figures visiting scenarios they comment on by means of jokes. This characterization of Allen as alien to the plot is more evident in narratives bearing an ensemble structure (*Hannah and Her Sisters, Crimes and Misdemeanors* [1989], *Shadows and Fog* [1991], *Husbands and Wives, Everyone Says I Love You* [1996]); when Allen shares the centrality of the narrative with female partners (*Love and Death, Annie Hall, Manhattan Murder Mystery* [1993], *Small Time Crooks* [2000], *The Curse of the Jade Scorpion* [2001]); or when he simply plays a secondary role (*Anything Else* [2003], *Scoop* [2006]). But even when incarnating the protagonist, Allen often bears an outsider's look, as we have seen. Incorporating the "right to confuse" and to parody (Bakhtin 163) characteristic of both the fool and the stand-up comic, the director undertakes the role of a commentator who sometimes sets himself apart from the narrative—a trait that he shares with Godard, as the next section shows, but that causes the diegesis to constantly readapt to his "foreign" presence, as if wanting to assimilate the auteur to the point of dissolution—even though, as I stated earlier, Allen's image resists full immersion. However disturbing, Allen's disruptions are at the service more of comedy than of structural or political transgressions. Therein lies the main difference between the two directors.

What Allen does share with Godard is the taste for citations, which open the film to a dialogue with other works and other authors. In step with Roland Barthes's description of the author as orchestrator of preexisting discourses ("Death" 211), the citing director positions himself at the center not of production, but of reception. As we know, in "The Death of the Author," Barthes replaced the waning figure of a controlling, self-expressing writer with that of the "scriptor" who does not precede the writing, existing rather in the here and now of the enunciation (211). Citation thus defines the image of the author not as unified, but as dispersed. The resulting patchwork aesthetic echoes in the fool's theatrical rendition of a dissipated self. The characteristic lack of motor coordination in slapstick comedy, for example, points to an understanding of boundaries separating body from mind, movement from intention, thus constituting the individual not as unified, but as uncoordinated—the clown is constantly faced with the challenge of orchestrating his own body parts, as well as his movements. If in the works by Godard this sense of dissipation is magnified by the aesthetics of citation and extends to the film as a whole, Allen contains its destabilizing effect. However alienating the tributes he pays to directors such as Fellini, Eisenstein, Kubrick, and Bergman, the resulting distraction is only momentary because, unlike Godard, Allen does not allow for much digression. Still, his use of one-liners brings an element of fragmentation to his discourse that is transferred onto the films. Even if the jokes are not always exclusive to the characters played by the director, when voiced by other actors, they come across as a ventriloquism of sorts, as if Allen sometimes chose to express himself through characters other than the ones he plays. In any case, though integrating the director's fools with other characters, thereby lending a degree of uniformity to the diegesis, the instances in which actors mimic the director's gag style do not undermine the author's impulse to supersede boundaries. On the contrary, it is as if Allen bled into other characters, refusing to stay within the boundaries of his own body.

Allen's similar refusal to stay within the confines of the diegesis and his need to constantly surpass, in addition, the borders of the frame and look at the extra-filmic also take the form of self-conscious references to the workings of the apparatus. Brecht, of course, is as important a link between Godard and Allen as the Bakhtinian fool—they both follow the teachings of the German dramatist through the use of the direct address and the deconstructionist approach to the medium. The two directors create as much tension as harmony between image and sound tracks—but whereas Godard proceeds by dissonance and asynchrony, Allen contrasts the contents of each track so as to create contradictions, irony, and unreliable narrations. Alvy's voice-over discourse at the opening of *Annie Hall* calls attention both to his account's untrustworthiness and to the support of visual and verbal material in the making of films. Alvy openly admits his "trouble between reality and fantasy" while also addressing the coexistence of image and sound tracks—"showing" us his father ("There he is, and there I am"), thus assuming our viewing of the image. By the same token, in *Radio Days* (1987), Allen's voice-over narration alerts us that Rockaway, which he also admits romanticizing, "wasn't always as stormy and rain-swept like *this*," confident that we see the neighborhood in the visual track.

This form of direct address typically adopted by voice-over narrators constitutes the cinematic version of what in literature Gérard Genette calls author's metalepsis, "which consists of pretending that the poet [the narrator] 'himself brings about the effects he celebrates'" (234) through phrases indicating the author's control over the narrative.[11] In fact, the metalepsis grants such narrators the right to transition across diverse narrative levels. In the words of Genette, "any intrusion by the extradiegetic narrator or narratee into the diegetic universe (or by diegetic characters into a metadiegetic universe, etc.), or the inverse … produces an effect of strangeness that is either comical (when, as in Sterne or Diderot, it is presented in a joking tone) or fantastic" (235). It is through the comic use of such a device that Allen's fools are given free pass across the different spaces and the different temporalities separating the act of narrating from the narrative itself—as a result, the author's image crosses also the borders between narrative levels. For that matter, the conflation of temporalities in scenes depicting Alvy physically revisiting the space of his childhood at the opening of *Annie Hall* constitutes the visual rendition of metalepsis. It should be said, however, that despite Allen's refusal to stay within fixed territories, his creative processes are clearly placed in the realm of plot and do not completely obstruct narrative closure. In what follows I discuss how the foreignness embodied by Godard's fools constitutes a more radical break with the diegesis, to the extent that his characters render the frame malleable, expandable, and sometimes breakable.

"WHERE AM I?" GODARD'S FOOLS AND THE SPACE OF THE AUTHOR

In the works by Godard, the fools refer to the author's dispersed sense of self, as well as to his trajectory toward an increasingly marginal position in the film market. This dissipation of the self is partly the consequence of the director's aforementioned love of quoting, which often produces a collage effect manifested on the level of both the image (insert shots of paintings, photographs, or other films) and sound (dissonance, cacophony, juxtaposition of discourses and bits of music). As we know, Godard quotes indiscriminately, rarely distinguishing cited from original discourse and sometimes anarchically disposing of the works of others, as in the misattribution of Michel Mourlet's statement to Bazin at the beginning of *Contempt* (1963).[12] Following the lessons from "The Death of the Author," Godard's prac-tices point not so much to the demise, but to the refashioning of authorship. Godard gives body to the "scriptor" by presenting himself as receiver—an idea brilliantly explored in Kaja Silverman's study of *JLG/JLG: Self-Portrait in December*. Silverman sees this 1995 film as the maturation of a Godardian movement toward authorial divestiture that can be traced back to his shift to collective authorship in the late 1960s. It is well known that Godard has frequently tried to disappear as one type of author so as to be reborn in a different guise. The famous title "End of Cinema," which closed *Weekend* in 1967, labeled the closing of a stage in the director's career. *Weekend* passed into history as Godard's first last film, announcing his move from cinephilia to political militancy, soon to be followed by the transition from auteurism to collective authorship in his collaborations with the Dziga Vertov group. On the other hand, Godard has a number of first films, including *Breathless, Tout va bien,* which in 1972 marked his failed attempt to come back to mainstream cinema after the Dziga Vertov enterprise, and then *Numéro Deux* (1975), deemed Godard's "second first film," and *Slow Motion* (1980), which marked his return to the cinema after the video and television experiments with Anne-Marie Miéville. One could see *Carmen* (1983) as Godard's second last film: the director's quarrels with the crew gave material for dramatic statements about his retirement from the world of cinema, which nonetheless did not happen (MacCabe 286). The director's trajectory is thus marked by departures and comebacks, and though the consistency of his pursuits and meditations makes him an auteur par excellence, Silverman is right in defining his constant questioning and reshaping of his practices as a form of dying, as an altruistic impulse to define the author as receptacle. But this authorial divestiture, in Silverman's words, "is better understood as an ongoing process than as a realizable event." "The crucial question to ask Godard," she goes on to say, "is whether he is able to sustain himself there and elsewhere in the mode of dying" (34). The drama of authorial processes, the idea of the author as a principal actor in the battle for expression and communication, brings us back to "The Death of the Author." Writing, said Barthes, should be understood no longer as the "operation of recording, notation, representation, 'depiction,'" but as "a performative, a rare verbal form (exclusively given in the first person and in the present tense) in which the enunciation has no other content ... than the act by which it is uttered" (211). It is this emphasis on process that endows authorship with a dramatic dimension, positing the author as central actor. It follows that Godard's fools caricature the director's conception of his authorial self as dispersed, as a patchwork of influences, rather than as a fixed identity. Godard's fools are hence the embodiment of this disjointed self. But like Allen's characters, this fragmented being assumes a recognizable appearance whose immutability contrasts with narrative progression, setting him apart from the filmic universe. It is as if the auteur's image coagulated, refusing to dissolve in the narrative flow.

Furthermore, Godard's fools embody the director's casting of himself as maverick: marginality defines not only his particular place in the world of cinema but also the necessary condition of a true artist. As we move between the concept of the author as receiver and Godard's buffoonish performances in *Carmen, Soigne ta droite,* and *King Lear,* we find a contrast between elusiveness and exaggeration, disembodiment and the bodily lower stratum (to use another Bakhtinian idea), sublimation and caricature, introspection and externalization. *Carmen,* for example, transfers to the plot one of Godard's main struggles—the one against the film system. This is mirrored in the filmmaker's relative foreignness to the story, which is far more radical than Allen's. The director appears in the guise of Carmen's Uncle Jean, also referred to as Monsieur Godard. His body bears an aggressive quality resulting first from his grotesque behavior and vulgar language and second from his inability to fit in the narrative.[13] Further setting Godard's character apart is the generational gap between the director and his young cast—the designations "Uncle" and "Monsieur" indeed accentuate Godard's relative seniority, forging (however prematurely) his character's senility and by extension his isolation. Uncle Jean confines himself in a hospital so as to avoid contact with the real world. Based on Prosper Merimée's novel about a Spanish soldier who embarks on a life of crime for the love of a young gypsy, *Carmen* is about deception. The film's heroine belongs to a criminal gang that "fools" the character of Godard into helping them shoot a documentary that is nothing but a ploy, their real intention being to rob the rich. The central plot involves Carmen's relationship with a policeman, Joseph, whom she seduces during a robbery.

Uncle Jean's foreignness to the plot comes as a result of his way of disrupting narrative progression in each of his appearances. Like the traditional fool, he behaves in unusual and often vulgar ways that caricature the director's otherness to real and fictional worlds alike. This disruptive quality is partly due to grotesqueries that bring comic relief to the drama between Carmen and Joseph. But this fool's inappropriateness, which renders him alien, can be attributed also to the fact that his marginality functions as a reminder of Godard's biography, or of the realm of the extra-filmic. In one of the sequences mostly charged with biographical references, Uncle Jean meets with the leader of Carmen's gang, who poses as a film producer trying to con Godard's character into helping them with what he believes is a documentary, but which is actually a plan to kidnap a big manufacturer. During this meeting, which takes place in a Parisian café, Uncle Jean and the "producer" carry a conversation marked by a lack of communication to be blamed on the old man's elusive and nonsensical discourse, as well as on his inability to engage with plot elements—the details about the supposed shoot and Monsieur Godard's official agreement. Concurrently, the lack of chemistry between the characters echoes Godard's feelings of isolation in the world of cinema, the director's own battle to make himself understood. Uncle Jean's abrupt and unmotivated references to Van Gogh's search for the right tone of yellow, for example, and the insistence that one must always keep searching contribute nothing to the plot, but evoke Godard's own effort to find the "just image"—and are, of course, a reminder of the recurrence of Van Gogh's paintings in Godard's films. By the same token, the reference to Mao as a great cook (who "fed all of China") brings to mind his flirtation with Maoism in 1968. There is also, of course, the questioning of the boundaries between documentary and fiction when Uncle Jean momentarily scares the gang leader by asking if the documentary is really "true," indulging in a theoretical question (all documentaries are fiction) rather than suspecting the other's real intentions. Most importantly, Uncle Jean evokes Godard's directorial role when he provides us with scene and take numbers at the beginning of the sequence, as well as when he reprimands his actor for not finishing his dialogue, stopping him as he gets ready to leave the table. Finally, Godard's most clearly autobiographical statement is to explain, under the mask of his fool, that he has been "banished" from the "cinematographer" (in a typical tribute to Robert Bresson)—even though his temporary exile was voluntary.

Soigne ta droite shows Godard as equally foreign, this time as a character inspired by the protagonist of Dostoevsky's *The Idiot*. Introduced by a voice-over narrator as the Idiot, but addressed as Prince by the film's characters, Godard's fool is assigned the absurd mission of writing, shooting, and releasing a film in one day in order to be "forgiven" for an unnamed sin. The Idiot's task, however, is not exactly central—though apparently setting a goal for the narrative, this mission is dislodged by the appearance of "the Man" (played by comic actor Jacques Villeret), who takes up more screen time than Godard's fool, and by scenes of the musical group Les Rita Mitsuko rehearsing and recording songs.

Much like Uncle Jean and Dostoevsky's hero, the Idiot is sometimes grotesque, yet he is also simple and innocent in an unjust world that condemns him to exclusion. Like Dostoevsky's Myshkin, the part played by Godard constitutes a positive "other," who in the film calls attention to complexities overlooked by the rather absurd figures that populate his universe. Citing Baudelaire, the Idiot theorizes, for example, on "the smiling regret" to an incredulous grandmother sitting next to him on a plane.[14] Godard's character is also fond of wordplays, which the director has always deployed as an alienating device. In step with Godard's penchant for both puns and translation, the Idiot conflates, for example, an airline's "manager" (which the French designate by the English word) with the French *ménagère* (housewife). The generational gap addressed in *Carmen* is also hinted at in this sequence—after addressing the airline employee as "Mademoiselle," the Idiot is told that this title is no longer in use. Douglas Morrey reads this dialogue as a symptom of Godard's alleged remarks about the postfeminist "discomfiture of the male" (166), which again suggests the director's (and his character's) sense of exclusion. Most significantly to the feeling of estrangement, the Idiot also enacts slapstick routines, creating

Figure 3.7. Godard's grotesque and uncoordinated Prince/Idiot in *Soigne ta droite* (1987).

chaos from actions as simple as getting into a car, thereby giving life to the uncoordinated, dispersed body.

The same sense of alienation that involves Uncle Jean is manifested also in *Soigne ta droite,* this time through the use of titles and in the absence of proper names. The film's opening credits give us only surnames and, in addition, group male and female crew-members under the categories of "Messieurs" and "Mesdemoiselles," instituting a ceremonial, formal element to the credit sequences and perhaps unintentionally associating the director (singled out as "Monsieur Godard") with his homonymous roles in *Carmen* and *King Lear.* This humorous formality reverberates in the lack of character names in the narrative, where individuals are designated by generalizing labels such as the Man, the American, the Passenger, the Golfer. The emptying of identities that comes with this lack of individuation attests to the binary reasoning that opposes essence and surface, inner and outer selves, soul and body—the very same reasoning that is behind the challenges to self-expression and sincerity as the author's defining features. Referring to the Man, whose centrality to the narrative and sense of inadequacy turn him into the Idiot's double, the voice-over narrator describes this character's "last creative effort to get outside the dream, outside of fate, outside of chance, outside of form, outside of himself." This sense of imprisonment that calls for a desire to exceed one's body is what unites the Man and the Idiot—or, better still, what creates them as two manifestations of the same essence. Indeed, this yearning for extrapolating boundaries extends to the relationship between the character and the film; it brings together Godard's fools in *Carmen, Soigne ta droite,* and *King Lear,* all of whom exist in excess to the narrative, as if wanting to lie outside of it, or at least stand between the film and the real world. Not coincidentally, the main space occupied by the Idiot is the airplane he takes in order to deliver the finished film, which confines the fool to a site of transition—one that may be claustrophobic in its tightness, but which is nonetheless conveniently removed, unanchored, and unstable.

Like the Idiot, *King Lear*'s Professor Pluggy bears the burden of setting the goal for the film's narrative. But here Godard is turned into the object of desire for the real protagonist, Shakespeare the 5th (Peter Sellars), who while trying to write a new version of Shakespeare's play goes into a journey to find Pluggy, his purpose being to learn the secret of montage. But just as with the other Godardian fools, Pluggy takes up little screen time, remaining at the periphery. Further emphasizing his marginality is the fact that, as with Uncle Jean, Pluggy also has been locked away from the world, this time in an editing studio.

In *King Lear* the disjointed quality of Godard's fool is best epitomized by his character's untidy dreadlocks, made with wires and cables. In turn, Godard's authorial presence is felt in spite of his peripheral position and the lack of clarity about his narrative role; after all, the mad editing guru is a constant reminder of the director's existence. In fact, Godard evokes the author's separate identity when at the beginning of the film he gives away some production notes as a narrator named Godard, but who nonetheless speaks in the foolish, buffoon-like voice of Pluggy. Later in the film Godard and Pluggy are once again conflated by Shakespeare the 5th, who refers to him as a man named "Godard, Pluggy or something," at once equating artist and character and revealing the character as artifice. Finally, like Uncle Jean, Pluggy eventually voices Godard's famous takes on the cinema, such as the concern with the primacy of the image over the word and the meditations on the revelatory potential of film. Godard goes as far as to establish a connection between Pluggy and the revealing power that, in the director's view, constitutes the essence of cinema. At the end of the film, Godard sacrifices his fool, repeating another recurring aphorism, this one borrowed from Saint Paul, which says, "the image will reappear in the time of resurrection."[15] Pluggy's sacrifice echoes the near death of the Idiot in a fall from the aircraft's open door and Uncle Jean's declared desire to go to the moon in order to finance his movie. Godard's fools thus lend their awkward bodies to what appears to be a lost cause—the production of films at the margins of society.

After all, these fools become vehicles for the author's inquiries about his own place. When Carmen first visits Uncle Jean in the hospital, he startles as she knocks on his door, asking, "Where am I?" This is too brief a moment in the film; indeed, Uncle Jean promptly rephrases his question, saying, "I mean, who is it?" However, this Freudian slip encapsulates Godard's self-conscious questioning of his position in the world of cinema and also in the world of the very film in which he acts. The hospital, the airplane, and the editing suite function as allegories for the entr'acte, the space of transition, including the one between Godard's real and screen images. But these spaces are also allegories of Godard's self-imposed exile, the equivalent of the Swiss town of Rolle, the place where he retreated when he refused to participate in the commerce of films and where to this day he indulges in his right not to understand. We find also a carnivalesque inversion where the work's creator and main authority figures as marginal and where costumes and role-play become vehicles for the uncensored expression of the self. *Carmen, Soigne ta droite,* and *King Lear* dramatize the tension between exposure and masking. To be sure, the mask typically allows for the full expression of the artist who wears it—here it allows for the expression of Godard's frustrations.

Nevertheless, even if these fools evoke the author's biography, they are far from finalizing, from organizing the author's life in a logical series of causally linked events. The biographical author in Godard's films could not be more removed from Barthes's worst fear, that biography "would exceed the body, give a meaning to life, forge a destiny" (*Pleasure* 56). Quite the opposite—Godard's fools might evoke autobiography, but they do not narrate the man. They become, instead, the very instrument for the negation of closure—for that matter, the fact that all fools bear slash names, some of which embed the director's own, further dramatizes their instability as independent entities. Godard's mode of self-inscription questions his own authority, as well as the autonomy of the texts he produces. To borrow Jacques Rivette's expression in his call for a move away from a supposedly self-involved and introspective cinephilia in the early 1960s, the self-inscribed author may very well "unframe" the film, opening it up to the outside world. Far from emptying the author's function—far from rendering him abstract—this disjointed body gives him a corporeal existence.

RESISTING DISSOLUTION

If in Woody Allen's films the struggles that define the author as a protagonist in the saga to communicate inner feelings and worldviews are narrativized, Godard's fools persistently sidestep from the narrative grid. In other words, Allen transfers his artistic concerns to the story, experiencing them through his characters. Allen's fools blend more easily with his costars and with the overall narrative than do Godard's unadjusted buffoons—what is more, Allen's resistance to staying within boundaries is intermittent. His fools seem to visit the entr'acte only once in a while, whereas Godard's characters never leave this transitory space—there are variations in quality and degree separating the American and French filmmakers. It is therefore worth asking again the extent to which reality and fiction really mix in Allen's films, which brings me once more to the position of the author in relation to the film: does Allen bridge the film and the outside world, or is he swallowed by the text?

I have suggested that Allen's films keep readjusting to his foreign body, allowing for a sense of closure of which Godard completely deprives us. Still, like with his French counterpart, Allen's relative foreignness reconnects the film author's textual and phenomenological beings; the dynamics akin to both the Bakhtinian fool and the mode of stand-up comedy restore indexicality to this figure. However, though by connecting the film with the real artist, these directors may establish the author as origin, and however consistent may be their understanding of film as a legitimate tool for individual self-expression, the dramatization of their creative and identity crises shuns traditional conceptions of control and authority. In fact, Allen and Godard use their "foolish" bodies as instruments for the disruption of closure, as they disturb any sense of completeness and fixedness, even if to different degrees. This openness, in turn, seals the connection between the film and the outside world; the authors' bodies are agents allowing for the interpenetration between the image and the real. The spatial in-betweenness characteristic of the fool suggests its refusal to let itself be framed or contained by the fiction, to fully belong to the depicted universe. The authors' constant evocation of biographical elements, historical events, the present time, and other films is what defines them as the Bakhtinian fool and, in the case of Allen, as a stand-up comic, both of which are "other" to the universes they comment on and also to the realm of classical film narrative. It is as elements foreign to the depicted world that the self-inscribed directors open this world up to what lies beyond the diegesis, transgress the borders of the screen, and unframe the film.

ENDNOTES

I would like to thank Carla Marcantonio and Peter Stanfield for their inestimable comments and suggestions and Robert Stam for his insights on an earlier and unpublished version of this article. I also would like to thank Moses Malekia for his help with the images.

1. For an account of the origins of stand-up comedy and fools, see Mintz 71–80.
2. I should note that we can find an earlier version of Godard's fools in *Vladimir et Rosa*, which he directed with the Dziga Vertov Group in 1971, and a later one in *Les enfants jouent à la Russie,* from 1993.
3. Godard was born in 1930, Allen in 1935.
4. This interview is punctuated with appearances of Godard as an unnamed fool-like figure very similar to his character in *King Lear*—which incidentally features a Woody Allen cameo.
5. I would like to thank Robert Stam for pointing this out to me in the aforementioned earlier version of this article.
6. Allen's stand-up routines, for that matter, used to include tales that bordered on the absurd.
7. Incidentally, see Carla Marcantonio for discussion of the sense of an authorial presence in the entr'acte of Max Ophuls's *Letter from an Unknown Woman.*
8. See Bailey 59.
9. For a very interesting discussion of the audience's perception of this film, see Sobchack 258–85.
10. See Baxter and Lax.
11. Genette lists a number of examples, including Diderot's *Jacques le fataliste,* where the narrator inquires, "What would prevent me from *getting the Master married* and *making him a cuckold?*" and, addressing the reader, says, "If it gives you pleasure, *let us set* the peasant girl back in the saddle behind her escort, *let us let* them go and *let us come back* to our two travelers" (234).

12. In *La Cinéphilie,* Antoine De Baecque attributes *Contempt's* opening statement that "[t]he cinema substitutes for our gaze a world more in harmony with our desires" to Michel Mourlet's "Sur an art ignoré" (216). Godard's voice-over narration attributes it to Bazin.
13. Illustrating Uncle Jean's vulgarity is the scene in which, hoping that a fever will allow him to stay indefinitely in a clinic, he tells a young and attractive female nurse that the fever will come if he sticks his fingers up her ass.
14. See Morrey 167.
15. This sentence appears also in *Histoire(s) du cinéma.*

REFERENCES

Bakhtin, M. M. *The Dialogic Imagination.* Trans. Caryl Emerson and Michael Holquist. Austin: U of Texas P, 2001. Print.

Barthes, Roland. "The Death of the Author." *Theories of Authorship: A Reader.* Ed. John Caughie. London: Routledge & Kegan Paul in association with the British Film Institute, 1981. Print.

———. *The Pleasure of the Text.* Trans. Richard Miller. New York: Hill and Wang, 1975. Print.

De Baecque, Antoine. *La Cinéphilie: Invention d'un regard, histoire d'une culture 1944–1968.* Paris: Fayard, 2003. Print.

Bailey, Peter J. *The Reluctant Film Art of Woody Allen.* Lexington: UP of Kentucky, 2001. Print.

Baxter, John. *Woody Allen: A Biography.* London: HarperCollins, 1998. Print.

Deleuze, Gilles. *Cinema 2: The Time-Image.* Minneapolis: U of Minnesota P, 1989. Print.

Denby, David. "Imitation of Life." *New York* 21 Sept. 1992: 60. Print.

Double, Oliver. *Getting the Joke: The Inner Workings of Standup Comedy.* London: Methuen, 2005. Print. Genette, Gérard. *Narrative Discourse.* Ithaca: Cornell UP, 1980. Print.

Lax, Eric. *Woody Allen: A Biography.* New York: Knopf, 1991. Print.

MacCabe, Colin. *Godard: A Portrait of the Artist at Seventy.* New York: Farrar, Straus and Giroux, 2003. Print.

Marcantonio, Carla. "Letter from an Unknown Woman." *Senses of Cinema.* N.p., 5 May 2006. Web. 27 Aug. 2009.

Mintz, Lawrence E. "Standup Comedy as Social and Cultural Meditation." *American Quarterly* 37.1 (Spring 1985): 71–80. Print.

Morrey, Douglas. *Jean-Luc Godard.* Manchester: Manchester UP, 2005. Print.

Pogel, Nancy. *Woody Allen.* Boston: Twayne, 1987. Print.

Silverman, Kaja. "The Author as Receiver." *October* 96 (Spring 2001): 17–34. Print.

Sobchack, Vivian. *Carnal Thoughts: Embodiment and Moving Image Culture.* Berkeley: U of California P, 2004. Print.

MARILYN FABE

FEMINISM AND FILM FORM: PATRICIA ROZEMA'S *I'VE HEARD THE MERMAIDS SIGNING*

All of the films I have considered thus far have been made by male directors. What difference might it make—in a film's style, content, or representation of women—when a woman directs? To consider this question, I turn to an exceptional film written and directed by a woman, the Canadian director Patricia Rozema's *I've Heard the Mermaids Singing.* The film, made on a tiny budget, had limited distribution by Miramax and is rarely seen now outside of college film courses, but it was the surprise hit at the Cannes Film Festival in 1987, and winner of the Prix de Jeunesse for the best first feature film that year. The film was subsequently voted one of the ten best Canadian films ever made by one hundred international critics, filmmakers, and scholars.[1] Rozema's offbeat, innovative style and the psychological themes she explores in her film reflect a keen consciousness of the issues raised by feminist critics regarding the way women have been represented in films directed by men.

FEMINIST FILM CRITICISM

Most feminist approaches to film share a common assumption: the ways women are represented in mainstream commercial films reflect, justify, reinforce, and naturalize what Molly Haskell in her pioneering book *From Reverence to Rape* calls "The Big Lie" of patriarchy, that women are

Marilyn Fabe, "Feminism and Film Form: Patricia Rozema's I've Heard the Mermaids Singing," *Closely Watched Films: An Introduction to the Art of Narrative Film Technique*, pp. 207-227, 266-267. Copyright © 2014 by University of California Press. Reprinted with permission.

inferior to men and rightly occupy a subordinate place in culture. Feminist film critics work to raise our consciousness about the negative images of women in film in order to denaturalize these images, to expose them as cultural constructs, not mirror reflections of the way women really are.

The first feminist film critics took a sociological approach to the subject, exemplified by two books that came out simultaneously in the early 1970s, Marjorie Rosen's *Popcorn Venus* (1973) and the above-mentioned *From Reverence to Rape* (1974), by Molly Haskell. Both Rosen and Haskell persuasively demonstrate that women on the screen are often nothing more than cultural stereotypes of women—the flapper, the vamp, the virgin, the Madonna, the femme fatale, the gold digger, the hooker with a heart of gold. Moreover, despite the fact that the rise of the Hollywood film industry coincided with the crest of the first wave of feminism in America, when more and more women were entering the labor force, attending college, earning doctorates, and entering the professions, most movies still ended in marriage, which was presented as the only real fulfillment of the heroine's heart's desire. Marjorie Rosen in *Popcorn Venus* asks, "Why did screen heroines covet 'winning the love of another' above all else? Why did they not value themselves? Their work? An independent future? Or dedication beyond that of their hearts?" Hollywood, she concludes, was determined to "squash feminine self determination."[2] The result was the depiction of deplorably bad role models for those women in the audience who aspired to more than the most conventional, male-centered definitions of what a woman is and what a woman wants.

The sociological approach greatly contributed to an awareness of how restricted images of women in film often were, but it was limited. Academic feminist critics, influenced by semiology, the study of how meaning is produced in communication systems such as language, literature, and film, suggested a more sophisticated and nuanced approach. For these critics, the argument that women are presented as negative stereotypes or poor role models in film does not go far enough toward explaining how Hollywood films reinforce the idea of women's inferiority. What really matters is not so much the type of woman the fictive character in the film represents, but what she comes to signify within the whole textual system of the film's narrative. Hollywood, for example, can easily, and often did, serve up a strong, ambitious career woman—the kind Katharine Hepburn is famous for playing and the kind of woman Rosalind Russell plays in *His Girl Friday*. Yet at the same time, the image of the strong woman is undercut by subtle and not so subtle narrative effects. Rosalind Russell's Hildy, for all her talent as a newspaper reporter, remains distinctly inferior to Walter Burns. He knows from the start what is best for her, and the film brings her around to his point of view. In the end, she depends on him to rescue her from an inappropriate marriage and to teach her what she really wants—to be a newspaper reporter and remarried to him. Thus despite the positive image of Hildy as an ace reporter, she remains *his* girl Friday.

An even better example of how a seemingly progressive Hollywood film has it both ways— presents a smart ambitious woman but ultimately contains and undercuts her—is George Cukor's *Adam's Rib* (1949). Here Katharine Hepburn plays Amanda, a feminist lawyer who successfully defends a woman on trial for shooting her husband point-blank when she catches him with another woman. Amanda wins the case by pleading that the woman is a victim of society's double standard. If a *man* had committed the same crime, that is, shot his unfaithful wife, she argues, society would sympathize with him and set him free. From a purely sociological perspective, *Adam's Rib* appears to be a subversive film.

So, what's wrong with this picture? If you look at the film from the perspective of how meaning or gender ideology is produced in the text, it is apparent that *Adam's Rib* is profoundly negative in its attitude toward its bright, ambitious heroine, proving that even if the heroine seems progressive, the movie need not be. Although Amanda convinces the jury and wins the case, the film's narrative is constructed in such a way that the spectator feels the jury is wrong. This point is not subtle. My son, who was seven years old when we watched the film together, said right after the jury's verdict was announced, "They made a mistake, didn't they, Mommy?"

The film's plot is constructed in such a way that we never doubt that Amanda is wrong-headed in her defense of the outraged wife. The first sequence of the film shows us the crime. We see an emotionally distraught, hysterical woman (Judy Holliday in her best dumb blond mode) stalking her husband and compulsively eating. When she catches him in his love nest with another woman, she shoots at him point-blank, failing to kill him only because of her incompetence. She doesn't know how to use the gun and she closes her eyes when she shoots. This account, which the film presents as the "real" event—it is presented not as a flashback through a character's point of view but from the perspective of an omniscient narrator—is distorted by Amanda's reconstruction of it during the trial. She coaches the defendant to tell the story in a way that makes it seem as if she was just trying to scare her husband, not kill him. Since the audience has seen the "truth," it is clear that Hepburn wins her case only by lying. Amanda also literally turns the courtroom into a circus when, in order to prove that women are equal to men (a point that has nothing substantive to do with the case), she instructs one of her witnesses, a female circus "strong man," to lift up her husband (Spencer Tracy), the prosecuting attorney in the case, who is made to look ridiculous as he dangles helplessly over the courtroom.

Hence, despite the characterization of the film's heroine as a smart, ambitious, successful lawyer, the deeply conservative ideological subtext of the film asserts that putting women in positions of power is dangerous to our legal system and society. It means chaos over order, lying over the truth, and the humiliation of men. Man-killers will be set loose on society. Like the title *His Girl Friday,* the very title *Adam's Rib* reflects a condescending attitude toward women. The title refers to Amanda, Adam's wife, reducing her to the body part the biblical Adam had to sacrifice for the sake of Eve's creation. In this light, Amanda can be read as a modern-day Eve moving onward and upward in her ruination of the male sex. From the way she humiliates (ribs) her husband and compulsively competes with him in a man's world, it is not too hard to guess what part of his anatomy she is after next.

CINEMA-SPECIFIC APPROACHES TO WOMEN IN FILM

Thus far we have been discussing the way meaning is constructed through narrative strategies that undermine or qualify seemingly progressive images of women in film. But, since this kind of analysis can apply not only to film but to literature and drama as well, academic feminist film critics went beyond considerations of the ways female characters appear within film plots to address the way women's inferior secondary position in culture was inscribed in the use of the film medium itself. Drawing upon and extending the theories of French psychoanalytic film theorist Christian Metz, feminist film theorists came up with even more subtle and sophisticated tools of analysis to demonstrate how film's unique means of representation and specific appeal help construct or naturalize denigrating ways of looking at women.

Christian Metz theorizes that the primal pleasure of cinema lies in its satisfaction of a primal urge—our *scopophilia,* or love of looking. In the live theater, Metz observes, we watch actors who are aware of and hence implicitly give consent to our presence. At the cinema, the actors on the screen are in a time and space radically elsewhere. Even when looking directly into the lens of the camera, the actors can never really return our gaze. Hence we can look at them to our heart's content, but they can never see us looking. At the root of cinema's appeal, Metz believes, is a license for a lawless looking, a guiltless, because safe, voyeurism.[3] The very first cinema spectators viewed moving pictures through Edison's Kinetoscope, a peephole device, which foregrounded the voyeuristic appeal of the images. As Alfred Hitchcock made evident in *Rear Window* (1954), the rectangle of the cinema screen is like a window on the world through which we often peer at the private lives of people with prurient fascination. At the cinema we are all peeping Toms.

The voyeuristic pleasure offered at the cinema, however, is distinctly inflected by gender. (Even my use of the term "peeping Tom" genders the peeper male.) The thrust of much feminist film criticism, influenced by Laura Mulvey's formative essay, "Visual Pleasure and Narrative Cinema," has been that most mainstream films assume a male spectator and play to male pleasure by visually objectifying and eroticizing the women on the screen.[4] Whatever happens to be the heroine's function in the plot, a necessary component of her appeal is usually sexual: her appearance pleases the man on the screen and the men in the audience who identify with the camera's eroticizing gaze. Often the narrative action is suspended as the woman on the screen becomes primarily an erotic object to be looked at.

In *Coma* (Michael Crichton, 1978), for example, the heroine (Genevieve Bujold) is a physician in a major hospital who lives with her fiancé, who is also a doctor. Soon after she conducts major surgery, we see her at home arguing with him over whose turn it is to get dinner. As the two quibble, the man is standing fully clothed at the bathroom door gazing at the woman, who is standing stark naked in the shower. Later in the film, as the heroine perilously searches the ventilation system of the hospital for clues that will expose a crime that led to her friend's death, she is obliged to remove her pantyhose to achieve a more secure footing, an action captured by a voyeuristic camera looking up from below. Feminist film critics argue that the apparatus of the cinema extends and intensifies an enduring tradition in Western art, a tradition which the art historian John Berger sums up in his famous dictum: "Men act and women appear."[5] These conventions of looking in film, which give activity to male characters and passivity to female characters, are replicated on the level of a film's plot. Male characters are traditionally the heroes, the doers, the rescuers, or even the psychotic killers, whereas the women are traditionally the hero's reward, the rescuee, or the victim.[6]

In "Visual Pleasure and Narrative Cinema," Mulvey uses psychoanalysis as a political tool to investigate the psychic roots of why women are eroticized and disempowered in mass-media representation. At the root of the problem, she argues, is the male child's castration anxiety when he discovers that his mother lacks a penis. This, according to Freud, is a momentous discovery because it signals to the little boy that he could lose his too. The trauma of the boy's discovery of his mother's "lack," Freud believed, helps to catapult him out of his mother's sphere into an identification with his father (who has the valued penis) as well as into the cultural place of power and privilege which having the penis signifies in a patriarchal culture. But traces of castration anxiety forever remain in the boy's unconscious, making women ambivalent figures in the male psyche. They are objects of erotic desire but also of scorn and contempt (they lack something the boy has) and also fear and dread (they remind the boy of what he has to lose). Mulvey's main point is that for men, women signify castration, a disturbing idea which forever threatens to break through into consciousness and thereby interfere with their erotic pleasure.

In the medium of film, Mulvey goes on to argue, men have found a perfect system of representation which allows them both maximum erotic pleasure and the disavowal of their castration anxiety. In the large majority of mainstream films, Mulvey notes, the point of view or the gaze is predominantly filtered through the eyes of a male character. That is, we see the action through a male's eyes, and what he is looking at is often the figure of a sexy woman, as in the example of the woman in the shower observed by her fiancé in *Coma*. This eroticizing gaze, according to Mulvey, gives the male spectator who identifies with the male character on the screen a feeling of power, control, and heightened virility, counteracting male fear of women's lack. Women are also made nonthreatening in films through plots in which women are dominated, investigated, found guilty, and disempowered. The logic here is: "*She* is lacking, humiliated, guilty, weak—not me."

A final filmic strategy to counteract the threat of women's lack is to deny or disavow it by an extreme idealization of women on the screen. Only ravishingly beautiful women with perfect bodies and regular features become film stars, and these women are made even more perfect through an arsenal of special lenses and lighting techniques. The ultra-perfection of the female star, Mulvey theorizes, exists to disavow her imperfection, the lack of a penis, which makes her threatening to male viewers. In addition, costumes of female stars often include oversized hats, spike-heeled shoes, long black stockings or gloves, or flowing scarves, all of which, Mulvey suggests, are fetishistic phallic stand-ins, objects that symbolize the penis and reassure the male viewer that there is nothing about these women to fear and dread. The camera can play a role in disavowing the woman's lack by isolating parts of the woman's body in closeup shots, focusing on just her hands, her legs, her feet, or her breasts—all of which, like the fetish objects which adorn her body, stand in for the missing penis. The bodies of women on film tend to be seen in pieces, the camera focusing in on close-ups of body parts much more than it does in photographing the bodies of men, which are more likely to be seen in medium or full shots. The special (or specialized) treatment reserved for women in film demonstrates conclusively for Mulvey that films are cut to the measure of male desire.

Although it was criticized from a number of perspectives,[7] "Visual Pleasure and Narrative Cinema" was enormously influential, because it made viewers acutely aware of the prevalence of the male gaze in the cinema and the ways in which women, much more than men, were fetishized on the screen. One only needs to look at "The Lady in the Tutti Frutti Hat" number from Busby Berkeley's musical *The Gang's All Here* (1943), in which scantily clad chorus girls perform suggestive dances with giant bananas positioned at their crotches, to know that Mulvey was onto *something*.

Mulvey's article remains important because at the end she raises the issue of how women filmmakers can create alternative conventions to liberate cinema from male-centered practices of representation. At the conclusion of "Visual Pleasure and Narrative Cinema," she recommends the overthrow of the whole system of voyeuristic pleasure as the basis of narrative film:

> There is no doubt that this [the disappearance of filmic devices that invite voyeuristic pleasure] destroys the satisfaction, pleasure and privilege of the "invisible guest," and highlights how film has depended on voyeuristic active/passive mechanisms. Women, whose image has continually been stolen and used for this end, cannot view the decline of the traditional film form with anything much more than sentimental regret.[8]

Patricia Rozema's *I've Heard the Mermaids Singing* is an especially appropriate film to discuss in the context of Mulvey's call for a counter-cinema, because in a number of ways it does what Mulvey suggests. It subverts most male-centered conventions of female representation by refusing the voyeuristic pleasure of objectifying or fetishizing women and it also interferes with the male-active, female-passive dynamics of most mainstream films. At the same time, however, *Mermaids* is visually appealing, emotionally complex, and fun to watch, whether or not one is consciously aware of the conventions it is subverting.

I'VE HEARD THE MERMAIDS SINGING AS COUNTERCINEMA

The title *I've Heard the Mermaids Singing* is a quotation from T. S. Eliot's "The Love Song of J. Alfred Prufrock." In the poem, Prufrock is an alienated, painfully self-conscious ("Do I dare to eat a peach?"), middle-aged bachelor who senses beauty in the world but can never capture or create it. In the poem he laments, "I have heard the mermaids singing, each to each / I do not think that they will sing to me."[9] He is an outsider in the realms of love and art. Despite the gender, age, and class difference between Prufrock and Polly (Sheila McCarthy), the film's protagonist, Polly shares not only the first initial of Prufrock's name but his sad predicament. Still unmarried at age thirty-one, she refers to herself as a spinster. An orphan (her parents died when she was twenty-one), she supports herself by being a temporary part-time worker for a Person Friday agency, which places women in low-level positions, despite the politically correct update of the agency's name. Her real passion and pleasure in life, however, is photography. The walls of her small apartment are thick with her photos, images she has captured on film of things that she loves. Her problem is that she has no one other than herself with whom to share her rich internal world.

If this were a mainstream film, Polly's lack would most likely be filled by the narrative. She would find a man and the world would at last recognize her talent. Yet though Polly gains neither recognition nor a partner, the film has a genuinely feel-good ending, albeit not in the conventional Hollywood mode. Rozema was able to challenge mainstream film conventions because she was not aiming her film at a mass-market audience. In an interview she confides that "I hoped for the respect—very secretly and quietly—of Margarethe von Trotta, Wim Wenders, Woody Allen, or Bill Forsyth."[10]

Plot Synopsis

Polly's story, which is framed by a videotaped image of herself narrating her tale as if she were directly addressing the film audience, begins when her temporary agency sends her to assist Gabrielle St. Pères (Paule Baillargeon), the curator and owner of a small art gallery. Gabrielle is an attractive, wealthy, articulate, sophisticated older woman whom Polly greatly admires. Despite Polly's clerical inadequacies, the curator (the name by which Polly refers to Gabrielle throughout the film) enjoys Polly's presence and makes her position permanent. Polly's happiness is somewhat tempered by the return of Mary (Ann-Marie McDonald), a young artist and Gabrielle's ex-lover. But since Polly defines her love for the curator as platonic—"I just loved how she talked and wanted her to teach me everything"—she manages to coexist with Mary, still happy to have her job and to bask in the daily presence of her beloved mentor.

At her birthday party, the curator, having obviously had too much to drink, confides to Polly that she is depressed because she knows she will forever fail to achieve her greatest desire in life, which is to create one immortal and enduring painting. Recently, when she tried to sign up for an adult art course (the sort where housewives learn landscape painting), she was devastated when the instructor refused to admit her, deeming her work "simple minded." But when Polly sees the curator's work, she is dazzled by its beauty. "I didn't even have to pretend to like it," she tells us. When the curator falls into a drunken sleep, Polly takes one of her paintings home. Inspired by its beauty and feeling herself a kindred spirit (Polly too is insecure about the value of her work), she decides to send Gabrielle some of her photographs. "I kind of thought she just might like them," she says. To make the undertaking less risky, she mails the photographs to the gallery under a pseudonym.

While the curator is out sick, Polly, behind her back, displays her painting at the gallery. An art reviewer sees the painting and writes a rave review. The same day that the review appears in the newspaper, Polly's photographs arrive in the mail. After giving them a cursory glance, the curator dismisses them as "completely simple minded," and "the trite made flesh." When Polly asks if the photographs at least show potential, the curator replies that the photographer is going nowhere and "She just doesn't have it." Devastated, Polly burns her photographs and then, in a final act of self-loathing, pushes her beloved camera off a ledge. Later, she refuses solace from Mary who, happening upon one of Polly's photos (but not knowing its creator) questions the curator's harsh judgment.

Because of the curator's meteoric rise in the art world, she spends less and less time in the gallery and Polly is left desolate and alone. One night Polly gets drunk in the gallery in the presence of the curator's luminous work. Hearing Gabrielle enter the gallery with Mary, Polly hides behind a bench and overhears their conversation. It turns out that Mary, not the curator, is the real artist. The curator, afraid to show her own work even to her clerk, had shown Polly Mary's paintings, allowing her to surmise they were her own. When Polly exhibited them the next day under Gabrielle's name and they were enthusiastically received, Mary and Gabrielle decided to continue the deception. Mary despises the pretentiousness of the art world and has no desire to play the role of celebrated artist. "I paint, you talk," she says.

Gabrielle discovers Polly hiding and invites her to go along with the deception. But Polly's realization that Gabrielle is a fake at last enables her to unleash her long-pent-up rage at the curator's crushing dismissal of her beloved photographs. She flings a cup of scalding tea in the curator's face and, for the first time in a long while, feels wonderful. Then, she impulsively steals the gallery's surveillance camera and returns to her apartment. We understand in retrospect why Polly has been taping her confession into a video camera. She is trying to explain why she has to leave town ("before they send me to prison or sue me") to the person who will be making the arrangements to sell her furniture and rent out her apartment. "There it is," she says to the video camera, "That's what happened." The credits begin to roll.

However, to the surprise of those who have begun to leave the the-ater, the film is not yet over. The credits are intercut with the film's continuing action. There is a knock at the door and we see (from the point of view of the video camera) Mary and Gabrielle (with a bandaged face) enter Polly's apartment. Polly apologizes to the curator for hurting her. When Mary points out to Gabrielle that the photographs she so harshly dismissed were Polly's, the curator apologizes in turn. This sounds a little flat in the telling, but it marks a moment of powerful reconciliation. As the credits continue, Polly's voice-over says, "C'mon, I'll show you some more." In the final shot of the film, Polly opens a door which now magically leads out into a richly colored forest into which she invites Mary and Gabrielle. Before Polly joins them, she runs back inside, smiling triumphantly, and turns off the video camera. This signals the real end of the film.

Exploring Women's Desires

If we look at plot alone, the differences between *I've Heard the Mermaids Singing* and the films directed by the male directors discussed in this book are already manifest. *Mermaids* focuses on the concerns and desires of its female protagonist, while the protagonists of the previous films, from *The Birth of a Nation* to *Do the Right Thing,* focus on the concerns and desires of males.[11] At least five of the plots of the male-directed films I have considered involve the oedipal dynamic of two men vying for the love of a woman, reflecting the male child's rivalry with the father for the love of the mother. In the plot of *Mermaids* an oedipal triangle also exists, but all three of its members are women—Polly and Mary both love Gabrielle. What marks *Mermaids* as female-directed is not so much the fact that the plot is about women, but the depth with which it explores the dynamics of female psychology, specifically the inner worlds of women who compete with their sisters for the favors of their mothers, a theme rarely treated in mainstream cinema, but an important and resonant one for many female spectators.

The curator, an older woman whose job, as her name suggests, is care-taking, is like a mother with two daughters. She thinks one is beautiful, but the other is not. She thinks one is talented, and the other is not. Mary is the kind of daughter who fulfills the narcissistic needs of a depressed mother by allowing the mother to participate vicariously in her talent. The film makes this fantasy literal, as Gabrielle takes the credit for Mary's paintings. In this light, Gabrielle's excessive denigration of Polly's photographs can be understood as the loathing of the depressed mother for the daughter who reflects her self-doubt and vulnerability, rather than her grandiosity. Note that Gabrielle uses the same words in judging Polly's photos as the art instructor has used to dismiss *her* work, calling them "simple minded."

The film can also be read as a feminist fairy tale, a playful, slightly tongue-in-cheek reworking of the Cinderella story. Polly, like Cinderella, is an orphan who has to do all the drudge work at the gallery, unlike the favored "sister" Mary, whom Gabrielle thinks is too talented to work. But unlike Cinderella, Polly is neither beautiful nor even good at being a drudge. And no prince comes to her rescue. Rather Cinderella reconciles with the evil stepmother and stepsister and the three of them live happily ever after. Polly needs no prince to redeem her. The happy ending comes when she learns to value herself and discovers kindred spirits with whom to share her work. This is exactly the kind of film heroine Marjorie Rosen called for in her 1973 book *Popcorn Venus*.

Just as *8 1/2* presents the conflicts and confusions of a male artist from the inside out, *Mermaids* presents the conflicts, difficulties, and inhibitions of a female artist. From this perspective, *Mermaids* can be read as a meditation on the difficulty women have in gaining confidence in a world in which they are defined as defective. Polly is the cosmic opposite of Guido in *8 1/2*. He suffers from too much adulation while she suffers from too little. An ex-boss, Polly tells us, once called her "organizationally impaired." The curator echoes Polly's male boss's judgment of her as fundamentally lacking when she says that the creator of Polly's photographs "just doesn't have it." Part of Polly's problem, which is the same problem of all women in a male-privileged culture, is having internalized these harsh judgments of herself as defective or impaired.

The character in the film who most ostensibly has "it," of course, is the curator. According to Rozema, in her original conception of the script the curator was a male. She changed the gender, she explains, because "I found that I seemed to be making an anti-masculine-authority statement, and all I wanted was an anti-authority message."[12] But while Gabrielle is a woman, she appears to be psychologically male-identified in the sense that she is a woman who has made it in a man's world and internalized male values. She owns an art gallery, has plenty of money, and trades on her power and mastery of words. This becomes evident when she convinces a client that a trite painting hanging in her gallery is trendy and profound. She even has an attractive, younger, female lover.

Gabrielle is also male-identified in her adherence to absolute, universal standards of value. She wants to create a work of art that is "undeniably, universally good," aligning her with the absolutist values of patriarchal culture which itself is based on the idea of the phallus as a universal symbol of all that is powerful, complete, and good. This system, which empowers men and denigrates women, is upheld by the authoritarian patriarchal institutions of church and state. It is no coincidence that Gabrielle's gallery is named "The Church Gallery." As Rozema remarks, "I wanted to point out the parallel paths of organized art and organized religion, because neither can exist without the assumption of absolute authority and infallibility of the reigning leaders. When in fact, the history of religion as well as art is a study of trends, fashions, and cycles."[13] Gabrielle's belief in an absolute standard of value which defines her as deficient (she unquestioningly accepts the authority of the male teacher who calls her work "simple minded") emotionally devastates her. She passes on this sad legacy to Polly, whom she emotionally devastates in turn. The film's happy ending involves Polly's triumphant recovery from her acceptance of Gabrielle as an ultimate authority.

To Gabrielle's absolutist way of thinking, Rozema counterposes a relativistic philosophy. Polly voices this viewpoint in a fantasy sequence in which she imagines herself, poised and wise, lecturing to Gabrielle. Polly's lesson is that no one has direct communication with some ultimate truth or knowledge. Truth is relative, and ultimately subjective. There is no one right way. When Gabrielle asks Polly how her relativistic philosophy applies to relationships, Polly (whose name reflects her philosophy) draws on Freud's concept of *poly*morphous perversity, which holds that all children are born open to a range of sexual preferences. There is no one right way to be. It is only society that pushes us to conform to set ways of expressing our sexuality. Since social norms are not based on any universal truths, Polly believes, one should actively cultivate rather than repress polymorphous inclinations, which she believes are natural and not perverse.

As Polly is intoning her wisdom to an enthralled Gabrielle (reversing their usual roles), Rozema pulls back the camera to reveal that Polly is walking on water. But, despite the authority these words are given by likening Polly to Christ, Rozema immediately reminds us that Polly's truth, too, is relative and subjective. When Gabrielle wonders how Polly has suddenly become so wise and articulate, Polly answers, "It is, after all, *my* vision." Rozema's belief in the importance of relativity and subjectivity, that there is no one right way, is reflected in the witty way she represents Gabrielle's (though actually Mary's) paintings. They are seen as luminous blank screens, and thus ripe for the projection of subjective responses based not on one universal standard of merit but on individual values. Rozema's relativistic vision has profound feminist implications. By undermining the idea of phallocentric universal standards of truth, Rozema empowers women who no longer need to be defined as deficient, just different.

Departures from Mainstream Cinema Style

Rozema's relativism is built into the very infrastructure of her film. Beginning with the opening credit sequence, she undermines the mainstream film convention that aligns the spectator with an all-seeing camera eye (the eye of God) with access to an unmediated reality unfolding on the screen before us. The reality in *I've Heard the Mermaids Singing* is mediated from the very beginning. The opening credits of the film are intercut with video images of Polly narrating the film's story before a video camera that she herself has set up. The bad quality of the video image makes us acutely aware that we are watching an image, not reality, and foregrounds the fact that we are seeing the events through one person's eyes. Then, even the authority of the pseudodocumentary window-on-the-world "reality" of the video image is undercut by being placed in dialogue with the film's credits. Here Rozema broadcasts loud and clear that what we are seeing is a constructed fiction, made to seem like reality, not real life.

When Rozema cuts from the video image of Polly narrating to a visualization of the events of her story, the film becomes more conventional. The film stock is standard 35mm color film, the kind used to give an illusion of unmediated reality in most mainstream films, and, in fact, we do get drawn into the fiction in these portions of the film, identifying with Polly in all her painful predicaments. Yet Rozema keeps undermining this illusion by continually cutting to Polly's fantasy visions of impossible actions in which she is flying, climbing up the side of a huge skyscraper, or walking on water. These visions are photographed in black and white with a grainy film stock, calling attention to the film medium. The juxtaposition of three kinds of film stock in one film—videotape, 35mm color film, and grainy black-and-white film stock—renders every "reality" we witness in the film relative. Rozema manages to have it both ways. Much of the film is in the style of mainstream cinema with the viewer an "invisible guest" looking in. At the same time her juxtaposition of multiple film stocks (and the constant use of freeze-frames whenever Polly snaps a picture) makes us aware of the artifice of this seeming reality and hence aware of the fact that we are always seeing her (Rozema's) vision and not some ultimate truth.

Rozema departs most noticeably from the conventions of mainstream cinema in *I've Heard the Mermaids Singing* with her creation of a radically different kind of film heroine. Polly's very appearance goes counter to the way heroines look in mainstream films. A birdlike little person with flaming red hair that sticks up, she could never be mistaken for a star. Nor does the camera idealize her through the use of flattering lights and lenses. Just the opposite. The poor-quality video image in which she appears throughout much of the film is harsh and unflattering. Even the position of her head is awkwardly decentered in the frame. Nor is she given star visual treatment in the body of the film. Mostly she looks awkward and unattractive, especially in comparison with the more conventionally beautiful Gabrielle and Mary. By the end of the film, however, she becomes extremely appealing to look at. This is not because Rozema has begun to photograph her in a more flattering way, but simply because we have gotten to know and like her. Thus Rozema demonstrates that women need not be fetishized or idealized to be attractive, appealing film heroines.

Not only is Polly not idealized, she is not objectified in this film by appearing as the passive object of the camera's (male) gaze. As I noted earlier, when we first see Polly, she is setting up a camera to film herself. At least within the fiction of the film's narrative, she is in control of the visual apparatus, simultaneously the subject and object of the camera's look. The form of the surveillance camera in the gallery wittily mirrors this theme. The camera is placed inside a TV monitor where the head should be on a bust of a nude woman. Hence the nude body cancels out its objectification by itself becoming all-seeing. Nor in *Mermaids* does the audience have the illusion that we are "uninvited guests" peering at someone who is unaware that we are watching them. Instead, Polly directly addresses her words to the camera and hence, it would appear, to the film audience. She knows we are out there. Occasionally she even addresses us directly.

Rethinking Cinematic Voyeurism

Perhaps the most innovative aspect of *I've Heard the Mermaids Singing* is the way it self-consciously plays with the concept of cinematic voyeurism. Mulvey, as you will recall, decreed in her conclusion to "Visual Pleasure and Narrative Cinema" that in order to be nonsexist, films must eliminate the pleasures of voyeurism. Rozema, it would appear, is too much of a relativist to sanction such extreme measures. Voyeurism abounds in Rozema's film, but it is a different brand of voyeurism than that found in mainstream cinema. A major difference, of course, is that in *I've Heard the Mermaids Singing* the voyeur is a woman—not a peeping Tom but a peeping Polly. In scene after scene Polly engages in illicit looking, sometimes combined with illicit listening. She secretly watches the curator and Mary kiss when she turns on the surveillance camera in the Church Gallery. She snaps pictures of a couple making love until they discover her watching. She listens at the door as the curator mesmerizes a client with her words, talking him into buying her art.

She stands outside the window watching Mary and Gabrielle together on the night of Gabrielle's birthday party. Finally, hidden under a bench in the gallery, she overhears the conversation between Mary and Gabrielle that reveals that Gabrielle has deceived her about the paintings.

Polly can certainly be defined as a voyeur, but she is a voyeur with a difference. The kind of voyeurism Mulvey wanted to ban from women's cinema was the controlling, objectifying sort, in which women are reduced to the status of sex objects for the delectation of male viewers. Polly's voyeurism derives from curiosity, the curiosity of a young child who wants to know what adults do together when they are alone, a curiosity that transcends gender. Something about the charged atmosphere between Mary and Gabrielle when Mary first appears at the gallery sends Polly rushing to the surveillance camera to find out more about just what is going on between them in the next room. She watches Gabrielle and Mary kiss with the wide-eyed fascination of a small child discovering sex for the first time. Part of Polly's astonishment, to be sure, comes from the fact that two women are kissing. In mainstream male-directed films such as *Personal Best* (Robert Towne, 1982) and *The Hunger* (Tony Scott, 1983), the camera lingers over scenes of women making love to make them as titillating as possible. Rozema refuses to provide this kind of voyeuristic satisfaction. Mary and Gabrielle move out of the monitor's range at the moment they begin to kiss. But even as Rozema denies us voyeuristic pleasure, she humorously makes us aware of our prurient desires by showing Polly peering beyond the edge of the monitor frame hoping to see more. Polly, who is munching crackers as she watches the love scene on the monitor screen, recalls the spectators in the audience munching popcorn as we too watch the cinematic screen in guilty fascination. In this brilliant and funny scene, voyeurism is not eliminated but foregrounded, contemplated, laughed at, and acknowledged as natural.

Rozema then juxtaposes the scene of Polly watching Gabrielle and Mary making love with images of Polly taking pictures of a young couple making love in the woods. The juxtaposition of the two incidents suggests a cause-and-effect relationship. Polly, odd woman out, is trying to master her hurt feelings by actively seeking images of couples making love and joining in vicariously with her camera. Polly is not taking pictures to gain some kind of sadistic control over objects in the world but to provide a kind of solace for herself. She becomes even more sympathetic when the couple spots her taking pictures and she lamely tries to pretend she is bird-watching.

A final way that sexual voyeurism is played with and transformed in *Mermaids* is the brief scene just after Polly sees Gabrielle and Mary kissing. Presumably from Polly's point of view, the camera begins at Gabrielle's feet and slowly moves up her body, almost as if the camera were caressing her. This frankly sexual gaze from the point of view of a woman is rarely seen in mainstream films, and Rozema is consciously playing against the convention in so many mainstream films of the sexualized female body seen from the point of view of a male character. Interestingly, the shot is accompanied by Polly's voice-over disavowing that her love for the curator is sexual. "I don't think I wanted kissing and hugging and all that stuff," she says. "I just loved her." But here a picture is worth a thousand words—Polly's inhibited desire is expressed by how she sees, not by what she says. Although she will later express the idea in a fantasy sequence that gender is irrelevant in matters of the heart, that is, that desire naturally follows love irrespective of the gender of the loved one, it is made clear by the counterpoint of word and image that Polly's sexual liberation lags behind her philosophical one.

Yet *I've Heard the Mermaids Singing* is not primarily about sex. It is equally about looking. While the film plays with the conventions of sexual voyeurism, Polly's voyeuristic impulses are seen as a natural continuum of her more generalized love of looking, the passion that has led to her hobby of photography. She likes to take pictures of things she loves—and not just images of people making love in the woods (though, of course, that too). Polly's passion encompasses a wide variety of subjects—from majestic skyscrapers to mothers holding babies. A film like *Mermaids* illustrates through its parade of stunning and surprising visual images, especially as they appear in Polly's fantasy visions of strange urban landscapes and waves crashing against cliffs, that the pleasures of looking need not involve sexual voyeurism to enthrall and engage us.

Patricia Rozema makes it clear in her film that women filmmakers do not have a monopoly on nonsexualized visual aesthetics. The scene in which Polly climbs a ladder to the top of a grain silo to take a picture is a quotation from Dziga Vertov's self-reflexive silent film masterpiece *The Man with a Movie Camera* (1928). Rozema's homage to Vertov suggests she feels an aesthetic kinship with him. Vertov's camera's gaze in *The Man with a Movie Camera* is by no means the sadistic, controlling, objectifying gaze deplored by Mulvey, but a playful, self-reflexive one that celebrates the capacity of cinema to reveal the world in a new and revolutionary way. This too is Rozema's goal. By including in her film an homage to Dziga Vertov's *The Man with a Movie Camera,* Rozema, a woman with a movie camera, proclaims that in the best of all worlds, gender is irrelevant in the creation of cinematic art. In this ideal world, whether a man or a woman is behind the movie camera makes no difference at all. But until that time comes, I am grateful for films like Patricia Rozema's *I've Heard the Mermaids Singing.*

ENDNOTES

1. Since *I've Heard the Mermaids Singing* Rozema has made five more feature films: *The White Room* (1990), *When Night Is Falling* (1995), *Mansfield Park* (1999), *Happy Days* (2000), and *Kit Kittredge: An American Girl* (2008). A collection of Patricia Rozema's works is available on DVD from Alliance Atlantis Home Video, 2003.
2. Marjorie Rosen, *Popcorn Venus: Women, Movies and the American Dream* (New York: Avon Books, 1973), 105.
3. These issues are discussed in "The Passion for Perceiving," in Christian Metz, *The Imaginary Signifier,* trans. Celia Britton et al. (Bloomington: Indiana University Press, 1982), 58–68.
4. Mulvey's article originally appeared in *Screen* 16, no. 3 (Autumn 1975), but was reprinted in numerous anthologies of feminist film theory and criticism. My subsequent references to the article are from Constance Penley, ed., *Feminism and Film Theory* (New York: Routledge, 1988), 57–68.
5. John Berger, *Ways of Seeing* (London: British Broadcasting Corporation and Penguin Books, 1975), 47. In *Ways of Seeing,* Berger writes of the way representations of men and women in Western painting have divided up certain attributes according to gender. Images of men connote power or the promise of power; images of women are seen and judged as sights, objects of erotic contemplation. Berger believes women are depicted in quite different ways from men, "not because the feminine is different from the masculine—but because the 'ideal' spectator is always assumed to be male and the image of the woman is designed to flatter him" (64).
6. I say traditionally because these methods of representation have obviously changed since the 1970s (when most of the pioneering feminist criticism was written), as the film industry responded to feminist critiques and the public's desire to see women play more active roles. Nevertheless, to quote Elizabeth Cowie in her extended article on *Coma,* a woman character can be written as "strong" while "as an actant within the narrative she is 'weak.'" ("The Popular Film as a Progressive Text—A Discussion of *Coma,*" in Penley, ed., *Feminism and Film Theory,* 125.)
7. Mulvey's article was controversial from the start, criticized as male-centered in its perspective because it did not explain or theorize in a very satisfactory way why women, if they were so objectified and disempowered in movies, nevertheless made up such a large proportion of the film audience. Women's pleasure in cinema, according to Mulvey, resulted from their narcissistic identification with the eroticized women on the screen, and their masochistic pleasure in the women's objectification and/or victimization. With feminist friends like this, one might well inquire, who needs enemies? Mulvey was also criticized for being heterosexist. All her theorized male spectators went to the movies to ogle women. She never took the male homosexual spectator into account. Nor did her theory acknowledge the pleasure lesbians might have in looking at the bodies of women on the screen.

    Moreover, as many critics pointed out, and Mulvey herself later acknowledged in an article entitled "Afterthoughts on 'Visual Pleasure and Narrative Cinema,'" in Penley, ed., *Feminism and Film Theory,* 69–79, women are not confined to same-sex screen identifications. Women can feel empowered identifying with the active males on the screen. Other critics, most notably Gaylyn Studlar, emphasized that male spectators, too, identify not just with the male characters but also with the women on the screen. The point is that movies provide more than sadistic pleasure for men by presenting the spectacle of female suffering. Men can also derive masochistic pleasure by identifying with the suffering woman. Studlar points to the prevalence of films, notably those by Joseph von Sternberg, in which men are victims of powerful women. Thus it is not only women on the screen who are punished and humiliated. See Gaylyn Studlar, *In the Realm of Pleasure: Von Sternberg, Dietrich, and the Masochistic Aesthetic* (Urbana and Chicago: University of Illinois Press), 1988.
8. Mulvey, "Visual Pleasure and Narrative Cinema," 68.
9. T. S. Eliot, "The Love Song of J. Alfred Prufrock," *Major Writers of America II*, ed. Perry Miller (New York: Harcourt, Brace and World, 1962), 770–3.
10. Quoted in Karen Jaehne, "*I've Heard the Mermaids Singing:* An Interview with Patricia Rozema," *Cineaste* 16, no. 3 (1988): 22.

11. Possible exceptions are *His Girl Friday* and *Notorious,* both of which divide attention between the male and female protagonists. Despite the title of Woody Allen's *Annie Hall,* this film is told from the perspective of Alvy Singer, not Annie.
12. Jaehne, "An Interview with Patricia Rozema," 23.
13. Jaehne, "An Interview with Patricia Rozema," 23.

KAREN A. RITZENHOFF

LISBETH SALANDER AS "FINAL GIRL" IN THE SWEDISH "GIRL WHO" FILMS

One of the most compelling protagonists in the Swedish films based on Stieg Larsson's Millennium trilogy is twenty-four-year-old psychologically damaged computer hacker Lisbeth Salander (Noomi Rapace), who takes control of her fate by retaliating against her abusers. In a key courtroom scene in the third and final film, Salander produces a video she made with a hidden camera that shows her legal guardian raping her. In lieu of the chainsaw, a favored implement of "final girl" vengeance, Salander uses new technologies—a Taser, a tattoo machine, a nail gun, the Internet—to protect herself and to exact revenge against those who would do her serious harm.

In the first two "Girl Who" films, Salander resembles the "final girl" described by feminist film scholar Carol Clover. In its simplest formation, the "final girl" is the lone survivor in a slasher or horror film. She must fend for herself, often using domestic utensils (such as a coat hanger) or outdoor equipment (such as a chainsaw) to destroy the monster, vampire, ghost, or serial killer who has wiped out all her friends. Salander is repeatedly attacked in the "Girl Who" films and we see her single-handedly fighting antagonists with her unusual arsenal of weapons. She returns to torture and humiliate her guardian, Nils Bjurman (Peter Andersson), using a tattoo machine to crudely brand his torso with the message, "I'm a sadist pig and a rapist." Having been maliciously controlled, violently sexually assaulted, and sadistically manipulated, Salander now controls Bjurman's life; her surveillance technologies and hacking abilities allow her to track his every move. In this way, she enforces justice on her own terms as a final girl acting alone.

Bjurman is respected as a public servant and his sadistic cruelty remains hidden until Salander turns his body into a testimony of abuse. She demonstrates that violence against women is not perpetrated by monsters, serial killers, or other bizarre characters, but by "normal" men hiding their acts in plain sight of society. As opposed to dark alleys, empty parking garages, or creepy cellars, the locations in which Bjurman rapes Salander are his office and his apartment—everyday places that aren't necessarily marked as dangerous for women. By showing Bjurman acting out his sadistic fantasies in ordinary settings, the violence is desensationalized, making it more realistic and allowing viewers to question their tendencies to see violence as entertainment.

In classic slasher films, the final girl is often physically abused and tortured to the point of death before she finally prevails and kills her assailant. Similarly, in the "Girl Who" films, we see Salander shot in the head, buried alive, and left for dead. We watch as she literally digs herself out of the grave to track down her father and her brother, who have tried and failed to annihilate her. Since childhood, she's also been systematically abused by corrupt political, legal, and mental health systems bent on controlling, discrediting, and silencing her. The audience is drawn to sympathize with Salander and cheer her on as she methodically exacts punishments against all her abusers. We are led to feel empowered as the would-be victim becomes a hero who embodies not only physical courage but technological skill, intelligence, and wit.

Throughout the films, audiences are reminded of the videotape of Salander's rape. We view the rape only once, but we hear the sound of the recording on multiple occasions, especially Salander's screams while being tortured. By framing the rape scene in this way, the filmmakers pose violence as entertainment in mainstream cinema as a problem. The recording of the rape gains significance because, deprived of images, the audience relies on its memory of the scene. By refusing to replay the actual rape in visual flashbacks (contrary to other scenes of abuse, such as Salander's traumatic childhood memories, which are evoked again and again), the filmmakers subvert the voyeuristic pleasure of visual violence so prevalent in mainstream film. In the third "Girl Who" film, we see Salander's lawyer and her trial judge—both women—turn away in horror from the video-graphic violence as it is displayed in court. The representation of rape in the "Girl Who" films is significantly opposite of mainstream depictions of abuse in slasher and action films: Lisbeth Salander's suffering is made real to audiences.

In a climate where video is increasingly used for surveillance in public life, watching Salander employ it for self-defense as an invaluable tool seems original and new in a film adaptation. Given her history and her experiences, Salander assumes that the police are corrupt and that they will reject or subvert the documentary evidence of her rape. She hacks into Bjurman's official files and discovers that even though he is a practicing sadist, his record is clean. In light of her encounters with coercive state-mandated psychiatric treatment and unsympathetic law enforcement, she mistrusts social institutions and believes she would never win a legal battle in court. Deemed psychologically unfit by state authorities, Salander comes across to the audience as highly effective, intelligent, self-reliant, and iconoclastic: she rejects social demands to find a heterosexual mate, pursue an education, have children, or settle for a conventional job, and that doesn't make her criminal or crazy in the audience's eyes.

In the third and final film, Swedish government officials and so-ciopathic criminals (including Salander's own father and brother) work to eliminate her once and for all. For most of the film, she is confined to a hospital bed and has to rely on others to help her survive. This complicates her final girl status dramatically. She is protected from harm only through the unrelenting support of her investigative journalist friend, Mikael Blomkvist (Michael Nyquist); his sister, women's rights lawyer Annika Giannini (Annika Hallin); a sympathetic emergency hospital doctor; her former boss; Dragan Armansky (Michalis Koutsogiannakis); a few decent cops; and a motley band of anarcho-hacker comrades. Through their efforts, she is eventually found to be innocent of murder, declared mentally competent, accorded full rights as an adult citizen, and finally set free to reclaim her life. No longer alone in the world, the final girl learns how to trust and accept help from supporters who care about her. Physical strength and solitary status no longer determine whether the final girl will survive, and viewers are led to conclude that broadly based collective support and access to twenty-first-century technologies can change the power differential between men and women.

In her groundbreaking analysis "Her Body, Himself: Gender in the Slasher Film," Clover (2008) argues that while brutalization of women was typical in American mainstream slasher films, what had not been studied was how the final girl heroically survived by developing masculine traits. Clover characterizes the final girl hero as "a physical female and a characterological androgyne: like her name, not masculine but either/or, both, ambiguous" (106). Noomi Rapace's appearance as Salander is striking in the "Girl Who" films. She has physically ambiguous traits that allow audiences to identify with her across gender lines, and she can be seen as transgressing stereotypes by exploring new boundaries of gender identity. She not only wears androgynous clothing (hoodies, T-shirts, jeans, and black Goth garments) and decorations (piercings, Mohawk hairstyles, and massive tattoos), she also acts in assertive and violent ways that help her develop "masculine" traits of strength and dominance without losing her identity as a woman. Clover analyzes horror and slasher films and detects a variety of "gender teasing" that can take many different forms (101). According to Clover, the final girl shows "signs of boyishness" (104) and frequently "acquits herself like a man" (102). At the same time, she argues, slasher films since Hitchcock's *Psycho* have showcased abject fear as gendered feminine. Salander eliminates her opponents without the "crying, cowering, screaming, fainting, trembling, begging for mercy" that according to Clover "belong to the female" (96). But Salander identifies as a woman, sleeps with women and men, fights on behalf of all women abused by men who hate women, and ultimately triumphs with the support of women and men who love women. She moves women cinematic heroes well beyond the limitations of the conventional final girl.

It is solidarity with women and men (who love and support women) that allows Salander to survive and triumph against the corrupt and sadistically misogynistic opponents who would have her eliminated. This twist allows audiences to view the final girl in new and innovative ways. The broad international appeal of the Swedish "Girl Who" films, and particularly of Noomi Rapace as Salander, seems to suggest that they are inaugurating a new kind of gender politics in cinema.

Clover, Carol. 2008. "Her Body, Himself: Gender in the Slasher Film." In *The Dread of Difference: Gender and the Horror Film*, edited by Barry Keith Grant, 66–113. Austin: University of Texas Press.

Girl with the Dragon Tattoo, The. 2009. Dir. Niels Arden Oplev. Music Box Films.

Girl Who Played with Fire, The. 2009. Dir. Daniel Alfredson. Music Box Films.

Girl Who Kicked the Hornet's Nest, The. 2009. Dir. Daniel Alfredson. Music Box Films.

Hutchings, Peter. 2004. *The Horror Film*. New York: Pearson Longman.

Ritzenhoff, Karen A. 2009. "The Frozen Family: Emotional Dysfunction and Consumer Society in Michael Haneke's Films." In *Sex and Sexuality in a Feminist World*, edited by Karen A. Ritzenhoff and Katherine Hermes, 71–88. Newcastle, UK: Cambridge Scholars Publishing.

Tasker, Yvonne, and Diane Negra. 2007. *Interrogating Post-Feminism: Gender and the Politics of Popular Culture*. Durham, NC: Duke University Press.

JANE GAINES

WHITE PRIVILEGE AND LOOKING RELATIONS: RACE AND GENDER IN FEMINIST FILM THEORY

This essay was originally conceived as a challenge to the paradigm that dominated feminist film theory in Britain and the United States for roughly ten years, from 1975 to 1985. Because that paradigm, introduced and developed in the British journal *Screen,* has since lost its exclusive position in the field, the combativeness of the original essay no longer seems appropriate. And yet, debates over the use of psychoanalytic theory have continued, now less heated in film studies than in African and African-American studies.[1] There is another development. Not only is a strong tradition of black feminist literary theory and cultural studies emerging, but we are about to see a parallel development in both critical and creative work on film and video art.[2] One key question remains, however, and I dedicate this reprinting of "White Privilege and Looking Relations" to the consideration of this issue. Yes, more work is being done by Asian, Hispanic, and African-American women. However, has feminist film theory, heretofore written exclusively by white women, shown signs of transformation?[3]

What I want to do here is to show how a theory of the text and its spectator, based on the psychoanalytic concept of sexual difference, is unequipped to deal with a film that is about racial difference and sexuality. The Diana Ross star vehicle *Mahogany* (Berry Gordy, 1975) immediately suggests a psychoanalytic approach because the narrative is organized around the connections between voyeurism and photographic acts and because it is a perfect specimen of the classical cinema, which has been so fully theorized in Lacanian terms. But as I will argue, the psychoanalytic model works to block out considerations that assume a different configuration, so that, for instance, the Freudian-Lacanian scenario can eclipse the scenario of race-gender relations in African-American history, since the two accounts sexuality are fundamentally incongruous. The danger here is that when we use a psychoanalytic model to explain black family relations we force an erroneous universalization and inadvertently reaffirm white middle-class norms.

By taking gender as its starting point in the analysis of oppression, feminist theory helps to reinforce white middle-class values, and to the extent that it works to keep women from seeing other structures of oppression, it functions ideologically. In this regard, bell hooks criticizes a feminism that seems unable to think of women's oppression in terms other than gender: "Feminist analyses of woman's lot tend to focus exclusively on gender and do not provide a solid founda-tion on which to construct feminist theory. They reflect the dominant tendency in Western patriarchial minds to mystify women's reality by insisting that gender is the sole determinant of woman's fate."[4] Gender analysis rather exclusively illuminates the condition of white middle-class women, hooks says, and its centrality in feminist theory suggests that those women who have constructed this theory have been ignorant of the way women in different racial groups and social classes *experience* oppression. Many of us would not dispute this. But exactly how should the feminist who does not want to be racist in her work respond to this criticism? In one of the few considerations of this delicate dilemma, Marilyn Frye, in her essay "On Being White," urges us *not* to do what middle-class feminists have historically done: to assume responsibility for everyone. To take it upon oneself to rewrite feminist theory so that it encompasses our differences is another exercise of racial privilege, she says, and therefore all that one can do with conscience is to undertake the study of our own "determined ignorance."[5] One can begin to learn about the people whose history cannot be imagined from a position of privilege.

I recall from graduate school in the late 1970s the tone of feminist film theory as I first heard it—firm in its insistence on attention to cinematic language and strict in its prohibition against making comparisons between actuality and the text. I always heard this voice as a British-accented female voice, and over and over again I heard it reminding me that feminists could only analyze the ideological through its encoding in the conventions of editing and the mechanics of the motion picture machine. This was the point in the history of the field when there were only two texts that had earned the distinction "feminist film theory" (as opposed to criticism), and in the United States we were very aware that they came out of British Marxism: Claire Johnston's "Women's Cinema as Counter-Cinema," and Laura Mulvey's "Visual Pleasure and Narrative Cinema."[6] In retrospect, we understand that the apparent intransigence of the theory of cinema as patriarchal discourse as it developed out of these essays is the legacy of the Althusserian theory of the subject. From the point of view of Marxist feminism the psychoanalytic version of the construction of the subject was a welcome supplement to classical Marxism; gaining a theory of the social individual, however, meant losing the theory of social antagonism.

The ramifications for feminism would be different on the American side of the Atlantic. The theory of the subject as constituted in language, imported into U.S. academic circles, could swell to the point that it seemed able to account for all oppression, expression, and sociosexual functioning in history. The enormously complicated developments through which European Marxists saw a need for enlarging the capacity of the theory of ideology were lost in translation, so that in the United States we heard that "representation reproduces the patriarchal order." Stuart Hall has described this tendency in both discourse theory and Lacanian psychoanalysis as the opposite of the economism these theories intended to modify—"a reduction upward rather than downward." What transpires in such movements to correct economism is, as he says, "the metaphor of x operates like y is reduced to $x = y$."[7]

This would happen with a vengeance in the U.S. university scene, where the theory of classical cinema as patriarchal discourse would appear at first quite alone and recently divorced from larger Marxist debates. On campuses where students could not hope to acquire any background in political economy, a film course introduction to the analysis of subjectivity and cinema might well be the only exposure they had to Marxist theory in an entire college career. We must now wonder, however, if the relatively easy assimilation of *Screen* theory into feminist studies in the United States had something to do with the way the radical potential of the theory was quieted with the very use of the psychoanalytic terminology it employed. We further need to consider the warm reception given to high feminist film theory in women's studies circles in terms of the new respectability of academic feminism in the United States, surely signaled by Peter Brooks's statement that "anyone worth his salt in literary criticism today has to become something of a feminist."[8]

Within film and television studies in the United States, the last three years have seen a break with the theory of representation that, it appears, had gripped us for so long. The new feminist strategies that engage with, modify, or abandon the stubborn notion that we are simultaneously positioned in language and ideology are too numerous to detail. In the United States, as in Britain, one of the most influential challenges to this theory posed the question of our reconstitution at different historical moments. How could the formative moment of one's entry into language be the one condition overriding all other determining conditions of social existence? This question would become especially pertinent as the theoretical interest shifted from the text that produced subjects to the subjects who produced texts; the "real historical subject" became the escape route through which theorists abandoned a text weighted down with impossible expectations.

In the United States, lesbian feminists raised the first objections to the way film theory explained the operation of the classic realist text in terms of tensions between masculinity and femininity. The understanding of spectatorial pleasure in classical cinema as inherently male drew an especially sharp response from critics who argued that this theory canceled the lesbian spectator, whose viewing pleasure could never be construed as anything like male voyeurism. Positing a lesbian spectator would significantly change the trajectory of the gaze. It might lead us to see how the eroticized star body might be not just the object but the visual objective of another female gaze within the film's diegesis—a gaze with which the viewer might identify. Following this argument, Marilyn Monroe and Jane Russell in *Gentlemen Prefer Blondes* are "only for each other's eyes."[9] Two influential studies building on the lesbian reading of *Gentlemen Prefer Blondes* suggested that the lesbian reception of *Personal Best* held a key to challenging the account of cinema as producing patriarchal subject positions, since lesbian viewers, at least, were subverting dominant meanings and confounding textual structures.[10]

Consistently, lesbians have charged that cultural theory posed in psychoanalytic terms is unable to conceive of desire or explain pleasure without reference to the binary oppositions male/

female. This is the function of what Monique Wittig calls the heterosexual assumption, or the "straight mind," that unacknowledged structure not only built into Lacanian psychoanalysis, but also underlying the basic divisions of Western culture, organizing all knowledge, yet escaping any close examination.[11] Male/female is a powerful, but sometimes blinding, construct. And it is difficult to see that the paradigm that we embraced so quickly in our first lessons in feminism may have been standing in the way of our further education.

The male/female opposition, seemingly so fundamental to feminism, may actually lock us into modes of analysis that will continually misinterpret the position of many women. Thus, women of color, an afterthought in feminist analysis, remain unassimilated by its central problematic. Feminist anthologies consistently include articles on black female and lesbian perspectives as illustration of the liberality and inclusiveness of feminism; however, the very concept of "different perspectives," while validating distinctness and maintaining woman as common denominator, still places the categories of race and sexuality in theoretical limbo. Our political etiquette is correct, but our theory is not so perfect.

In Marxist feminist analysis, race and sexuality have remained loose ends because as categories of oppression they fit somewhat awkwardly into a model based on class relations in capitalist society. Although some gay historians see a relationship between the rise of capitalism and the creation of the social homosexual, only with a very generous notion of sexual hierarchies—such as the one Gayle Rubin has suggested—can sexual oppression (as different from gender oppression) be located in relation to a framework based on class.[12] Race has folded into Marxist models more neatly than sexuality, but the orthodox formulation that understands racial conflict as class struggle is still unsatisfactory to Marxist feminists who want to know exactly how gender intersects with race. The oppression of *women* of color remains incompletely grasped by the classical Marxist paradigm.

Just as the Marxist model based on class has obscured the function of gender, the feminist model based on the male/female division under patriarchy has obscured the function of race. The dominant feminist paradigm actually encourages us *not to think* in terms of any oppression other than male dominance and female subordination. Thus feminists and lesbians, says Barbara Smith, seem "blinded to the implications of any womanhood that is not white womanhood."[13] For purposes of analysis, black feminists agree that class is as significant as race; however, if these feminists hesitate to emphasize gender as a factor, it is in deference to the way black women describe their experience, for historically, African-American women have formulated identity and political allegiances in terms of race rather than gender or class.[14] Feminism, however, seems not to have heard the statements of women of color who say they experience oppression first in relation to race rather than to gender, and for them exploitation can be personified by a white female.[15] Even more difficult for feminist theory to digest is black female identification with the black male. On this point, black feminists diverge from white feminists in repeatedly reminding us that they do not necessarily see the black male as patriarchal antagonist, but feel instead that their racial oppression is "shared" with men.[16] In the most comprehensive analysis of all, black lesbian feminists have described race, class, and gender oppression as an "interlocking" synthesis in the lives of black women.[17]

The point here is not to rank the structures of oppression in a way that implies the need for black women to choose between solidarity with men or solidarity with women, between race or gender as the basis for a political strategy. At issue is the question of the fundamental antagonism so relevant for Marxist feminist theory. Where we have foregrounded one antagonism in our analysis, we have misunderstood another, and this is most dramatically illustrated in applying the notion of patriarchy, have not been absolutely certain what they mean by patriarchy: alternately it has referred to either father-right or domination of women, but what is consistent about the use of the concept is the rigidity of the structure it describes.[18] Patriarchy is incompatible with Marxism when used transhistorically without qualification to become the source of all other oppressions, as in the radical feminist theory that sees oppression in all forms and through all ages as derived from the male/female division.[19] This deterministic model, which Sheila Rowbotham says functions like a "feminist base-superstructure," has. the disadvantage of leaving us with no sense of movement or idea of how women have acted to change their condition, especially in comparison with the fluidity of the Marxist conception of class.[20]

The radical feminist notion of absolute patriarchy has also one-sidedly portrayed the oppression of women through an analogy with slavery, and since this theory has identified woman as man's savage or repressed Other, it competes with theories of racial difference that understand the black as the "unassimilable Other."[21] Finally, the notion of patriarchy is most obtuse when it disregards the position white women occupy over black men as well as black women.[22] In order to rectify this tendency in feminism, black feminists refer to "racial patriarchy," which is based on an analysis of the white patriarch/master in U.S. history and his dominance over the black male as well as the black female.[23]

I now want to reconsider the film *Mahogany,* the sequel to *Lady Sings the Blues,* in which Diana Ross plays an aspiring fashion designer who dreams of pulling herself up and out of her Chicago South Side neighborhood by means of a high-powered career.

Mahogany functions ideologically for black viewers in the traditional Marxist sense, that is, in the way the film obscures the class nature of social antagonisms. This has certain implications for working-class black viewers who would benefit the most from seeing the relationship between race, gender, and class oppression dramatized. Further, *Mahogany* has the same trouble understanding black femaleness that the wider culture has had historically; a black female is either all woman and tinted black, or mostly black and scarcely woman. These two expectations correspond with the two worlds and two struggles the film contrasts: the struggle over the sexual objectification of Tracy's body in the face of commercial exploitation and the struggle of the black community in the face of class exploitation. But the film identifies this antagonism as the hostility between fashion and politics, embodied respectively by Tracy Chambers (Diana Ross) and Brian Walker (Billy Dee Williams); through them it organizes conflict and, eventually, reconciliation. Intensifying this conflict between characters, the film contrasts "politics" and "fashion" in one daring homage to the aesthetic of "attraction by shock." Renowned fashion photographer Sean McEvoy (Tony Perkins) arranges his models symmetrically on the back stairwell of a run-down Chicago apartment building and uses the confused tenants and street people as props. Flamboyant excess, the residue of capital, is juxtaposed with a kind of dumbfounded poverty. For a moment, the scene figures the synthesis of gender, class, and race, but the political glimpse is fleeting. Forced together as a consequence of the avant-garde's socially irresponsible quest for a new outrage, the political antagonisms are suspended—temporarily immobilized as the subjects pose.

The connection between gender, class, and race oppression is also denied as the ghetto photography session's analogy between commercial exploitation and race/class exploitation merely registers on the screen as visual incongruity. Visual discrepancy is used for aesthetic effect and makes it difficult to grasp the confluence of race, class, and gender oppression in the image of Tracy Chambers. The character's class background magically becomes decor in the film-it neither radicalizes her nor drags her down; instead it sets her off. Diana Ross is alternately weighted down by the glamour iconography of commercial modeling and stripped to a black body. But the *haute couture* iconography ultimately dominates the film. Since race is decorative and class does not reveal itself to the eye, Tracy can be seen as exploited only in terms of her role as a model.

One of the original tenets of contemporary feminist film theory-that the (male) spectator possesses the female indirectly through the eyes of the male protagonist (his screen surrogate)—is problematized in this film by the less privileged black male gaze. Racial hierarchies of access to the female image also relate to other scenarios that are unknown by psychoanalytic categories. Considering the racial categories that psychoanalysis does not recognize, then, we see that the white male photographer monopolizes the classic patriarchal look controlling the view of the female body, and that the black male protagonist's look is either repudiated or frustrated. The sumptuous image of Diana Ross is made available to the spectator via the white male character (Sean) but *not* through the look of the black male character (Brian), In the sequence in which Tracy and Brian first meet outside her apartment building, his "look" is renounced. In each of the three shots of Tracy from Brian's point of view, she turns from him, walking out of his sight and away from the sound of his voice as he shouts at her through a megaphone. Both visual and audio control is thus denied the black male, and the failure of his voice is consistently associated with Tracy's white world publicity image. The discovery by Brian's aides of the Mahogany advertisement for Revlon in *Newsweek* coincides with the report that the Gallup Polls show the black candidate trailing in the election. Later, the film cuts from the *Harper's Bazaar* cover featuring "Mahogany" to Brian's limping campaign where the sound of his voice magnified a microphone is intermittently drowned out by a passing train as he makes his futile pitch to white factory workers.

"The construction of the sexual self of the Afro-American woman," says Rennie Simpson, "has its roots in the days of slavery."[24] Looking at this construction over time reveals a pattern of patriarchal phases and female sexual adjustments that have no equivalent in the history of white women in the United States. In the first phase, characterized by the dominance of the white master during the period of slavery, black men and women were equal by default. To have allowed the black male any power over the black woman would have threatened the power balance of the slave system. Thus, as Angela Davis explains social control in the slave community, "The man slave could not be the unquestioned superior within the 'family' or community, for there was no such thing as the 'family' provided among the Slaves."[25]

If the strategy for racial survival was resistance during the first phase, it was accommodation during the second phase. During Reconstruction, the black family, modeled after the white bourgeois household, was constituted defensively in an effort to preserve the race.[26] Black women yielded to their men in deference to a tradition that promised respectability and safety. Reevaluating this history, black feminists point out that during Reconstruction, the black male, "learned" to dominate. Thus they see sexism as not original to black communities but more as a plague that struck.[27] One of the most telling manifestations of the difference between the operation of patriarchy in the lives of black as opposed to white women is the way this is worked out *at the level of language* in the formal conventions organizing the short stories and novels by African-American women. Particularly in the work of early writers such as Harriet E. Wilson,

Frances E. W. Harper, and Pauline Hopkins, the black father is completely missing, and, as Hazel Carby says, "The absent space in fiction by black women confirms this denial of patriarchal power to black men."[28] The position consistently taken by black feminists, that patriarchy was originally foreign to the African-American community and was introduced into it historically, then, represents a significant break with feminist theories that see patriarchal power invested equally in all men throughout history, and patriarchal form as color blind.

Black history also adds another dimension to the concept of "rape," the term that has emerged as the favored metaphor for defining women's jeopardy in the second wave of feminism, replacing "prostitution," the concept that articulated women's fears in the nineteenth century.[29] The charge of rape, conjuring up a historical connection with lynching, is inextricably connected in American history with the myth of the black man as archetypal rapist. During slavery, white male abuse of black women was a symbolic blow to black manhood, understood as rape only within the black community. With the increase in the sexual violation of black women during Reconstruction the act of rape began to reveal its fuller political implications. After emancipation, the rape of black women was a "message" to black men that could be seen, says one historian, as "a reaction to the effort of the freedman to assume the role of patriarch, able to provide for and protect his family."[30] Simultaneous with the actual violation of black women, the empty charge of rape hurled back at the black man clouded the real issue of black (male) enfranchisement, creating a smoke screen by means of the incendiary issue of interracial sexuality. Writing at the turn of the century, black novelist Pauline Hopkins unmasked the alibis for lynching in *Contending Forces:* "Lynching was instituted to crush the manhood of the enfranchised black. Rape is the crime which appeals most strongly to the heart of the home life…. *The men who created the mulatto race, who recruit its ranks year after year by the very means which they invoked lynch law to suppress,* bewailing the sorrows of violated womanhood!"[31] Here is a sexual scenario to rival the oedipal myth: the black woman sexually violated by the white man, but her rape repressed and displaced onto the virginal white woman, and thus used symbolically as the justification for the actual castration of the black man. It is against this historical scenario that I want to reconsider the connotations of sexual looking that at one time in history would have carried with it the threat of real castration against which symbolic castration must surely pale.

Quite simply, then, there are structures relevant to any interpretation of *Mahogany* that override the patriarchal scenario feminists have theorized as formally determining. From African-American history, we should recall the white male's appropriation of the black woman's body that weakened the black male and undermined the community. From African-American literature, we should also consider the scenario of the talented and beautiful mulatta who "passes" in white culture, but decides to return to black society.[32] Further, we need to reconsider the narrative convention of the woman's picture—the career renounced in favor of the man—in the context of black history. Tracy's choice recapitulates black aspiration and the white middle-class model that equates stable family life with respectability, but her decision is significantly different from the white heroine's capitulation since it favors black community cooperation over acceptance by white society. Finally, one of the most difficult questions raised by African-American history and literature has to do with interracial heterosexuality and sexual "looking." *Mahogany* suggests that, since a black male character is not allowed the position of control occupied by a white male character, race could be a factor in the construction of cinema language. More work on looking and racial taboos might determine whether or not mainstream cinema can offer the male spectator the pleasure of looking at a white female character via the gaze of a black male character. Framing the question of male privilege and viewing pleasure as the "right to look" may help us to rethink film theory along more materialist lines, considering, for instance, how some groups have historically had the license to "look" openly while other groups have "looked" illicitly.[33] Phrased differently, does the psychoanalytic model allow us to consider the prohibitions against homosexuality and miscegenation?

Feminists who use psychoanalytic theory have been careful to point out that "looking" positions do not correlate with social groups, and that ideological positioning is placement in a representational system that has no one-to-one correspondence with social experience. While I would not want to argue that form is ideologically neutral, I would suggest that we have over-emphasized the ideological function of "signifying practice" at the expense of considering other ideological implications of the conflicting meanings in the text. Or, as Terry Lovell puts it, "While interpretation depends on analysis of the work's signifying practice, assessment of its meanings from the point of view of its validity, or of its ideology, depends on comparison between those structures of meaning and their object of reference, through the mediation of another type of discourse."[34] The impetus behind Marxist criticism, whether we want to admit it or not, is to make comparisons between social reality as we live it and ideology as it does not correspond to that reality. This we attempt to do knowing full well the futility of looking for real relations that are completely outside ideology.

Thus, while I am still willing to argue, as I did in earlier versions of this essay, that we can see the *Mahogany* narrative as a metaphor for the search for black female sexuality, I see something else in hindsight. I would describe this as the temptation in an emerging black feminist criticism, much like an earlier tendency in lesbian criticism, to place sexuality safely out of patriarchal bounds by declaring it outside culture, by furtively hiding it in subcultural enclaves where it can remain its "essential self," protected from the meaning-making mainstream culture. *Mahogany,* then, is finally about the mythical existence of something elusive. We know it through what white men do to secure it, and what black men are without it. It is the ultimate substance to the photographer—Tony Perkins's character—who dies trying to record its "trace" on film. It is known by degree—whatever is most wild and enigmatic, whatever cannot be conquered or subdued—the last frontier of female sexuality. Although it is undetectable to the advertising men who can analyze only physical attributes, it is immediately perceptible to a lesbian (Gavina herself, the owner of the Italian advertising agency), who uses it to promote the most inexplicable and subjective of commodities—perfume.[35] Contrary to the suggestion that black female sexuality might still remain in excess of culture, and hence unfathomed and uncodified, it is worked over again and again in mainstream culture because of its apparent elusiveness, and in this context it is rather like bottled scent, which is often thought to convey its essence to everyone but the person wearing it.

To return to my main point, as feminists have theorized women's sexuality, they have universalized from the particular experience of white women, thus effecting what Hortense Spillers has called a "deadly metonomy."[36] While white feminists theorize the female image in terms of objectification, fetishization, and symbolic absence, their black counterparts describe the body as the site of symbolic resistance and the "paradox of nonbeing," a reference to the period in African-American history when black female did not signify "woman."[37] What strikes me still in this comparison is the stubbornness of the terms of feminist discourse analysis, which has not been able to deal, for instance, with what it has meant historically to be designated as not-human, and how black women, whose bodies were legally not their own, fought against treatment based on this determination. Further, feminist analysis of culture as patriarchal cannot conceive of any connection between the female image and class or racial exploitation that includes the male. Historically, black men and women, although not equally endangered, have been simultaneously implicated in incidents of interracial brutality. During two different periods of African-American history, sexual assault, "symbolic of the effort to conquer the resistance the black woman could unloose," was a warning to the entire black community.[38] If, as feminists have argued, women's sexuality evokes an unconscious terror in men, then black women's sexuality represents a special threat to white patriarchy; the possibility of its eruption stands for the aspirations of the black race as a whole.

My frustration with the feminist voice that insists on change *at the level of language* is that this position can deal with the historical situation described above, only by turning it into discourse, and even as I write this, acutely aware as I am of the theoretical prohibitions against mixing representational issues with real historical ones, I feel the pressure to transpose people's struggles into more discursively manageable terms. However, a theory of ideology that separates the levels of the social formation in such a way that it is not only inappropriate but theoretically impossible to introduce the category of history into the analysis cannot be justified with Marxism. This has been argued elsewhere by others, among them Stuart Hall, who finds the "universalist tendency" found in both Freud and Lacan responsible for this impossibility. The incompatibility between Marxism and psychoanalytic theory is insurmountable at this time, he argues, because "the concepts elaborated by Freud (and reworked by Lacan) cannot, *in their in-general and universalist form,* enter the theoretical space of historical materialism."[39] In discussions within feminist film theory, it has often seemed the other way around—that historical materialism could not enter the space theorized by discourse analysis drawing on psychoanalytic concepts. Sealed off as it is (in theory), this analysis may not comprehend the category of the real historical subject, but its use will always have implications *for* that subject.

ENDNOTES

Earlier versions of this essay in *Cultural Critique,* no. 4 (Fall 1986), and *Screen* 29 (Autumn 1988).

1. These debates can be traced through the following: Henry Louis Gates, ed., *Black Literature and Literary Theory* (New York: Methuen, 1984); "Critical Fanonism," *Critical Inquiry* 17 (Spring 1991); Homi Bhabha, "What Does the Black Man Want?" *New Formations* 1 (Spring 1987); Stephen Feuchtwang, "Fanonian Spaces," *New Formations* 1 (Spring 1987); Kobena Mercer and Isaac Julien, "De Margin and De Centre," *Screen* 29 (Autumn 1988).
2. See, for instance, Patricia Hill Collins, *Black Feminist Thought: Knowledge, Consciousness, and the Politics of Empowerment* (New York: Unwin Hyman, 1991); Cheryl A. Wall, ed., *Changing Our Own Words: Essays on Criticism, Theory, and Writing by Black Women* (New Brunswick, N.J.: Rutgers University Press, 1989); Michelle Wallace, *Invisibility Blues: From Pop to Theory* (New York: Verso, 1990); Valerie Smith, "Reconstituting the Image: The Emergent Black Woman Director," *Callaloo* 11 (Fall 1988); Martina Attille, "Black Women and Representation," *Undercut,* nos. 14–15 (Summer 1985); Alile Sharon Larkin, "Black Women Filmmakers Defining Ourselves: Feminism in Our Own Voice," and Jacqueline Bobo, "*The Color Purple,* Black Women as Cultural Readers," both in *Female Spectators: Looking at Film and Television,* ed. E. Deidre Pribram (London: Verso, 1988); Karen Alexander, "Fatal Beauties: Black Women in Hollywood," in *Stardom: Industry of Desire,* ed. Christine Gledhill (New York: Routledge, 1991); see also *Black American Literature Forum 25* (Summer 1991) and *Wide Angle* 13 (July 1991).
3. Consider, for instance, Mary Ann Doane, "Dark Continents: Epistemologies of Racial and Sexual Difference in Psychoanalysis and Cinema," in *Femmes Fatales: Feminism, Film Theory, Psychoanalysis* (New York and London: Routledge, 1991).
4. bell hooks, *Feminist Theory: From Margin to Center* (Boston: South End Press, 1984), 14.
5. Marilyn Frye, *The Politics of Reality* (Trumansburg, N.Y.: Crossing Press, 1984), 113, 118.

6. Claire Johnston, "Women's Cinema as Counter-Cinema," in *Notes on Women's Cinema,* ed. Claire Johnston (London: Society for Education in Film and Television, 1973); Laura Mulvey, "Visual Pleasure and Narrative Cinema," *Screen* 16 (Autumn, 1985): 6–18.

7. Stuart Hall, "On Postmodernism and Articulation: An Interview," *Journal of Communication Inquiry* 10 (Summer 1986): 57.

8. As quoted in Annette Kolodny, "Respectability Is Eroding the Revolutionary Potential of Feminist Criticism," *Chronicle of Higher Education,* May 4, 1988, A52.

9. Lucie Arbuthnot and Gail Seneca, "Pre-Text and Text in *Gentlemen Prefer Blondes" Film Reader 5* (Winter 1981): 13–23.

10. Chris Straayer, *"Personal Best:* Lesbian/Feminist Audience," *Jump Cut* 29 (February 1984): 40–44; Elizabeth Ellsworth, "Illicit Pleasures: Feminist Spectators and *Personal Best,"* *Wide Angle* 8, no. 2 (1986): 46–56.

11. Monique Wittig, "The Straight Mind," *Feminist Issues* (Summer 1980): 107–11.

12. Gayle Rubin, "Thinking Sex: Notes for a Radical Theory of the Politics of Sexuality," in *Pleasure and Danger,* ed. Carol Yance (Boston: Routledge and Kegan Paul, 1984), 307.

13. Barbara Smith, "Towards a Black Feminist Criticism," in *The New Feminist Criticism,* ed. Elaine Showalter (New York: Pantheon, 1985), 169.

14. Bonnie Thornton Dill, "Race, Class, and Gender: Prospects for an All- Inclusive Sisterhood," *Feminist Studies* 9 (Spring 1983): 134; for a slightly different version of this essay, see " 'On the Hem of Life': Race, Class, and the Prospects for Sisterhood," in *Class, Race, and Sex: The Dynamics of Control,* ed. Amy Swerdlow and Hanna Lessinger (Boston: G. K. Hall, 1983); Margaret Simons, "Racism and Feminism: A Schism in the Sisterhood," *Feminist Studies 5* (Summer 1979): 392.

15. Adrienne Rich, in *On Lies, Secrets, and Silence* (New York: Norton, 1979), 302–303, notes that while blacks link their experience of racism with the white woman, this is still patriarchal racism working through her. It is possible, she says, that a black first grader, or that child's mother, or a black patient in a hospital, or a family on welfare, may experience racism most directly in the person of a white woman, who stands for those service professions through which white male supremacist society controls the mother, the child, the family, and all of us. It is *her* racism, yes, but a racism learned in the same patriarchal school which taught her that women are unimportant or unequal, not to be trusted with power, where she learned to mistrust and hear her own impulses for rebellion; to become an instrument.

16. Gloria Joseph, "The Incompatible Ménage à Trois: Marxism, Feminism, and Racism," in *Women and Revolution,* ed. Lydia Sargent (Boston: South End Press, 1981), 96; the Combahee River Collective, "Combahee River Collective Statement," in *Home Girls: A Black Feminist Anthology,* ed. Barbara Smith (New York: Kitchen Table: Women of Color Press, 1983), 275, compares their alliance with black men with the negative identification white women have with white men: "Our situation as Black people necessitates that we have solidarity around the fact of race, which white women of course do not need to have with white men, unless it is their negative solidarity as racial oppressors. We struggle together with Black men against racism, while we struggle with Black men about sexism."

17. "Combahee River Collective Statement," 272.

18. Michele Barrett, *Women's Oppression Today* (London: Verso, 1980), 15.

19. For a comparison between radical feminism, liberal feminism, and Marxist and socialist feminism, see Alison Jaggar, *Feminist Politics and Human Nature* N.J.: Rowman and Allenheld, 1983).

20. Sheila Rowbotham, "The Trouble with Patriarchy," in *People's History and Socialist Theory,* ed. Raphael Samuel (Boston: Routledge and Kegan Paul, 1981), 365.

21. Frantz Fanon, *Black Skin, White Masks,* trans. Charles Lam Markmann (Paris, 1952; reprint, New York: Grove Press, 1967), 161.

22. Simons, "Racism and Feminism," 387.

23. Barbara Omolade, "Hearts of Darkness," in *Powers of Desire: The Politics of Sexuality,* ed. Ann Snitow, Christine Stansell, and Sharon Thompson (New York: Monthly Review Press, 1983), 352.

24. Rennie Simpson, "The Afro-American Female: The Historical Context of the Construction of Sexual Identity," in *Powers of Desire,* 230.

25. Angela Davis, "The Black Woman's Role in the Community of Slaves," *The Black Scholar* (December 1971), 5–6.

26. Omolade, *Powers,* 352.

27. Joseph, "The Incompatible Ménage à Trois," 99; Audre Lorde, *Sister Outsider: Essays and Speeches* (Trumansburg, N.Y.: Crossing Press, 1984), 119, says:

    Because of the continuous battle against racial erasure that Black women and Black men share, some Black women still refuse to recognize that we are also oppressed as women, and that sexual hostility against Black women is practiced not only by the white racist society, but implemented within our Black communities as well. It is a disease striking the heart of Black nationhood, and silence will not make it disappear.

28. Hazel Carby, "'On the Threshold of Woman's Era': Lynching, Empire, and Sexuality in Black Feminist Theory," *Critical Inquiry* 12 (Autumn 1985): 276; Harriet E. Wilson, *Our Nig* (1859; reprint, New York: Random House, 1983); Frances E. W. Harper, *Ioia Lerpy, or Shadows Uplifted* (1892; reprint, New York: Oxford University Press, 1988); Pauline E. Hopkins, *Contending Forces* (1900, reprint, New York: Oxford University Press, 1988).

29. Linda Gordon and Ellen DuBois, "Seeking Ecstasy on the Battlefield: Danger and Pleasure in Nineteenth Century Feminist Sexual Thought," *Feminist Review* 13 (Spring 1983), 43.

30. Jacquelyn Dowd Hall, "'The Mind That Bums in Each Body': Women, Rape, and Racial Violence," in *Powers of Desire,* 332; See also, Jacquelyn Dowd Hall, *The Revolt against Chivalry* (New York: Columbia University Press, 1979), and Angela Davis, *Women, Race and Class* (New York: Vintage, 1983), chap. 11.

31. As quoted in Carby, "'On the Threshold of Woman's Era,'" 275.

32. See, for instance, Jessie Fauset, *There Is Confusion* (New York: Boni and Liveright, 1924), and *Plum Bun* (1928; reprint, New York: Routledge and Kegan Paul, 1983); Nella Larsen, *Quicksand* (1928), and *Passing* (1929; reprint, New Brunswick, N.J.: Rutgers University Press, 1986).

33. Fredric Jameson, in "Pleasure: A Political Issue," *Formations of Pleasure* (Boston: Routledge and Kegan Paul, 1983), 7, interprets Mulvey's connection between viewing pleasure and male power as the conferral of a "right to look." He does not take this further, but I find the term suggestive and at the same time potentially volatile.

34. Terry Lovell, *Pictures of Reality* (London: British Film Institute, 1980), 90,

35. Richard Dyer, *"Mahogany,"* in *Films for Women,* ed. Charlotte Brunsdon (London: British Film Institute, 1986), 135, Suggested this first about Gavina.

36. Hortense J. Spillers, "Interstices: A Small Drama of Words," in *Pleasure and Danger,* 78.

37. Ibid., 77.

38. Davis, "The Black Woman's Role," 11.

39. Stuart Hall, "Debate: Psychology, Ideology and the Human Subject," *Ideology and Consciousness* (October 1977), 118–19.

1. In what way did early screwball comedies "reappraise" and challenge the institution of marriage?

2. How did early screwball comedies define love relationships in terms of dramatic conflict?

3. In what way have film critics disagreed on how to "label" film noir?

4. According to *The Maritorious Melodrama: Film Noir with a Female Detective*, what differences persist in traditional film noir with male protagonists and those with female protagonists, that would prompt a writer like Donald Phelps to coin the term 'cinema gris'?

5. In what way did film noir tropes and storytelling conventions address threats to patriarchal rules in America?

A constructivist approach to film theory is to a film student reconnaissance into the uncharted sphere of cinema. What greater joy exists than to uncover the magic behind the trick—the man behind the curtain? One needs to look no further than the confines of a childhood dream for this universal curiosity. For the rest of us, J. Dudley Andrew's assertion of the "sheer pleasure of knowing," might be reason enough.

The authors in this section deal primarily with the minds behind production, or more specifically, the thought process that goes into creating the individual shots in a film—the composition, the staging, and the lighting of which seasoned directors, production designers, and cinematographers are so acutely cognizant. Robert Spadoni's didactic yet necessary analysis of mise-en-scène provides the fundamental components to a film's look. His thorough breakdown of the terminology and visual language encompasses not just design and staging, but also cinematography. He also goes on to reflect upon cultural perceptions of stylization as it pertains to costume and lighting. John

THE WAY WE LOOK

Mateer's treatise on mainstream production methods sheds light on changing perspectives amongst cinematographers who once worked in the "old" system of physical film and who currently work in a digital medium. The act of embracing a new tech is thus ostensibly an intolerable relinquishing of creative control. Hsiu-Chuang Deppman's essay balances two approaches from contrasting Chinese directors—Chen Guofu (Kuo-Fu Chen) and Cai Mingliang (Ming-Liang Tsai) and how each filmmaker depicts his female protagonists in similarly-fashioned films. Particularly interesting in this reading is how Deppman contrasts the concept of male gaze with female "scrutiny." Lovorka Grmusa and Keine Wurth's impressive work *Cinematography as a Literary Concept in the (Post)Modern Age*, while an essay largely theoretical in scope, finds a home amidst a discussion on the visual appeal of cinema itself. Throughout, the parallels between cinematographic language and textual language are drawn—perhaps with the suggestion that cinematic language possesses transformative properties absent in literary text.

ROBERT SPADONI

MISE-EN-SCÈNE

Originally a French theatrical term meaning "put in the scene," **mise-en-scène** is everything in front of the camera. If we imagine our basic building block, the shot, as a box, mise-en-scène is everything inside this box. Mise-en-scène splits into four main categories—and let me stress that starting now, we really begin to move systematically through a large set of terms. I'll continue to remind you where we are in the big picture—what umbrella term we're underneath and what term that term is underneath—but your efforts will pay off if you review these relationships as you go. The four categories of mise-en-scène are *setting, costume and makeup, lighting,* and *staging.*

Once a space is filmed, it is transformed in ways that we'll look at in this chapter. This space, before it's transformed, is called **profilmic space.** Think of profilmic space as the visual raw material a camera takes in and turns into mise-en-scène. The notion of profilmic space might seem increasingly quaint as, more and more in mainstream films, there may be no profilmic space at all, or less of it anyway, as filmmakers create new spaces and modify existing ones on computers. Still, thinking about profilmic space as something captured and transformed by the camera continues to be a useful way to think about film art, for as we look at this "stuff in the box," we'll be asking how the elements in front of the camera resolve into images on a flat screen. When we do, we'll be considering *composition* and asking questions of a sort that, if you've studied painting or photography, you may have asked before. Much of the art of cinema lies in this transformation from three dimensions into two.

STYLIZATION

One last idea to introduce before we move into the specifics of mise-en-scène is that an element in a film can be more or less *stylized*. This is a useful term because stylization is the other side of the coin of "realism," and it can be easier to describe how something is stylized than to describe how it is "realistic." (Realism might seem like a straightforward idea, but what people mean by it varies considerably.) **Stylization** pushes an element in a film outside the bounds to which we might expect the element, if we encountered it in daily experience (or perhaps another film), to conform. It's not, strictly speaking, how much the element differs from "reality" that is most important. In a viewer-centered approach, stylization is more a matter of perception than of objectively measuring a film element's deviation from the real thing. And yet while the standards of judgment will be subjective, most would agree that Fred Flintstone's prehistoric car is more stylized than the Batmobile (pick your version) and that the Batmobile is more stylized than a Toyota Prius.

Stylization is a matter of perception and also one of degree. Consider the Disney film *The Princess and the Frog* (Ron Clements and John Musker, 2009). How stylized is this film? Surely its characters and settings look more "cartoonish" than the ones seen in most live-action movies. But consider the moment when, in the scene pictured, a character bursts into song and the look of the film changes dramatically. The color scheme shifts to a brighter palette; finer details of face, costume, and setting vanish; and the figures seem to be less bounded by gravity and the limits of human anatomy than they did moments ago. If the film was stylized before, it has become more so with the start of this number. Stylization is a matter of degree.

Figure 7.1. *The Princess and the Frog.* Tiana (right) and her mother visit the old sugar mill where Tiana hopes one day to open her own restaurant.

Figure 7.2. As she begins singing "Almost There," imagining herself running the restaurant, the film becomes more stylized. The art deco look of the number mirrors an illustration, torn from a magazine, on which her father wrote "Tiana's Place" years ago, when she was a little girl and he taught her to work hard for her dreams.

SETTING

Our first component of mise-en-scène is **setting,** which is the physical environment wherein a film's action takes place. Broadly, we can speak of two pairs of options.

LOCATION AND STUDIO FILMING

First, filmmakers can use an actual setting ("shot on location in the Florida Everglades") or build one—and, increasingly in mainstream film-making, building a setting can mean creating one, wholly or in part, digitally with computers. Using an existing locale can be associated with notions of realism—and also with low-budget filmmaking, since it's usually cheaper to shoot in, say, an actual diner than to build one. Or, if it's a hard-to-reach place, location shooting can be associated with *big*-budget filmmaking. During the Hollywood studio era (roughly 1917 to 1960), the increased costs of building sets versus going on location were often judged to be worth the corresponding gain in control. No need to worry about rain pelting the diner window and delaying shooting or ruining a take if the diner is inside a soundstage, and the rain will only fall if the filmmakers wish it. Today, computer-generated environments afford filmmakers greater control than ever before.

Parts of the Soviet Montage film *Storm over Asia* (aka *The Heir to Genghis Khan,* Vsevolod Pudovkin, USSR, 1928) were shot on the Mongolian plains. This historical fiction film shows, in documentary fashion, landscapes, indigenous dwellings, and rituals that remain fascinating today for the rare glimpses of remote locations, peoples, and cultural practices they provide. Location shooting contributes to impressions of this film's realism, while settings in *Frankenstein* (James Whale, 1931) practically flaunt their studio-built artificiality, a quality that some admirers of the film find contributes to its nightmarish atmosphere.

STYLIZED AND UNSTYLIZED SETTINGS

Second, a setting can be more or less stylized. That is, the degree to which it meets our expectations based on our sense of such a place in the real world, or perhaps another film, can vary. This might seem like a rewording of the "built versus found locale" distinction above, but in fact built sets can be rendered indistinguishable from found ones, and a found setting, filmed from certain angles and with certain lighting, can be made to appear strange and unreal. Examples of stylized settings are in *Careful* (Guy Maddin, Canada, 1992), a contemporary film with a deliberately antiquated look and sound.

Figure 7.3. *Storm over Asia*. Location shooting.

Figure 7.4. *Frankenstein*. Studio-built "exteriors."

Figure 7.5. *Careful*. A stylized setting.

PROPS

A film's setting includes props. A **prop** is an object that serves some function within the narrative. The spinning top at the end of *Inception* is a prop. The ring that Frodo bears in the *Lord of the Rings* movies is a prop. So is the diary the woman reads in *The Curious Case of Benjamin Button*. Recall from chapter that anything can be a motif. This includes props. In *The Seventh Seal* (Ingmar Bergman, Sweden, 1957) a character plays chess at different points in the story with a figure representing Death. The chess set is a prop and a motif. So are the knives in *Secrets of a Soul*.

COSTUME AND MAKEUP

An unstylized Civil War Confederate soldier costume would match, as accurately as possible, the cut, stitching, buckles, fabric, color, and wear and tear of an actual uniform as far as can be determined from drawings, photographs, and other archival sources. Or suppose some aspect of the original uniform has not been copied in Civil War films very often; a costume that duplicates *this* original aspect might strike some viewers as stylized. (In ancient Rome a thumbs-down gesture from the emperor meant *Let the defeated gladiator live;* in every gladiator film it means the opposite.) Notions of realism are shaped, like everything else in a film, by conventions. Still, if stylization is to an extent subjective, most viewers would nevertheless agree that the formal attire worn by the title character in *Willy Wonka & the Chocolate Factory* (Mel Stuart, 1971) is more stylized than that worn by the title character in *Lincoln* (Steven Spielberg, 2012).

What if there exists no direct real-world reference for comparison? Can we still call a character's costume or makeup stylized or unstylized? Consider the costumes in the science

Figure 7.5. *Killer of Sheep* (Charles Burnett, 1979). A woman checks her reflection in a pot lid, a prop in the film.

fiction horror film *Alien* (Ridley Scott, 1979). The wrinkled jackets and greasy caps of the spaceship crew, like the lived-in look of the ship's interior—the coffee cups and general clutter—would strike many viewers as less stylized than the brightly colored costumes and interiors in the cartoonishly futuristic *Flash Gordon* (Mike Hodges, 1980).

Like the other aspects of mise-en-scène, a character's costume or makeup can pick up colors or other details that play into a motif, provide clues to a character's nature or psychology, and contribute in striking or subtle ways to a shot's composition. A costume can also act as a disguise that a viewer might or might not see through. In *All about Eve* (Joseph L. Mankiewicz, 1950) the title character waits every night outside a Broadway theater stage door in the hopes of meeting her idol, Margo Channing. One night she manages to get backstage, where she quickly demonstrates her eagerness to pick up what crumbs of wisdom she can from this grande dame of the stage and to help out in every way that's asked of her. At this first meeting Eve wears a buttoned-up trench coat and frumpy hat. This plain, diffident girl is the picture of abject humility and fan worship. But it's all an act, for Eve is actually a treacherous, ruthlessly ambitious aspiring actress. Over the course of the story Margo, her friends, and we will learn all about Eve. Or consider, conversely, how one could argue that Eve's costume at this first meeting *does* tell us about her, since it covers up nearly every part of her body (she's even wearing gloves). This character, her costume seems to be announcing, is about nothing if not concealment and camouflage.

A shot's **lighting** can come from diegetic sources of illumination (the sun, candles, lamps) within the setting, nondiegetic ones located outside the frame, or a combination. Two ways we can speak about lighting are in terms of its *quality* and *direction*—but first, to consider lighting is to consider shadows. Here are two kinds.

TWO KINDS OF SHADOW

An **attached shadow** is a shadow cast by something onto itself because it's not fully illuminated. The side of a planet that's facing away from the sun it orbits is in darkness; this is an attached shadow. Noses cast attached shadows on faces. This kind of shadow helps to make objects appear more three dimensional. A **cast shadow** results when something is placed between an object and a light source such that a shadow of that something—tree branches, a person—falls on the object. A film may use shadows for expressive purposes, suggesting a character's interior state or foreshadowing events. In *Kiss Me Deadly* (Robert Aldrich, 1955) a character accuses private investigator Mike Hammer of taking the law into his own hands, saying that anyone who does that "might as well be living in a jungle." This accusation plays into a motif that draws on the way Hammer prowls around his apartment when he suspects that someone is hiding in it; the curiously treelike column in this space; and, in his building lobby, vine-patterned wallpaper and crisscrossing shadows that make the lobby resemble a dark animal lair.

LIGHTING QUALITY AND DIRECTION

Lighting quality can be *hard* and even harsh, such as in sunlight at noon or under an interrogator's lamp. Shadows are sharp-edged under this intense sort of lighting. Or lighting can be more *diffuse*, softening shadows and decreasing *contrast*—which is the amount of difference between an image's darkest and lightest tones.

The image from *The Scarlet Empress* is also useful for talking about **lighting direction**. Can you see where the light is coming from in this image? A way to tell is by looking at the direction in which the shadow of the nose is falling and at how the cheek hollows are darkening. These tell us the light is coming from above and to the right. Less flattering is **bottom lighting** (or underlighting). Characteristically seen in horror films, this lighting comes from below and can cast grotesque shadows on faces and walls. Lighting from above is **top lighting**.

Sticking with direction, also evident in the *Scarlet Empress* image, is **backlighting,** which comes from behind. Backlighting commonly serves two purposes. First, it can make figures glow in a glamorous fashion, giving them a halo that renders them luminously unlike the ordinary people who populate the real world. Second, and especially important in black-and-white films, it helps

Figure 7.6. *The Graduate* (Mike Nichols, 1967). Attached shadows on Benjamin's face.

Figure 7.6. He takes a few steps, and now the cast shadows of window blinds fall across him. This character is about to begin an affair with an older married woman that will plunge him into self-loathing and shame. Here, in the hotel room, cast shadows suggest the surreptitious nature of the encounter and also that Benjamin has walked into a trap.

Figure 7.7. *High Noon* (Fred Zinnemann, 1952). In this shot of this figure, who's about to face a band of killers alone, harsh daylight sets him off starkly against the empty background.

Figure 7.8. *The Scarlet Empress* (Josef von Sternberg, 1934). Diffuse lighting complements and accentuates the facial features of actress Marlene Dietrich.

Figure 7.9. *Dracula* (Tod Browning, 1931). A lamp seen in another shot motivates gruesome bottom lighting on the vampire as he closes in on his next victim.

Figure 7.10. *Shaft* (Gordon Parks, 1971). Top lighting on the title character as he stands in a phone booth.

Figure 7.11. *Osama* (Siddiq Barmak, Afghanistan/Ireland/JP, 2003). Silhouette lighting in a shot of demonstrators fleeing Taliban soldiers who have turned fire hoses on them.

separate figures from backgrounds, making them easier to pick out with the eye. Backlighting set to these purposes is sometimes called **edge lighting** (or rim lighting). When backlighting leaves figures entirely or predominantly in shadow, this is **silhouette lighting**.

LIGHTING IN CLASSICAL HOLLYWOOD CINEMA

The style of filmmaking that characterizes mainstream narrative films is **classical Hollywood cinema,** which has been around since the late 1910s and has since spread around the world. In this style backlighting combines with two other kinds in what is known as the **three-point lighting system.** A second of these lights is the **key light,** which is a shot's main lighting source, the one that, in *The Scarlet Empress*, comes from above and to the right. This light is usually motivated by a diegetic source, even if it's not the actual source of the lighting we see. Third is the **fill light,** which softens the shadows created by the key light and helps create a generally more flattering look for faces.

We can distinguish two major kinds of three-point setup. **High-key lighting** is relatively even, tends to be bright, and minimizes shadows. **Low-key lighting** provides little or no fill light, increases contrast, and results in darker and crisper shadows. Different genres are associated with each setup—comedies and musicals with high key; horror films, thrillers, and film noirs with low. But like the variations within these broad configurations, their possible applications are endless, and one must be cautious when making generalizations.

As with the other components of mise-en-scène, lighting can exhibit varying degrees of stylization. The shimmering lighting in the *Scarlet Empress* image is an example of stylized lighting. The more extreme lighting in *Careful* is another. The image from *Shaft*, a gritty urban crime drama, shows an example of unstylized lighting.

Figure 7.12. High-key lighting in the comedy *Monkey Business* (Howard Hawks, 1952).

Figure 7.13. Low-key lighting in *Blue Velvet* (David Lynch, 1986), a dark and disturbing thriller.

STAGING

Staging refers to what the figures in front of the camera do. We can think about staging in two ways: (1) acting and performance and (2) how the figures combine with other elements in the mise-en-scène to form patterns on the screen.

ACTING AND PERFORMANCE

Unlike other aspects of film style, acting can be hard to analyze because we lack the terminology to describe exactly what, say, Marlon Brando is doing in the drama *On the Waterfront* (Elia Kazan, 1954) versus what Steve Martin is doing in the comedy *The Jerk* (Carl Reiner, 1979). Still, the concept of stylization can help. Martin engages in broad physical comedy, which no one expects to look real as long as it's funny. He grimaces, leaps around, balletically twists his body into ludicrous positions, and telegraphs his emotions in the most hyperbolic fashion. Brando, in contrast, keeps his gestures small and grounds everything he does in the psychology of his character. In this film's most famous scene, the washed-up boxer, feeling bitterly let down, and grieving over what might have been, pours his heart out to his brother, telling him, "I could've been a contender." The scene remains a benchmark, even a cliché, for great (that is, realistic) film acting. Whether or not one considers it great, Brando's performance is surely less stylized than Martin's.

Incisive close reading rests on a foundation of common sense, yet vivid, description of what is happening on the screen. Practicing this skill will serve you well as you consider the mercurial art of film performance in your formal analysis.

SHIFTING PATTERNS ON THE SCREEN

Staging also refers to the actors' positions and movements in front of the camera. Again, three dimensions resolve onto two, so moving figures will disappear behind other ones and behind objects in the setting and grow larger or smaller as they get closer to or farther from the camera. Staging is a delicate and underappreciated cinematic art. Tracing it as it unfolds from one moment to the next can lead you to discoveries of virtuoso orchestrations of figural movements and cinematic effects.

Figure 7.14. *Ugetsu* (Kenji Mizoguchi, JP, 1953). A desolate and abandoned woman staggers into a frame crowded with branches, posts, grass, and shadows. We easily pick her out as she steps first into one aperture frame …

Figures can be arranged shallowly, strung laterally across the frame, or they can be set into the depth. When staging unfolds in a setting that has significant depth, and utilizes this depth, this is **deep-space staging.** We haven't covered editing yet, but in general, a film that relies less heavily on editing will rely more on staging to control its narrational flow and aesthetic appearance. Editing provides a means to guide viewers, but staging, whether or not a film minimizes editing, does this as well.

Figure 7.15. … and then another.

Figures can draw attention to themselves by moving or, conversely,

Figure 7.16. In *Raise the Red Lantern* (Yimou Zhang, CH/HK/Taiwan, 1991) a household's servants and wives live within a rigid and oppressive social hierarchy. This geometric composition, one of many in the film (and so a motif), sorts the characters into their boxes, with the lowliest servants, further down the pecking order than the wives, occupying the compartments nearer the fringes.

Figure 7.17. *West Side Story.* Tony sneaks into Maria's bedroom.

by holding still in a shot in which other elements are in motion. Or the eye can be drawn to a figure when it turns to face us or when it comes closer to the camera so that it fills more of the frame. A figure turning its back to the camera can encourage us to look elsewhere, including at something we shouldn't miss—or we might become riveted to the rear-facing figure as we wonder what this person, whose face we can't see, is thinking. Another way to focus attention is through a device called **aperture framing,** in which windows, doors, and other enclosing shapes embedded in the mise-en-scène section off portions of the frame. Placing or moving a figure into one of these visual pockets will draw the eye to it, and the device can be set to other purposes as well.

Figure 7.18. The two embrace …

Figure 7.19. …. and sing "Somewhere." Lighting places them in separate zones within the frame.

Figure 7.20. Then a piece of furniture in the foreground does the same.

Figure 7.21 Then they stand, and a thick line on the wall behind them does it again. The more emphatically these two cling to each other and pledge their love, the more the film hints that they have no future together.

Last, staging can be more or less stylized. The image from *Careful* provides a hint of the stiffly artificial staging in that film.

MISE-EN-SCÈNE IN A SCENE FROM *WEST SIDE STORY*

The four components of mise-en-scène can come together in rich and intricate ways. In *West Side Story* (Jerome Robbins and Robert Wise, 1961), a modern musical retelling of *Romeo and Juliet,* Tony is on the run after killing Maria's brother in a gang fight. He slips into Maria's bedroom through her window, and she, despite her shock and grief, lovingly welcomes him. In this scene they'll sing a duet titled "Somewhere."

A glass door motivates expressive lighting later in the scene. Tony assures Maria, "We're really together now," but lighting splits the frame and portends otherwise for these star-crossed lovers. Seconds later, mise-en-scène separates them again as we view them through the ironwork footboard of Maria's bed. In the same shot, as they continue singing "There's a place for us … ," the two stand, and the scene sets a divider between them for a third time. There is no place for these two. One needn't know the outcome of Shakespeare's play to intuit that this young love is doomed.

HSIU-CHUANG DEPPMAN

CINEMA OF DISILLUSIONMENT: CHEN GUOFU, CAI MINGLIANG, AND TAIWAN'S SECOND NEW WAVE

Although the study of Taiwan Cinema has recently been gaining momentum, the specific strengths and attractions of the Second New Wave (1987–present) have received only sporadic critical attention. This movement deserves study, however, not least because it includes such renowned directors as Ang Lee (Li An) and Cai Mingliang, whose global reputations have helped solidify the international appreciation and sponsorship of Taiwan's film industry. These two have also helped pave the way for a range of other key figures including the more locally based Wang Xiaodi, Wu Nianzhen, and Zhang Zuoji. The sprawling diversity of aesthetic visions and philosophical positions mean that there is no simplistic way to summarize the movement's signature innovations. Yet a focused comparative study of two key filmmakers, Chen Guofu and Cai Mingliang, who are very different and yet equally important to the Second New Wave, can illuminate some of the movement's most salient features.

Chen Guofu and Cai Mingliang are two of Taiwan's most significant contemporary filmmakers. Chen's *Guozhong nüsheng* (*Schoolgirl*, 1989) and Cai's *qingshaonian nuozha* (*Rebel of the Neon God*, 1992) were highly acclaimed debuts marking a recognizable break between the New Taiwan

Hsiu-Chuang Deppman, "Cinema of Disillusionment: Chen Guofu, Cai Mingliang, and Taiwan's Second New Wave," *positions: asia critique*, vol. 17, no. 2, pp. 435-437, 441-454. Copyright © 2009 by Duke University Press. Reprinted with permission.scène," A Pocket Guide to Analyzing Films, pp. 71-88. Copyright © 2014 by University of California Press. Reprinted with permission.

Cinema (1982–87) and the Second New Wave. Aesthetically, the two directors experiment with structural repetition, play-within-the-play, and symbolic mise-en-scène, with Cai, in particular, testing the possibilities of antinarrative. Thematically, they investigate the experiences of urban dystopia, especially the paradoxes of postmodern individualism. Lauded for their sensitive treatment of provocative issues like sex, rebellion, and alienation, their films are full of confused youths and independent-but-lonely urbanites lost in Taipei's urban jungles, simultaneously disdaining and yearning for companionship.

To consider Chen and Cai together is to synopsize the cinematic possibilities of the Second New Wave, for they represent the movement's different strengths. Chen is a notable critic-turned-director,[1] while Cai began his career as a screenwriter.[2] The difference in training shows: Chen has been deeply involved in theorizing, constructing, and evaluating the critical discourse of Taiwan Cinema. Cai, however, like his famous New Taiwan Cinema predecessor Hou Hsiao-hsien (Hou Xiaoxian), is a film practitioner who speaks mainly through the experiments of film art and the aesthetics of his camera.

Although many international film festivals have affirmed the cinematic achievements of Taiwan's Second New Wave, the movement, with the exception of Ang Lee, faces questions about its marketing viability and its undefined relationship with Taiwanese history and politics. It is no wonder that audiences often ask whether these films should be interpreted as reflections of or on Taiwan's postcolonial identity crisis. Is there, for example, any causality between the directors' attachment to urban disorientation and Taiwan's turbulent politics? Is it possible to understand the relationships between aesthetics and ideology that have enabled this movement to reenergize and market Taiwan Cinema?

These questions are closely related to the directors' own conceptions of how Taiwan cinema should be situated in the global political economy. Chen and Cai readily appreciate Taiwan's complex situation: while it is a de facto island state ideologically and economically aligned with "first-world" powers like the United States and Japan, it is sometimes also seen as politically and geographically akin to "third-world" states. Taiwan's adaptability to be neither, both, and between worlds—I will simply call this "transworldliness"—endows its artistic productions with a stylistically potent but anxious malleability. Speaking from the periphery of a nonpopulist cinema in the marginalized state of an atypical nation, contemporary Taiwan cinema embodies a true-to-itself creative freedom, obliged neither to adhere to political ideology nor to defend aesthetic autonomy. Indeed, for those who see those options as mutually opposed, Taiwan cinema can be surprising. This is especially clear in the case of the two Second New Wave works under discussion in part 2 of this essay, Chen Guofu's *Zhenghun Qishi* (*The Personals*, 1998) and Cai Mingliang's *Ni nabian jidian?* (*What Time Is It There?* 2001).

These two films have been instrumental in the revival of Taiwan Cinema both at the box office and on festival circuits. *The Personals* broke attendance records for all recent domestic films and has garnered five domestic and international film awards.[3] *What Time Is It There?* was also an important market success (one of the few in Cai's illustrious career), received eleven impressive awards, and was nominated for the *Palme d'or* at the 2001 Cannes Film Festival. For both critical and public audiences, these two films managed to speak seriously and entertainingly about love, life, and the confounding reality of Taiwan's shifting identity politics. Departing from their New Taiwan Cinema's predecessors in tone, style, philosophy, and theme, Chen and Cai create what I call a "cinema of disillusionment," a minimalist, naturalist combination of romance and dark comedic humor that presents a disenchanted but realistic view of life on the island.

[...]

LOCATING SEXUAL POLITICS

Synopses

Chen's *The Personals* records a series of monologues of a lonely, educated, and attractive female ophthalmologist with the answering machine of her absent lover and her dialogues with dozens of respondents to her newspaper ad seeking a marital partner. Du Jiazhen (René Ruoying Liu) is fearful that her married lover has left her to return to his wife. Acting upon a complex impulse of revenge, worry, and risk, she interviews a wide range of respondents in an empty, upscale tea house in Taipei. Every day she gets on the bus to attend a "meeting" and her routine takes on the monotonous regularity of a work schedule. At night, she keeps a voice journal on her lover's answering machine, from which the viewer learns about such matters as her pregnancy, abortion, and opinions of the various suitors. Her daytime meetings never yield a promising result and her voice journal abruptly ends when her lover's wife picks up to inform Du of her husband's sudden death.

In contrast to Chen's monologues and dialogues, Cai combines theater of the absurd with silent comedy. Xiaokang (Lee Kang-sheng), a quiet, asocial vendor of wristwatches, is single and lives with his parents. After the death of his father, he encounters an obstinate female customer, Xiangqi (Chen Xiangqi), who insists on buying the watch he is wearing. Despite initial resistance, Xiaokang relents; the woman takes the watch and later embarks on a solitary journey to Paris. The film then divides into a parallel surveillance of the lonely lives of these two people in far-apart cities. The watch provides a transcontinental connection between them and when Xiaokang obsessively begins to change all the time-keeping devices into Paris time, he eventually misleads his newly widowed mother (Lu Yijing) into believing in the untimely return of her husband's ghost. She then seeks help from a traditional Taiwanese priest to establish communication with her deceased husband. The film concludes with three disappointing sexual encounters: Xiaokang with a thieving prostitute, his mother with an imaginary ghost, and the woman in Paris with an unresponsive lesbian lover.

Both films parody love stories by having soulless one-night stands replace soul mates, true love, and marriage. Chen Guofu explains that *The Personals* "reveals a crisis of communication in today's urban society where modern men and women want to be loved, but are too scared to begin any potential relationship."[17] Despite the ubiquitous cell phones, Internet, and other means of instant connection in the age of media, there is little communication. To what extent, Chen wonders, can a postmodern relationship provide the security of companionship without compromising individual freedom?

Cai's characters reverse the priorities of these concerns. Not only do his protagonists feign no desire for communication despite the proliferation of communicative tools at their disposal, but they are quite willing to sacrifice personal freedom for a Platonic relationship that offers no tangible companionship. This is especially evident in Xiaokang's temporal "pursuit" of Xiangqi and Xiaokang's mother's "waiting" for her deceased husband. In making *What Time Is It There?* Cai wanted "to put people in situations where they do not have love." This narrative situation enables us "to know how much love we need, and what kind of relationships we want."[18] In order to pursue his quasi-epistemological experiments in the first phase of a postromantic society, Cai constructs and compares three kinds—one might say species, to emphasize his cool scientism—of intrigues: a tenuous transcontinental intertemporal fusion of unlike souls; an ersatz human-ghost "reunion" between a wife and her dead husband; and a half-hearted, unsuccessful search for same-sex comfort.

Camera and Sexual Politics

Chen Guofu and Cai Mingliang destabilize the traditional relationship between the camera and their female stars in a way that challenges the camera's existential and narrative control over the image of women. Instead of being eroticized as objects of desire, women in their films question, undermine, and contradict the desirability of their images. This is an important stylistic and ideological statement against traditional commercial films, because their camera "castrates" the eye's autocratic phallus in ways that remove erotic pleasure from the voyeurism of female bodies.

Chen and Cai begin by reconfiguring women's relations with their own private spaces. In such intimate locations as bathroom and bedroom, the camera is often deliberately paralyzed in a position that makes it unable either to disclose women's physical secrets or advance a spectator's sexual fantasy.

1) Bathroom

Both films include scenes in which the female protagonist is alone in a bathroom. In *The Personals*, the scene occurs after Du Jiazhen posts the marriage ad in the newspapers and her future seems to be wide open. The voyeuristic camera, accompanied by the narrative exposition of her matter-of-fact voice-over, moves ever so slowly to close in and sneak up on the protagonist from outside the window (fig. 8.1). This is a classic setup that frames the woman in a passive, unknowing, and vulnerable position. Mary Ann Doane, in her essay "Film and the Masquerade," characterizes the act of peeping as "a pleasure in seeing what is prohibited in relation to the female body. The image orchestrates a gaze, a limit, and its pleasurable transgression."[19] However, Chen's camera refuses to oblige this traditional anticipation. His next shot is an extreme close-up of Jiazhen's blurred face reflected in the bathroom's misty mirror (fig. 8.2). This blurry image shows the failure of the transgressive gaze to capture its prey; it is itself being trapped inside the immobilized camera lens. Chen's radical shift of camera angles from outside to inside, from peeping to being stared back at, reverses (or tries to reverse) the power dynamic between the woman and the camera: she is no longer a passive object of gaze; she may not control the visibility and meanings of her image, but

Figure 8.1. Window View of Jiazhen's Bathroom

Figure 8.2. Blurred Mirror Reflection of Jiazhen

Figure 8.3. Clear Mirror Reflection of Jiazhen

Figure 8.4. Xiangqi's Bathroom

she is not without an awareness that may imply agency, embodied by her refusal to engage in the coy give-and-take cinematic performance of desire. Indeed, Jiazhen's own ambition for ownership of the view becomes even more pronounced in the next shot in which she wipes off the steam on the mirror/camera lens to unveil an expressionless face (fig. 8.3). This disclosure through the screen of a mirrored reflection exposes neither her body nor her inner secrets. Instead, it is the camera that is being caught looking by Jiazhen's intense gaze into the mirror/lens/audience.

This is a transformative moment. Not only has Jiazhen quit her job, published a marriage ad, and decided to start interviewing candidates, she also has changed her appearance and assumed a false identity. Her struggle for control of her own image—in the mirror as well as in the lens—reflects her larger, perhaps societally emblematic, desire to take control of reconstructing the meanings of life.

Similarly, Cai Mingliang sets important limits on the intimating capacity of the voyeuristic camera. In one of the most strident scenes of her self-scrutiny, Xiangqi traces her steps back to the hotel's semi-private bathroom to look for her dual time-zoned watch. After retrieving the lost object, she casually stops to look at herself in the mirror (fig. 8.4). The camera quite noticeably looks in from outside and stays detachedly still in the duration. The medium long shot of her mirror image generates a sense of distance and even hostility between her self-gaze and the audience to render her ambivalent look inscrutable. Unlike Chen, Cai often prefers medium shots to close-ups. His resistance to zoom in to provide the viewer with a more detailed scrutiny of the protagonist's (lack of) expression defies the convention in narrative cinema of using the camera movement to dictate audience response. Instead, he favors a distance and ambiguity that leave ample room for interpretation.

Although Xiangqi is in a bathroom—a cinematic locale replete with sexual expectations—Cai's staging disrupts any erotic fantasy. Fully clothed in a generic black overcoat, Xiangqi's self-gaze in a well-lit space is asexual because, like Jiazhen, she does not mobilize any feminine guise to charm herself or the camera/audience. Furthermore, Cai's lighting frames the focus of the view on her face alone and, as a result, creates a reflection of a disembodied gaze that defies the camera's power of objectification.

Despite the camera's voyeuristic intrusion into the protagonist's private moment of reflection, Cai gives Xiangqi profuse physical and metaphorical space to stay independent from the control of both the plot and the camera. This is a first indication that, like Jiazhen, Xiangqi has an aesthetic, narrative, and physical autonomy that suggests, if not exactly defines, the postmodern experience of existing precariously between worlds (e.g., Europe and Asia), gazes (e.g., camera/spectator and self), and genders (e.g., feminine, amorphous, and masculine).

More fantasy-destroyers than fantasies themselves, these women resist the imperial power of both camera and audience; the bathroom scenes show how, subtly but unmistakably, Chen and Cai widen and complicate women's subjectivity.

2) Bedroom

If the reflection in the bathroom glass mimics the limitation and "paralysis" of the camera, denying both pleasure and knowledge to its collusive gaze, scenes of the bedroom expose a sublimation of libido. There are many important bedroom views in both films. In *The Personals*, Jiazhen repeats her bedtime ritual—the voice recording—six times, and during the course of these repetitions, her relationship with the bed evolves to symbolize her increasing isolation. In *What Time Is It There?* all three key characters are defined by their clandestine activities in the bedrooms (i.e., Xiaokang's urination, his mother's masturbation, and Xiangqi's compulsive eating). Strikingly, with the exception of Xiangqi's brief aborted affair, all of the characters appear alone in their boxed-in space, indulging in the personal idiosyncrasies that are symptomatic of their unfulfilled sexuality.

Among Jiazhen's six bedroom scenes, the first sets the tone of illustrating her diminished physical presence and psychological need for love in her own fortified bubble (fig. 8.5). Chen constructs the mise-en-scène in a way that deliberately obscures and obstructs the view of the protagonist. From the shadowy lighting and camouflaged clothing, to oversized glasses and enormous mosquito net that takes up more than half of the screen, the visual disorientation of the setting transforms Du Jiazhen into an inconspicuous part of the background. This eclectic collection of visual clues speaks of a retreat, a disappearance, a deiconization, as well as a refusal to make the woman on screen an erotic object of scrutiny. Notably, the blue lighting on the set (as reflected in the window) further adds to the audience's imagination a colored, otherworldly view of her repression and anxiety. Jiazhen communicates with a machine that seldom rings or speaks back. She monopolizes a conversation that never reaches its intended listener.

If Chen treats the desexualized bedroom scene with a focus on the character's look of diminishment, Cai reduces the function of bedrooms to a shelter where necessities of basic human survival are met. Xiangqi eats, drinks, and sleeps in a hotel room that evokes little of the tourist image of the City of Lights (fig. 8.6). The dark space suggests a generic ordinariness devoid of cultural characteristics, an "anyplaceness" reinforced by Xiangqi's makeshift dinner in a plastic bag: banana, water, crackers, and pears. Cai combines this mundane setting with an everyday routine to utterly deromanticize Xiangqi's Occidental adventure: there is no French-speaking lover, delicate wine or cuisine, or even graceful hotel furniture to greet Xiangqi's return from guidebook days of Parisian adventure. She gets Beckett's Paris of necessity, not enjoyment: a drab room with some groceries that she devours ravenously. And Cai's camera sits in a nonintrusive position to provide a full view of how she copes with her postmodern solitude matter-of-factly

Figure 8.5. Jiazhen's Bedroom

Figure 8.6. Xiangqi in a Parisian hotel

and without self-pity. Preserving "a true to life feeling," Cai is able to show Xiangqi's minimum interaction with her environment without theatrical sentimentality.[20]

3) The Sex Which Is Not Fun

But if both stories are about individuals' search for love, where is sex? One of the films' most provocative theses is the unsexiness of urban love life. Many sex acts are initiated by incidental encounters that prioritize physical impulses over romantic companionship. Hence, they often take on an air of being temporary, hasty, and cheap. Chen and Cai meticulously deeroticize the setting to stage an anticlimactic view of the characters' own disappointment in their pursuit of sexual adventures.

There is only one brief sex scene in *The Personals*. It occurs after Xiangqi interviews one of the marriage candidates—Chen Wuxiong (Chen Zhao-rong)—an excon. They go shrimp-fishing and then engage in sex in an unspecified hotel (fig. 8.7). Chen introduces this scene with an abrupt cut from the artificial shrimp-fishing pond—a commercial space—to the medium close-up of their entangled bodies and faces. The lack of any tangible romantic transition makes their physical involvement as unnatural as the well-lit space that spotlights Jiazhen's ashen white face and establishes a laboratory style of scrutiny. Looking from above, the camera angle presses down upon the characters in a way that boxes them in on the screen. Her hands, clenching the pillow's corners, seem to suggest an emotional detachment from her physical activity. She appears to endure, rather than enjoy, the physical intimacy, as further suggested by her closed eyes—a refusal to confront the reality of joyless sex.

Jiazhen's genteel demeanor, visible vulnerability, and sense of guilt have led critics to consider her a nostalgic construct that reaffirms, as Nick Kaldis states, "a patriarchal desire for [a return to] a traditional type of gender ideal."[21] Her conservatism is most noticeable in her class and sexual biases: she is homophobic, narcissistic, and class conscious. However, Chen carefully differentiates her position from that of the film by exposing and ridiculing her prejudices: her actions are constantly watched and documented by others. On the whole, the movie paints a complex psychological picture of her oscillation between confidence and insecurity, liberal and traditional, unreflective and philosophical, as evidenced by her initiation of the casual sex that later triggers a wave of regret. Since, in the sex scene, Chen projects Jiazhen's psychological agony through the use of the harsh white light glaring lovelessly and intrusively on her face, we are encouraged to see the encounter as a foreshadowing of the disclosure of her darkest secret: Jiazhen confesses to her absent lover's voicemail that she regrets her earlier abortion of their child. Chen's camera consistently uses both medium long shots and close-ups to identify these varying psychological

Figure 8.7. Jiazhen's Joyless Sex

Figure 8.8. Xiangqi's Unrequited Love

Figure 8.9. Xiaokang with a Prostitute

Figure 8.10. Xiaokang's Mother's Self-Love

Figure 8.11. Xiaokang's Mother's Bedroom

states: she is a character of becoming, who falters, evolves, and then adapts. In this way, Chen's Jiazhen represents the modern independent woman who, despite having financial security and a room of her own, has not buried the ghost of past cultural burdens.

In *What Time Is It There?* sex appears to be a desperate attempt to produce existential meaning for oneself. Cai interweaves three encounters that show the main characters in their most revealing and most compromising positions. Xiangqi overdoses on French coffee and runs into a woman from Hong Kong while vomiting violently in the toilet of a coffee shop. She makes sexual advances, but is ultimately rejected (fig. 8.8). This aborted affair explains, to some extent, the shadowy, cultural ghost that trails Xiangqi's transcontinental sojourn. Her sexual orientation seems to make her a perpetual exile who remains on the periphery of a society still dominated by heterosexual expectations. From a position of supplication, Xiangqi looks up to the Hong Kong woman with a diminished ego: she seeks nothing but equal access to the pursuit of sexual pleasure. Her pathos is all the more palpable when we remember the careful play of steady distancing Cai negotiated between Xiangqi and the camera/audience earlier in the film. Rarely do we see a close-up of Xiangqi. It is not until the exposition of her sexual frustration that the viewer is drawn closer in, to the fine-grained expression of her emotional wounds.

Through cross-cutting, Cai simultaneously presents two other ongoing sex scenes. Xiaokang is spending the night in his car after falling out with his mother who is obsessed with the idea of conjuring his dead father's ghost. After drinking and eating alone in the car, Xiaokang picks up a streetwalker (fig. 8.9). Their transaction seems routinely mechanical and hasty. In the dark winter night, the blue-tinged face of the prostitute shown in the reflected streetlight appears ghastly. While Xiaokang is running away from the expectant return of a familiar ghost, he is here entangled with another "ghost" living in the shadow of society.

The theme of the ghost is literally brought to the screen in Xiaokang's mother's desperate sexual longing that reaches a climax in the bedroom scene where she masturbates with her deceased husband's wooden pillow (fig. 8.10). Sitting prominently in the candle-lit foreground, Miao Tian in the enlarged picture seems to wear a contrived and mocking expression. This ascetic space, equipped with a single bed and wooden pillows, sharply contrasts with the mother's own femininely adorned bedroom in a more ornamental and luxurious setting (fig. 8.11). There, sitting on her vanity, are bottles of age-defying cream and cosmetics that promise an illusory fountain of youth. Her aggressive self-preservation makes her in figure 8.10 seem distinctly out of place: lying uncomfortably in an affected position, she looks small and pitiful as she attempts to reignite a passion that perhaps never existed, as suggested by the presence of their separate bedrooms. Sex is a wretched exercise of a creative but delusive imagination.

All three scenes use the contrast between shadows and deflected lights to create a color scheme (blue and soft yellow) of otherworldly alienation. Cai's camera remains subtly still in a way that lets the audience stay in a neutral position and witness these characters' painful revelations of secrets: Xiangqi is a lonely lesbian, Xiaokang prioritizes physical needs over a romantic fantasy, and Yijing is experiencing a midlife sexual crisis. Instead of pleasure, solace, or escape, sex leads all three characters, and the audience as well, to the uncomfortable realities of physical frailty and psychological disillusionment.

CONCLUSION

The films of Chen Guofu and Cai Mingliang are honest about the disappointments of urban life. With the possible exception of Xiaokang, the watch vendor who keeps irregular hours, none of the main characters are shown in the context of work that sustains the capitalist operation of social machinery. They are idle people living on the social fringe and (futilely) exploring (unpromising) channels of connections. They miss each other because they move, unwittingly, in circles rather than lines. The films quietly insist that the narrative arcs of such postmodern lives coexist unnaturally with the political and economic teleologies prized by the industrialized societies that produced them.

Chen's and Cai's cinema of disillusionment is not so much pessimistic as realistic. Their representations of modern women neither inflate the liberation of the second sex from social constraints nor advocate any kind of nostalgic return. On the contrary, both directors are committed to exploring the Jamesonian "private subjectivities" of urbanites that reflect complex intersections of Taiwanese politics and history, as well as apprehensions about the future. On an ideological level, the films' respect for each character's individualism mimics the shifting identity politics of the island eager to recognize the diversity of its many vibrant subcultures. Chen Guofu's democratizing parade of Jiazhen's suitors from all walks of life and Cai Mingliang's exploration of different hangouts for modern youth in Taipei and Paris all contribute to our understanding of how Taiwan has embraced its role as a multicultural state.

Thus the disillusioned cinema of Chen Guofu and Cai Mingliang has purposefully developed what Jameson has criticized as the excessive "psychologism and the 'projections' of private subjectivity,"[22] a trait especially visible in the way the directors studiously reconfigure a topic Jameson often overlooks: cinema's relation with sexual politics. However, both directors clearly tell individual stories in ways that invite interpretation, even allegorical readings, as "the experience of the collectivity itself."[23] Such paradoxes make it clear that, however marginalized it may be, a cultural production like the Second New Wave is well positioned to articulate aesthetic and ideological intersections between worlds. Or perhaps, since the vocabulary of worlds so clearly misfits Taiwan, this cinema is poised to open up larger questions about how to describe cultural identity without reference to it, while searching for new language and reference points. In this sense, Taiwan's Second New Wave is not only transworldly but post- or other-worldly, and the cinema of disillusionment is an avant-garde art form that is both representing and propelling the evolution of a postmodern urban culture. Disillusionment is its leading edge.

ENDNOTES

1. Chen Guofu is one of Taiwan's most influential film critics. For years he edited the popular film magazines *Yingxiang* (*Influence*) and *Dianying xinshang* (*Film Appreciation*). His works include a collection of film commentaries titled *Pian mian zhi yan* (*Partial Reflections*) and translation of *Dianying lilun* (*Film Theory*). He also edited *Buleisong* (*Bresson*) and *Xiqukaoke yanjiu* (*Studies of Hitchcock*).
2. See Michael Berry, "Tsai Ming-liang: Trapped in the Past," in *Speaking in Images* (New York: Columbia University Press, 2005), 363–97.
3. Ru-shou (Ruxiu) Robert Chen, "Marketing *The Personals*: New Strategies Pay New Dividends," *Cinemaya* 45 (1999): 38–39.
4. Chen Guofu, in *Pian mian zhi yan*, theorizes Taiwan's ambivalent relations with other cinematic markets and traditions. Chen Guofu, *Pian mian zhi yan* (*Partial Reflections*) (Taipei: Dianying Tushu Chubanshe, 1985). Cai Mingliang also states his concerns about Taiwan's film market in an interview with Michael Berry and one with Shujen Wang and Chris Fujiwara. See Berry, "Tsai Ming-liang," 363–97; and Shujen Wang and Chris Fujiwara, "My Films Reflect My Living Situations: An Interview with Tsai Ming-liang on Film Spaces, Audiences, and Distribution," *positions* 14 (2006): 219–41.
5. Fredric Jameson, "Third-World Literature in the Era of Multinational Capitalism," 15 (1986): 67.
6. Jameson cites Lu Xun and Ousmane Sembène to argue that in third-world texts, the telling of "the individual story and the individual experience cannot but ultimately involve the whole laborious telling of the experience of the collectivity itself" (ibid., 85–86). However, some critics question the basic validity of his three worlds formation, and others note the naiveté of treating the third world as an undifferentiable cultural Other. Aijaz Ahmad points out that "the ideological conditions of a text's production are never singular but always several," in "Jameson's Rhetoric of Otherness and the 'National Allegory,'" *Social Text* 17 (1987): 24. Rey Chow questions Jameson's "hegemonic reading of the third world cultures" as an "*oppositional* alterity to the West only." Refusing to see the third world as some "pure space with a distinctive 'otherworldly' aesthetic," she describes it as an ethnic construct that perpetuates "a *cross-cultural* commodity fetishism" and argues that third-world fetishism has controlled the reception of many Fifth-Generation films. Films such as Zhang Yimou's *Ju Dou* (1990), for example, are often characterized as the Western Other that functions as a "reflection, an alterity that gives (back) to the 'first world' a sense of 'its' freedom and democracy." Rey Chow, *Primitive Passions* (New York: Columbia University Press, 1995), 56, 59, 60 (italics in original). Taiwan's Second New Wave, however, defies Chow's logic. Western critics cannot use its films to produce a narcissistic reflection of a free "first-world" self, for they do not offer an alluring, oppositional Other. Unlike the attractive images in many of the Fifth Generation's films—beautiful, heroic, romantic, nostalgic, and patriotic (Zhang Yimou's most recent historical action drama *Man cheng jin dai huang jin jia* [*Curse of the Golden Flowers*] [2006] is a case in point), the ordinary, ugly, conflicted, and *inter*-national pictures of Taiwan cinema require a different interpretation.
7. Although the Taiwan/China "split" in some ways resembles post–cold war divisions in other countries (e.g., Korea and Vietnam) that seek national legitimacy after having been colonized, Taiwan's situation remains more precarious because so few other nations offi-cially recognize it. According to the Web site of the U.S. State Department, "as

of Septem-ber 2008, Taiwan had formal diplomatic ties with 23 countries." www.state.gov/r/pa/ei/bgn/35855.htm (accessed on March 31, 2009).Generally, despite sharing with many countries a history of colonial experience and concerns about first-world cultural and political imperialism, Taiwan remains a special case for postcolonial theory.

8. Chen, *Pian mian zhi yan*, 57. Unless noted otherwise, translations of Chen's writings are mine.

9. Ibid., 57–58.

10. Ibid., 58.

11. Ibid., 69.

12. Berry, "Tsai Ming-liang," 394.

13. Ibid.

14. See Shelly Kraicer, review of "*The Personals*," 1999, www.chinesecinemas.org/personals.html.

15. Fredric Jameson, "Third-World Literature," 69. Italics in original.

16. Fredric Jameson, "Remapping Taipei," in *The Geopolitical Aesthetic: Cinema and Space in the World System* (London: BFI Publishing, 2000), 148.

17. Chen Ruxiu, "Marketing *The Personals*," 38.

18. Mark Peranson, "Interview: Cities and Loneliness; Cai Mingliang's 'What Time Is It There?'" Indiewire, January 22, 2002, www.indiewire.com/article/interview_cities_and_loneliness_tsai_ming-liangs_what_time_is_it_there.

19. Mary Ann Doane, "Film and the Masquerade: Theorizing the Female Spectator," in *Feminism and Film*, ed. E. Ann Kaplan (Oxford and New York: Oxford University Press), 421.

20. Berry, "Tsai Ming-liang," 373.

21. Nick Kaldis, "Monogamorphous Desires, Faltering Forms: Structure, Content, and Contradictions in *The Personals* (*Zhenghun Qishi*) (Taiwan, 1998)," *Asian Cinema* 15 (2004): 41.

22. Jameson, "Third-World Literature," 85.

23. Ibid., 86.

JOHN MATEER

DIGITAL CINEMATOGRAPHY: EVOLUTION OF CRAFT OR REVOLUTION IN PRODUCTION?

The debate concerning the impact of the introduction of digital technologies into the filmmaking process and the emergence of digital cinema has been raging for well over a decade. "Evolutionists," as exemplified by John Belton's 2002 article "Digital Cinema: A False Revolution," view new technology and associated methodologies as a natural progression consistent with other technical advancements in cinema (100). "Revolutionists," including Ganz and Khatib, argue that these technologies have not only irrevocably altered filmmaking practice but have fundamentally changed the nature of cinematic storytelling (and thus the viewer experience) as well (Ganz and Khatib 21). What is interesting to note in both Belton's article and Ganz and Khatib's article is that there is a presupposition that the relevant technological evolution had plateaued at the time of writing such that the question of the impact of digital technologies on cinema could effectively be answered. Yet it can be argued that the most significant advancements in filmmaking technology have occurred since these articles were written. Recently released camera systems such as the Red One and Arri Alexa are claimed to have created a brave new world of data-centric production. A recent interview in *Variety* with Michael

John Mateer, "Digital Cinematography: Evolution of Craft of Revolution in Production?" *Journal of Film and Video*, vol. 66, no. 2, pp. 3-14. Copyright © 2014 by University Film and Video Association. Reprinted with permission. Provided by ProQuest LLC. All rights reserved.

Cioni, owner of Light Iron Digital, a postproduction facility catering specifically to data-centric production, sums this up: "You can't make film smaller. You can't make 35mm be 8K resolution no matter what you do. You can't have a [film] camera be four pounds. You can't fit a 400-foot magazine in a smaller space. It can't improve at the rate Moore's Law says we can predict technical improvements [in digital systems]" (qtd. in Cohen).

No longer does a camera department require light-tight temperature-controlled spaces to load camera magazines or store reels of film. Workstations with multiple RAID arrays and linear tape backup systems have taken their place. Dailies, so called because of the time it took to develop the film and create one-light prints to check the quality and aesthetics of a day's shoot, now take mere minutes to create, no longer requiring the specialist skills of a photochemical lab. But for all of this change, has the process of filmmaking been fundamentally altered? Is this truly a new era in which the cinematographer has become more of a data-capture specialist than a visual artist? Or do these advances in camera systems simply represent the latest chapter in the evolution of filmmaking as Belton originally argued? This article sets out to explore these questions by looking at the craft of cinematography for current mainstream production and how it has been affected by technological innovation.[1]

WHAT IS A CINEMATOGRAPHER?

Cinematography is an art-form but at the same time it's a craft, and it is definitely a combination of the two … You have to light, you have to compose and you have to create movement. Those are the three elements of cinematography.

—Owen Roizman (qtd. in Fauer 1: 234)

Roizman's definition arguably represents the most common view of cinematography. Cinematographers work with a director to develop a visual means of interpreting the story. In narrative film, this process typically includes the breaking down of scripts first by acts, then by scenes, and finally by dramatic beats. At each stage, primary and secondary themes are interpreted in terms of tone and desired audience response. From this, details of setting and basic production design begin to emerge, leading to a definition of a visual style. For the director, this serves as the backbone of the production bible, providing a framework for more detailed dramatic analysis. For the cinematographer, it represents the beginning of a blueprint to enable physical production to realize the look of the piece. As the process continues, some form of visualization usually takes place. Working methodologies can differ significantly from project to project and director to director, with the cinematographer's control over visuals ranging anywhere from being a slave to dictated camera positions (such as Hitchcock's reputedly definitive storyboarding or the tight requirements of visual effects–based work) to holding nearly free reign over position, composition, and even blocking (as in Woody Allen projects). Irrespective of the amount of creative freedom granted, the cinematographer will ultimately determine the position of lighting sources and the quality of that light (e.g., color, hardness of shadows, and opacity) to achieve the desired dramatic objectives.

The lesser-known side of the cinematographer's role is more mundane but no less important. Commercial film and television productions are expensive, so it is imperative that principal photography be successful. For the cinematographer, this means that light levels need to be calculated precisely to ensure proper reproduction and exposure within the latitude of the recording medium. Film stocks and electronic image sensors vary in their sensitivity to light and ability to reproduce certain visual spectra, so understanding the technical attributes of these is vital not only for production but for also ensuring that image quality is suitable for the postproduction process and mastering. Related to this, the cinematographer must be certain that the recording medium has sufficient robustness to cope with shooting conditions—be they dust, moisture, or vibration—which can affect recording. These conditions also dictate which specific camera systems and accessories are needed to enable shooting, which in turn can affect the cameras' mobility and the viability of complex shots. All of these logistical considerations must be considered with respect to the time it will take to prepare and shoot and, most importantly to producers, with respect to the overall cost. The modern professional cinematographer is part artist, part scientist, and part businessperson, and technology has always been a key tool in supporting his or her ability to fulfill all three roles.

THE ROLE OF FILM

Film stock has been revered as the gold standard for feature film and narrative broadcast-television projects for decades. Modern-day stocks are very sensitive and can handle a significant range of brightness within one frame (known as "latitude" measured in f-stops). Film is also remarkably durable, which is a prime consideration for cinematographers, studio executives, and archivists alike. But for all of its strengths, film is far from a perfect recording medium. Because it is a physical system, the duration of shots is directly linked to the length of the strip of film itself. Film relies on photochemical reaction to capture light, so a chemical process is required to render images in a finished form. This means that specialist equipment must be used to process the negative and print the footage. As a light-sensitive material, stock must be kept in controlled conditions prior to exposure and development (Kodak). Because of their mechanical nature, film cameras must be continually checked for light-tightness and cleanliness as well as calibrated for physical registration to ensure the film is accurately and securely stopped for each frame of exposure. Professional film cameras are expensive, and this, coupled with the cost of the film stock itself and secondary processing, means that shooting with film can be costly, particularly in comparison to other types of image recording.

THE EVOLUTION OF DIGITAL MOTION PICTURES

Although digital recording of moving images first began to appear in the 1970s, it was not seen as viable for any type of commercial work until the mid-1980s ("Grass Valley"). The television industry began to embrace these technologies once it was shown that digital cameras could out-perform their tube-based predecessors and that savings could be made with a digital workflow.[2] However, from a cinematographic perspective, even the newest systems of that time were woefully lacking in their technical capabilities. Standard-definition digital video has too low a resolution (about 0.4 megapixels), too little latitude (about six to eight f-stops compared with film's thirteen to fourteen), and insufficient color depth, making it unsuitable for anything beyond stylized low-budget cinema work. Although initial digital systems did provide freedom for small independent filmmakers, the technology was not yet developed enough to support mainstream film-making. Studios have long had strict requirements with regard to image quality and thus a conservative approach to new technologies.

In the late 1990s, Sony and Panavision engaged in a formal collaboration to explore how digital video technology might be utilized for film-style production. The first system emerging from this collaboration was the Sony HDW-F900 24p camera, which recorded to a new type of tape deck known as HDCAM (Kalley). Both components evolved from Sony's broadcast television systems, with the camera utilizing charge-coupled device (CCD) sensors to record images. For the first time, a digital camera could offer resolution approaching 16mm film stocks, with improved latitude and color fidelity. Likewise, the adaptation of traditional cinema lenses from Panavision allowed optical characteristics such as depth of field to be controllable in a way similar to the control granted by film cameras. Despite the advances, take-up of this new system was initially limited. This changed when George Lucas decided that he wanted a completely digital workflow for *Star Wars Episode II: Attack of the Clones* ("Sony and Panavision about to Deliver"). For that picture, Sony and Panavision refined their systems, ultimately leading to the commercial introduction of HDCAM SR in 2003, which represented a significant enhancement to HDCAM. The success of the film showed the industry that digital high-definition (HD) recording technologies were approaching the color fidelity and latitude of film.

At the same time, the digital intermediate (DI) process—where film negatives are scanned into digital form for editing, compositing, and picture finishing—was becoming standard practice in Hollywood. By the time HDCAM came onto the market, the notion of working in a completely digital postproduction environment, though not universally embraced, was becoming understood and accepted. The ability to copy or alter digital data an infinite number of times without any degradation or loss in quality demonstrated the advantages that digital systems could provide. HD digital video systems have a resolution of $1{,}920 \times 1{,}080$, which is not appreciably less than 2K (2048×1556), which is common for DI. This meant that workflows established through the evolution of the DI process could be adapted to HD material. As a result, the introduction of these new HD systems into the production pipeline represented a logical evolution in the application of digital technologies to the filmmaking process.

From an "on set" perspective, working with HD systems does not differ radically from standard film or television production methodologies and represents a hybrid of the two. The "look" of the project is effectively burned in to the tape recording—that is to say it cannot be fundamentally altered—in the same way it would be in film. Exposure is still determined based on the dramatic requirements of the scene, with limitations in latitude and other recording characteristics of the HD system taken into account, as would be the case for film. Unlike film, recorded output of HD systems can be played back on set. Aside from confirmation that recording has been successful, there is little difference between this and video assist systems. From a camera assistant's perspective, focus pulls and other during-shot activities are completely unchanged. Off set, cans and reels of film are replaced with magnetic tape cassettes, but the rules of storing and cataloguing footage are similar, again borrowing from TV workflows. The only significant handling difference is that tape is reusable, so it is vital that camera assistants ensure that recording tabs are switched off, so that tapes are not accidentally recorded over. From a practice perspective, it is evident that shooting with HD, though somewhat different from film, does not represent a new paradigm but the amalgamation of existing technique, albeit with additional considerations related to the technology. According to Victor Nelli Jr., "[m]ost of the procedure is the same. The equipment is much harder to troubleshoot. It no longer is a piece of film passing by a hole. There are so many things to the HD format. [Crew] do need to be up to date" (qtd. in Rogers).

Sony was by no means the only manufacturer to develop digital camera systems targeted at high-end production during this period. Panasonic and Thomson (the latter drawing on expertise from its acquisition of Technicolor in 2000) also created systems based on CCD imaging sensors; the VariCam and Viper are still used for television and feature film work, though neither is viewed by the industry as definitive. From a financial perspective, the costs associated with these systems—both the costs of procuring the equipment for production and the associated postproduction costs—are not appreciably lower than those of film. Despite straightforward workflows and advances in digital imaging technologies, many veteran cinematographers remained (and some still remain) skeptical as to whether these digital systems could ever truly supplant film. In large part this is due to CCD technology, which has a different look from film. The following remark by Oscar-winning cinematographer Wally Pfister typifies the view: "The range of colors that you can record with the best digital cameras is also a joke when put head-to-head with 35mm negative … Why anybody would replace a proven image capture system with vastly inferior technology is beyond my comprehension" (qtd. in Fisher).

Film processes light in a fundamentally different way from CCDs. It records more information in shadow and highlight areas, with less in mid-tones. This nonlinear approach means that it is better able to capture and reproduce detail at extreme areas of brightness. On the other hand, CCDs and other digital systems are designed such that light is processed linearly, giving equal weighting to dark, mid, and bright tones. In order for footage shot with a CCD-based system to look like film, a data transformation process is required to simulate the nonlinear distribution of luminance. Because this effectively means redistributing data and introducing information that was not originally present, artifacts are generated that would not be present in film. Likewise, once light levels reach a certain threshold, all data is capped at that point. If the brightness is greater than the CCD can handle, the signal is "clipped," that portion of the image goes pure white, and all detail is lost. The opposite is true with dark areas going to pure black ("crushed").

Negative film is much more forgiving at extreme ranges of brightness. It too can clip whites or crush blacks, but the change is usually much less pronounced. Other differences, such as the look of visual noise (e.g., chrominance or luminance artifacts compared to film grain) and the grid-based nature of CCD sensors, mean that a true film look can only ever be approximated through this type of technology.

THE ADVENT OF DIGITAL CINEMA

The emergence of digital cinema is arguably linked to technological advancements in image reproduction systems in parallel with significant increases in performance and decreases in costs for computer systems. The two are related in that high-quality image data requires significant storage space as well as computer processing capability to render finished footage. Cinematographically, advances in CMOS (complementary metal-oxide semiconductor) imaging technology have enabled a more efficient path to an all-digital workflow. CMOS sensors can respond more rapidly to light than CCDs, and they also have the benefit of requiring less external processing of the raw digital data. Although both of these imaging sensors started development at roughly the same time (the late 1960s), it was not until comparatively recently that CMOS technology matured to a point where its image reproduction capability reached that of CCD ("CCD vs. CMOS"). Three CCD chips are typically used—one each to capture red, green, and blue picture data—but only one CMOS chip is required to capture full-color information. This means that CMOS sensors work in a manner that more closely resembles film. Indeed, one of the major early shortcomings of CMOS technology when used in cameras was its slow shuttering, such that fast-moving vertical objects in a frame could appear distorted—the dreaded "rolling shutter" effect that also plagued early film-camera systems (as exemplified by Lartigue's classic 1913 photo, *Car Trip*). Wheeler gives a good overview of the technical aspects of digital cinema systems in his book *High Definition Cinematography* (43).

In 2005, seeing the emerging take-up of HD systems to replace film for television projects, Arri was the first of the traditional film camera manufacturers to utilize a CMOS chip for a "digital film" camera. The D20 represented a middle ground between film and HD video systems. The active recording area of its CMOS sensor was equivalent to super 35mm film, so it had similar optical characteristics to film systems (in areas such as depth of field, for example). It also featured a resolution of 2,880 × 2,160 pixels, which is approximately the same as 2K film scans for digital intermediate. Operationally, the D20 had an adjustable mechanical shutter just as Arri film cameras do, and many of the accessories and basic components of Arri's cameras were directly compatible with the D20. In Filmstream mode, the recorded data was captured in logarithmic form, mimicking the way film responds to light. This data output would be transferred either to tape (using HDCAM SR) or to proprietary data cartridges. The data itself was handled using methods not unlike those for scanned film in DI workflows. However, production and post with the D20 was cumbersome. Given that there were comparatively few D20s in the field, no clear consensus emerged regarding workflows. This led to a view among cinematographers (and producers) that the D20 was best utilized only in specific situations that lent themselves to digital production, such as stylized looks (as in Guy Ritchie's *RocknRolla*, shot by David Higgs) or visual effects work (as in the ferryboat fire sequence shot by Sam Nicholson for ABC's *Grey's Anatomy*). Indeed, at the time Arri itself conceded this point in its publicity, looking at digital not as a replacement for film but as simply another supporting tool. Bill Lovell, digital camera project manager for Arri, stated, "Film will continue to be the preferred acquisition format when its benefits are paramount, but if digital is the tool for the job, then we have a camera here for you to do it" (qtd. in "ASC Technology").

At roughly the same time, a start-up company also launched, proclaiming that they would "[change] the face of the motion picture industry" ("Red History"). Red Digital Cinema was founded by businessman Jim Jannard, a keen amateur photographer and film buff who was dismayed by the high cost and technical conservatism of industry film and HD camera systems and thought he could do better. Rather than develop cameras from a classical cinematography perspective, Jannard drew inspiration from the data-centric design of the then-emerging DSLR systems. He assembled a team of electronics experts to develop a CMOS chip that could effectively duplicate how film reacts to light but could be packaged in such a way that postproduction could be accomplished using commonly available computer desktop tools such as Apple's Final Cut Pro. From the start, Jannard and his followers proclaimed this to be a revolution, and the company structure reflects this. Red Digital Cinema's Ted Schilowitz, known as the "Leader of the Rebellion," explains:

> The company does not work in a normal hierarchy … There are some really brilliant people that work on the team that don't fit into the normal convention of who you might think would build a camera … [We envisioned] a 4K future that would be affordable, logical and accessible for a lot of people, and a lot of people were highly sceptical … ("HD Expo")

The first commercial Red system, Red One, was released in 2007. Although technologically it was not radically different from the Arri D20, a number of key differences did represent a shift from conventional film and HD systems. The CMOS chip developed by Red, Mysterium, had a full resolution of over 4K, which was significantly larger than Arri's and was the largest commonly available imager format made (similar to Super 35mm film). Likewise, the chip had extended latitude and sensitivity similar to mid-level film stocks. Rather than using tape recorders or bespoke data cartridges, the Red One could record to commonly available CompactFlash cards and portable hard drives. This reliance on established data technologies ensured that production and postproduction support could be accomplished through time-tested IT methods. A very low price point for the camera body itself ($17,500 on release) meant that the overall cost for a Red system was significantly less than HD systems and a fraction of the cost of a film system.

To give an example, the following table details the costs of a one-week shoot in Los Angeles for a total of ten hours of footage (including videotape-based dailies) shot using different systems (prices are from a survey of Los Angeles suppliers conducted in August 2011).[3]

At first the industry was highly skeptical. Wild claims of increased performance and low cost ran rife at trade shows, but Jannard was canny in promoting his new systems to filmmakers he knew to be tech-savvy. Peter Jackson became the first "name" director to shoot with a Red. A self-proclaimed early adopter of new filmmaking technologies, he heard about the development of the Red One and expressed his interest in the company. In preparation for NAB 2007, the annual trade show of the National Association of Broadcasters, Jannard asked Jackson if he would be interested in making a short film as a demonstration (reportedly on an unpaid basis). Intrigued by the system, Jackson agreed and created *Crossing the Line*, a twelve-minute period World War I drama, in only two weeks ("Ready for Takeoff"). The film was well received at NAB, and the

Table 9.1 Cost Comparison for One-Week Shoot in Los Angeles for Ten Hours of Footage

	Arri 435 ES (35mm film)	Sony SRW-9000 (HD video)	Arri Alexa (digital cinema)	Red One (digital cinema)
Package Rental Cost (based on three-day charge)	$8,145	$9,360	$8,610	$6,360
Recording Media	$24,920 (Kodak 5260)	$900 (HDCAM SR tape)	$0 (included)	$0 (included)
Processing	$4,800 (0.12/ft)	$0	$0	$0
Duplication/Backup	$0	$1,900 ($100/hr + tape)	$300 ($100/hr)	$300 ($100/hr)
Telecine/DataCine (supervised, for dailies)	$6,750 ($225/hr)	$6,750 ($225/hr)	$6,750 ($225/hr)	$6,750 ($225/hr)
Total	$44,615	$18,910	$15,660	$13,410

industry took notice, with other established directors, including Steven Soderbergh, soon looking to try the new camera. Given such directors' clout within the business, the system gained legitimacy, and industry take-up began. Producers became particularly enamored of Red because they could see the financial advantages of the system.

By 2010, more than 9,000 Red One systems had been sold. To put this in perspective, Sony produced approximately 2,500 CineAlta F900s (and variants) between 2002 and 2010, so Red's market penetration was truly remarkable for a specialist professional system. Mainstream feature films, including *Ché* (parts 1 and 2, both shot by Soderbergh), *The Book of Eli* (Don Burgess), and *The Social Network* (Jeff Cronenweth), as well as US network television series such as *Southland* (NBC), *Leverage* (TNT), and *Sanctuary* (Syfy), demonstrated the viability of Red to the Hollywood studios.

This did not go unnoticed by Arri, which launched Alexa in 2010 in response. Alexa has a very similar architecture and workflow to the Red One but a more filmic image quality. Not to be outdone, Red introduced a new 5K camera, the Epic, in 2011. Which camera is the more effective tool is a matter of debate—Reds are more affordable; Alexa has greater image reproduction capability—but there is no disputing that Arri, with its rich and comparatively conservative history in the development of film cameras, has recognized and embraced the notion that digital cinema represents the future of acquisition. As noted by Michael Cioni, digital has now surpassed film as the recording medium of choice for mainstream film and television production (Cohen).

NEW DIGITAL CINEMA TECHNOLOGIES AND THE CINEMATOGRAPHIC PROCESS

Even with the significant technological advances that Red and Alexa represent, the core tasks of cinematography have remained unchanged. Lens choice, shot composition, and means of facilitating camera movement are still the same. The relationship between the exposure index of the recording medium, the aperture setting, the exposure time, and the required level of illumination is also unaltered. Lighting design still needs to consider the latitude of medium as well as the dramatic requirements of the scene. That is not to say that there are not operational differences.

By definition, digital cinema production systems are data-centric. Recorded images are nothing more than computer files, so they must be handled using IT procedures, similar to other digital data. This has led to the creation of new roles for on-set production such as the digital imaging technician (DIT). The DIT's chief responsibility is to ensure the integrity of the data (i.e., to confirm that the recordings are correct) as well as to archive it to ensure that there are reliable backups in case of loss or corruption of the original recording media. In the film realm, these would have been the duties of the clapper/loader. He or she would have been responsible for loading film magazines, storing and cataloguing exposed reels, and maintaining the camera components. Now the focus of this role is centered on shooting tasks—marking actor positions, recording camera notes, and so on—allowing the DIT to handle most technical camera matters.

Changes in the cinematographic process lie in the nature of exposure and recording. Unlike film or tape, exposure for Red or Alexa is not "burned in" to the medium. As a result, so long as brightness falls within the recording range of the image sensor, the captured data can be altered without any loss in quality. In other words, if a shot appears to be overexposed to the naked eye, but distinct data is present for all areas in the shot (i.e., the brightest parts are not just one shade of white but actually consist of a subtle range of tonalities), the brightness can be changed in postproduction to provide correct exposure. Setting exposure for these systems is about capturing as much data as possible rather than creating the exact look per se. That is not

Figure 9.1. Red One Footage Pre-Grade

to say that differences in contrast between areas within a shot are ignored, but rather, in order to give the maximum amount of control over the image in grading, the cinematographer purposefully exposes the image using as much of the exposure range as possible without clipping white highlights even if the "look" of the shot is intended to be moody and dark. By creating a rich data set—akin to a "thick negative" in film—the cinematographer is able to utilize the entire dynamic range of the camera. However, this approach means that control over the final look of the image now rests with the grader of the project. It has always been the case that color timers could alter color balance and brightness of film footage, but the nature of data-centric image capture is such that much more extreme and fundamental changes can be made.

Following is an example of a properly exposed shot from a Red One using the "thick negative" model. Shadow areas are purposefully overexposed to preserve detail: the histogram at the bottom represents the amount of data captured at different brightness levels. Left represents pure black and right pure white, with the height representing the amount of picture with that level of

Figure 9.2. Red One Footage Post-Grade

brightness per color channel. Note that none of the data goes to either extreme, so that as much of the image information is recorded as possible. In the finished, graded image, the exposure has been manipulated digitally such that it is now correct. The contrast has been increased and brightness extended to enhance the dynamic range of the image.

To many cinematographers, the notion that someone in postproduction has final control over the look of their work is untenable and threatens their art. Mark Sawicki's remarks typify this view:

> Unfortunately, after a century of cinema the art of cinematography is threatened by the rush of technological change and the ease of digital capture…. Highly sensitive sensor chips that can shoot by starlight have brought about the erroneous conclusion by some producers that you don't need to light anymore as if the art of lighting amounts to merely obtaining an exposure…. Camerawork is so much more than so called "product acquisition."

Yet others, even those with traditional backgrounds, have recognized the imaging power that digital cinema systems can provide irrespective of protocol. Vilmos Zigmond says, for example, "After seeing *The Girl with the Dragon Tattoo* shot on the new Red Epic camera … the only thing I could think was that this looked like it was shot on 65mm film or with an IMAX camera. The latitude and detail was incredible. I was so impressed that I will be shooting my next feature on Epic" (qtd. in Jannard).

It is clear that the cinematographer's role has evolved with the introduction of digital cinema systems but does this represent a fundamental change in the role?

CONCLUSION: REVOLUTION OR EVOLUTION?

Revolutionists, as described by Kirsner in his discussion of "innovators" (5), claim that the rise of digital technologies, including Red and Alexa, represents a fundamental change in feature film production. No longer are individual, discrete frames recorded to a frame of film or specific location on a magnetic tape. Now, image data generated by the camera is captured using traditional computer hardware. As mentioned earlier, this meant the establishment of a new DIT role and changed the responsibilities of the clapper/loader. Likewise, post-production has seen the introduction of data wranglers, who take the raw data and convert it into the different formats required for different stages of postproduction—for example, small QuickTime files for off-line editing, DPX files for visual effects and grading work, and so on. The tremendous quantity of data means that new methods of asset management have had to be developed to catalogue and index footage to ensure easy access. Because the entire program is digital, editing and grading are no longer tied to specialist equipment or facilities. Shows can be edited, graded, and even finished on laptop computers, representing a freedom in working that has never been seen before. Likewise, digital content is easily repurposed from one platform to the next. Platform variants for DVDs, Blu-Ray, mobile phones, and other devices can be created directly and at low cost. The availability of professional-caliber equipment at a greatly reduced cost has meant that barriers to entry have been lifted.[4] Greater access to equipment has enabled independent filmmaking to flourish. The last argument put forth is simply that of commerce. All major equipment manufacturers—Arri, Panavision, Sony, Panasonic, and others—have modified or developed new designs based on technologies and methodologies used by a previously unknown start-up company. To many, Red has indeed fulfilled its promise of revolution.

Evolutionists counter that although there are new roles associated with production and post using new digital cinema systems, the fundamental aspects of cinematography—script interpretation, visualization, lighting design and planning, lens choice, camera movement, and so on—have remained virtually unchanged. Roles have adapted as technology has developed, but this has been an evolutionary process. Systems used in the creation of motion pictures have been emerging and changing for well over a century: hand-cranked cameras gave way to motorized systems; film stocks grew in gauge and sensitivity; color systems were introduced, developed, and refined, as was sound; wide-screen formats have come and gone in a wide range of aspect ratios; and the list goes on. It could be said that the only constant in feature film production is change. As such, digital cinema technologies simply represent the latest development, and there are bound to be others. The editing process is effectively unchanged as well, driven by the need to juxtapose shots as a story requires. New technologies and associated techniques make this easier and more efficient, but the editor's role is the same. Indeed, even the digital intermediate process evolved through the application of new technologies to existing postproduction techniques (namely, the replacing of physical optical printers with a digital counterpart).

For viewers, it is impossible to distinguish between films that utilize a DI process and those that do not. As Bill Pope notes, "[t]he point is, [DI] looks great and it's indistinguishable from film" (qtd. in "*Spider-Man 2* Set to Deliver"). The all-digital nature of the DI process is directly analogous to the all-digital production pipeline involved with cameras such as Red and Alexa. If the viewer cannot see a difference between movies shot on film and those shot digitally, how can the use of a digital technology be considered revolutionary? Of course, film-based, HD video–based, and digital cinema–based programs have different looks because each process introduces a different type of artifact into the recording. But this is arguably no different from variations in the grain patterns or color characteristics of standard film stocks.

Throughout the history of cinema, there have often been alternative platforms for showcasing film content—from audio soundtracks adapted for radio to versions cut for TV broadcast to videotape for videocassette distribution. This is nothing new. To evolutionists, the bottom line is that the essence of the filmmaking and film-watching experiences is unchanged, and thus, digital cinematography is simply yet another landmark in the evolution of cinema.

Much of the innovation with regard to film production and delivery systems has historically been driven by commerce. Producers and studios have always sought to create products attractive to the market in such as way as to maximize profit. In this sense, the evolution and take-up of digital camera systems is similar to the arrival of sound. As Douglas Gomery describes it, the adoption of sound technology was driven by economic benefit to the studios (1). For a period, limitations in the emerging technologies and related production methods had a negative effect on the presentation of story, but these issues were resolved fairly quickly, resulting in a greater number of higher-profile (and higher-budget) projects moving to sound. The slow take-up of the first HD and digital camera systems for mainstream film-making, leading to the current reliance on digital camera systems for network television and big-budget features (e.g., *Pirates of the Caribbean: On Stranger Tides*, budgeted at roughly $250 million and shot solely on Red Epic), mimics this. The effect of the introduction of digital camera systems in production has been far less obvious to the viewer, but the impact on the business of film is arguably the same. Hollywood studios are conservative by nature to ensure profitability. Thus, production methods have evolved with new technologies rather than completely changing when new systems are available. The mainstream cinematographer's role may be slightly different with the advent of digital technologies, but the importance of cinematographers' work to Hollywood's bottom line means that the role has not been (nor could it be) radically altered.

Kirsner explores the development of feature film technologies from the silent era to the present day just prior to the take-up of digital cinema systems. He categorizes industry attitudes and perceptions into three camps—innovators, those who adopt new technology and push it to its limits; preservationists, those who cling doggedly to established tried-and-true systems; and side-line sitters, those who will wait for a consensus to form once a new technology stabilizes (5). He demonstrates how these camps reappear on a cyclical basis as new systems are developed. Digital cinema can be viewed in the same light. Underpinning Kirsner's thesis is the idea that movies themselves have not fundamentally changed; the nature of cinema, the relationship between the screen and the audience, has evolved but is essentially the same. The same arguably can be said about cinematography and the cinematographic process.

The tools of the cinematographer have changed, and methods have been adapted accordingly, but fundamentally, the role is still centered on the creation of images through the understanding of light, optics, and story. Gabriel Bernstein sums up the introduction of digital tools to the cinematographic process nicely:

> I think cinematography will continue to be what it is.… For us, it will remain a discussion about lighting ratios, controlling our contrast ratios, our faces, trying to get enough detail in the shadow areas and trying to get enough detail in the highlights. For us, the art and technique of cinematography will continue. Our palette will still be there. Maybe our colors will change, but the film look will continue. Cinematography has not essentially changed in 100 years and it's not going to change. It is the process of artistry that will evolve. (qtd. in Fauer 2: 25)

ENDNOTES

1. This article was completed in August 2012.
2. "Workflow" refers to the step-by-step process of acquiring and manipulating picture and/or sound to create a motion picture (e.g., shooting, recording, editing, grading, mastering). In a digital context, this may require the use of specific file formats, software, and/or hardware systems at different stages. Not all systems are compatible, and thus, designing workflows is an important component of the technical side of filmmaking.
3. Data for the cost-comparison table was gathered on a like-for-like basis of production packages from established Los Angeles vendors that have a history of supporting commercial projects. Quotes for the Arri camera package were obtained from Otto Nemenz, and quotes for the other three packages came from Abel Cine. Lab and consumable prices are an average based on quotes from Los Angeles suppliers. All data was compiled in August 2011.
4. It is common for Red camera packages to be rented at heavily discounted rates that are significantly lower than those given for other camera systems. This, plus the ability to conduct postproduction on personal computer systems with comparatively inexpensive software such as Final Cut Pro Studio, represents a landmark shift in the accessibility of true theatrical-grade production tools for low-budget independent filmmakers.

"ASC Technology Committee Examines Arriflex D-20." *Arri Group*. ARRI, 11 Jan. 2005. Web. 14 Nov. 2011.

Belton, John. "Digital Cinema: A False Revolution." *October* 100 (Spring 2002): 98–114. Print.

"CCD vs. CMOS." *Teledyne Dalsa*. Teledyne DALSA, 2011. Web. 14 Nov. 2011.

Cohen, David. "Landmark Year for Digital." *Variety*. Reed Elsevier, 7 July 2011. Web. 14 Nov. 2011.

Fauer, Jon. *Cinematographer Style: The Complete Interviews*. 2 vols. Los Angeles: American Society of Cinematographers, 2008. Print.

Fisher, Bob. "Why 10 of the World's Top Cinematographers Have Still Not Bought into the Digital Revolution." *MovieMaker* 30 Nov. 2009. Web. 14 Nov. 2011.

Ganz, Adam, and Lina Khatib. "Digital Cinema: The Transformation of Film Practice and Aesthetics." *New Cinemas: Journal of Contemporary Film* 4.1 (2006): 21–36. Print.

Gomery, Douglas. *The Coming of Sound*. New York: Routledge, 2005. Print.

"Grass Valley: 50 Years of On-Air Innovation." *Grass Valley*. Grass Valley USA, 2011. Web. 14 Nov. 2011.

"HD Expo Presents Interviews with the Experts: Ted Schilowitz." *HD Expo*. Nielsen Business Media, 6 Mar. 2008. Web. 23 Sept. 2011.

Jannard, Jim. "Video: TED talks with Landmine Media at NAB 2011." *REDUser.net*. Landmine Media, 2011. Web. 7 July 2011.

Kalley, William. "Filmed in Panavision: An Interview with Sony Electronics' Larry Thorpe." *From Script to DVD*. N.p., 27 Sept. 2004. Web. 14 Nov. 2011.

Kirsner, Scott. *Inventing the Movies: Hollywood's Epic Battle between Innovation and the Status Quo, from Thomas Edison to Steve Jobs*. Seattle: CreateSpace, 2008. Print.

"Ready for Takeoff: Peter Jackson Takes the Time to Provide an Exclusive Update on *The Lovely Bones, The Dam Busters, Halo*, Wingnut Interactive, and a Great Deal More." *On Film*. Mediaweb, 1 May 2007. Web. 14 Nov. 2011.

"Red History." *Red Digital Cinema*. Red.com Inc., n.d. Web. 23 Sept. 2011.

Rogers, Pauline. "Cinematographers Discuss the Do's and Don'ts of Shooting in HD." *International Cinematographers Guild*. International Cinematographers Guild, Feb. 2005. Web. 14 Nov. 2011.

Sawicki, Mark. "A Plea to Preserving the Art of Cinematography." *MasteringFilm*. Focal Press, 2011. Web. 14 Nov. 2011.

"Sony and Panavision about to Deliver First Prototype 24 Frame Progressive High Definition Camera System to Lucasfilm." *All Business*. AllBusiness.com, 15 Nov. 1999. Web. 14 Nov. 2011.

"Spider-Man 2 Set to Deliver the Sharpest, Clearest Motion Picture Images Ever." *eFilm*. eFilm, 3 Sept. 2004. Web. 14 Nov. 2011.

"Technical Information Bulletin: Storage and Handling of Unprocessed Film." *Kodak*. Eastman Kodak, 2002. Web. 14 Nov. 2011.

Wheeler, Paul. *High Definition Cinematography*. 3rd ed. Oxford: Focal Press, 2009. Print.

Wright, Steve. *Digital Compositing for Film and Video*. 3rd ed. Oxford: Focal Press, 2010. Print.

LOVORKA GRUIC GRMUSA AND KIENE BRILLENBURG WURTH

CINEMATOGRAPHY AS A LITERARY CONCEPT IN THE (POST) MODERN AGE: PIRANDELLO TO PYNCHON

> Long live the Machine that mechanizes life!
>
> Do you still retain, gentlemen, a little soul, a little heart and a little mind?
>
> —Luigi Pirandello, *Shoot!*

> In the Zone, all will be moving under the Old Dispensation, inside the Cainists' light and space: not out of any precious Gollerei, but because the Double Light was always there, outside all film.
>
> —Thomas Pynchon, *Gravity's Rainbow*

Since long before the invention of cinema, literary writing has been engaged in the mediation of moving images. Indeed, as Sergei Eisenstein once intimated, literary writing has in crucial ways premediated cinematographic techniques, especially that most cinematographic of arts: montage.[1] Montage may be tied to D. W. Griffith, but as Eisenstein famously observed, "Griffith arrived at montage through the method of parallel action, and he was led to the idea of parallel action by—Dickens!"[2] The link between cinema and the realist novel has by now been well established. In the 1970s, Alan Spiegel proposed to read Gustave Flaubert's *Madame Bovary* (1857) as a protocinematic (or, more precisely, "scenographic")

Lovorka Gruic Grmusa and Keine Brillenburg Wurth, "Cinematography as a Literary Concent in the (Post)Modern Age: Pirandello to Pynchon," *Between Page and Screen: Remaking Literature Through Cinema and Cyberspace*, pp. 184-200. Copyright © 2012 by Fordham University Press. Reprinted with permission.

novel that anticipated the special visual effects of film.[3] Such special effects, Robert Stam has noted, include the detailed notation of objects, gestures, and attitudes in the novel, literary props, verbal long shots (the scene of the Rouen cab), and so on.[4] Eisenstein had, of course, already celebrated the famous scene of Emma and her lover Rodolphe at the Yonville agricultural fair as an instance of vertical montage: a technique allowing various impressions, movements, stories, or dialogues to become present at the same time, rather than one after the other.[5] Spiegel, however, tried to show how cinematographic techniques evolved in nineteenth-century fiction—not only in Flaubert, but also in Henry James and Joseph Conrad—and culminated in modernist works such as James Joyce's *Ulysses* (1922). Such techniques, for Spiegel, boiled down to showing instead of telling, and in particular a showing of how things are seen: This pertained to visualizations of objects *and* to the ways in which such objects are perceived.[6]

In the 1990s, critics such as Irina Rajewski and P. Adams Sitney continued to debate cinema and literature in terms of transmediation or the transfer of techniques among different media, arguing that filmmakers were just as much influenced by literary writing (and literary scopic regimes) as modernist writers were affected by film.[7] More recently, Susan McCabe's *Cinematic Modernism* and Laura Marcus's *The Tenth Muse* have mapped the tracks between film and poetry (Williams, Moore) and early twentieth-century literary (Woolf, Joyce) as well as critical writing respectively. How have film's techniques helped to shape literature in the modernist age—and how has modernist literature affected film?[8] Similarly, Julian Murphet and Lydia Rainford's *Literature and Visual Technologies* traces the impact of twentieth-century visual technologies on literature, showing how such technologies have informed "new" literary modes and techniques, and vice versa.[9]

As an alternative to such medial histories of analogy and transaction, critics such as Garrett Stewart and David Trotter have proposed to analyze modernist techniques in literature *and* film as parallel manifestations of a shared "textuality" ruled by automatism.[10] "Modernist writing," as Stewart argues, is "neither predominantly impressionist nor expressive (since both imply the intervening subjectivity of an author) but in some new way strictly technical, a prosthesis of observation in the mode of inscription."[11] In this approach, modernist literature and film share a discourse network, rather than being separate modes of art affecting each other: the discourse of technologically mediated, depersonalized realities and subjectivities.[12] In this chapter, we follow this framework of contiguity as suggested by Stewart and seek to add to it through a comparative analysis that extends beyond the modernist age into the sphere of the postmodern. As we show, the issue of prosthetic perception is foregrounded in modernist as well as key postmodernist texts that take film as their primary cue.[13] We focus on Luigi Pirandello's *Shoot!* (1915) and Thomas Pynchon's *Gravity's Rainbow* (1973) as representative twentieth-century "cinematographic" texts in Europe and the United States that critically incorporate the power of film not only to mechanize perception, but also to mechanize or substitute for the real.[14] This comparative analysis lays bare the modernist "cinematographic" mechanisms at the heart of the postmodernist simulacrum: The one cannot be thought without the other. The parallel is extended to Pynchon's *Vineland* (1990), which processes and addresses the medium of television: Does this domestic mass medium signal a change, a radicalization, or an undermining of the patterns and discourse of automatized perception?

MEDIATED WORLDS, MEDIATED SUBJECTS: CAMERATIC PERCEPTION IN *SHOOT!*

The emergence of the modernist novel is roughly contemporaneous with the birth of film—and with a modernist "frame" of mind that casts the mind as "cinematographic." In 1907, in the final chapter of *Creative Evolution*, Henri Bergson invoked the cinematographic apparatus to capture the ways in which the intellect approaches reality: as movement rendered static rendered dynamic once again, as in filmic recording and montage. Thus, the intellect re-renders reality-as-movement as a discontinuous continuity:

> Instead of attaching ourselves to the inner becoming of things, we place ourselves outside them in order to recompose their becoming artificially. We take snapshots, as it

were, of the passing reality.... We may therefore sum up ... that the mechanism of our ordinary knowledge is of a cinematographical kind.[15]

For Bergson, while the intellect thus freezes moments of the flux that reality embodies, it is by contrast through intuition that one may penetrate and participate in that flux, rather than capturing this flow in snippets and reassembling it as a mechanical whole.[16] The implication is that film, as an embodiment of mechanized perception, cannot cater intuition.[17]

Pirandello's *Shoot!* (first translated into English in 1927) enacts this association between film and "inhuman" mediations of reality flows through its first-person narrator who is at once a cameraman. Because of this double bind, narration is framed within a cinematically mediated focalization,[18] so that the distinction between writing and filming, between reading and viewing, is problematized from the start—however much the narrator wants to artificially uphold the distinction between paper and celluloid. *Shoot!* offers the fate of Serafino Gubbio, who negotiates between old and new media by being an "operator" or cameraman for the film studio Kosmograph by day, and the writer of his memoirs by night.[19] Yet, even as a writer he cannot disengage himself from his perspective as a cameraman. His hand, operating the handle of the camera and holding his pen, which records the melodramas unfolding before and behind the camera, becomes a prosthetic device, as if attached first and foremost to the machinery Gubbio is operating, rather than to his body. This is precisely what *Shoot!* is about: the relegating of perception to the focus of a machine, an adaptation of a special kind.

Like other major Italian authors in the early twentieth century, such as Giovanni Verga, Guido Gozzano, Marco Praga, and Gabriele D'Annunzio, Pirandello was engaged in the emerging Italian film industry as a writer. Of these writers, it was Pirandello who became specifically concerned with the aesthetics and cultural implications of film, and who also became a source of inspiration for film "authors" such as Jean-Luc Godard.[20] *Shoot!* draws on Pirandello's experiences in the film business, offering the familiar story-within-a-story (and more) that takes on the shape of a melodrama typical of silent film: There is a diva, the Nestor-off, her lover, Carlo Ferro, a jilted lover, Aldo Nutti, two other rejected lovers (Duccella and Giorgio Mirelli) and a suicide (Giorgio), a caged and condemned tiger, and two murders in the end. As a subplot, there is the case of scenario writer Cavalena and his jealous wife—and their daughter Luisetta who is secretly, and impassively, loved by Gubbio. One way or another, these characters are all fed to Gubbio's camera, voracious and vampiristic like the other machines of the modern age:

Long live the Machine that mechanizes life!

Do you still retain, gentlemen, a little soul, a little heart and a little mind? Give them. Give them over to the greedy machines, which are waiting for them! ...

The machine is made to act, to move, it requires swallowing up our soul, devouring our life. And how do you expect them to be given back to us, our life and soul, in a centuplicated and continuous output, by the machines? Let me tell you: in bits and morsels, all of one pattern, stupid and precise, which would make, if placed on top of another, a pyramid that might reach to the stars.[21]

In Gubbio's camera perspective, it is not only perception but also life as a whole, indeed the life of the soul, which is mechanized: devoured, partitioned, carved out, made to fit. It is as if Bergson's "cinematographic" knowledge has colonized experience, subjectivity, and materiality, and no room is left for intuition—however feeble the pyramid of morsel-souls may be.

This all-pervasiveness of the cinematographic outlook at once implies a blurring of the "given" and the "mediated"—the latter rather always already frames the former in a world where, as Gubbio suggests, the speed and noise of machination format our experience:

Do you hear it? A hornet that is always buzzing, forbidding, grim, surly, diffused, and never stops. What is it? The hum of the telegraph poles? The endless scream of the trolley along the overhead wire of the electric trams?... Of the cinematograph?

The beating of the heart is not felt, nor do we feel the pulsing of our arteries. The worse for us if we did! But this buzzing, this perpetual ticking we do notice, and I say that all this furious haste is not natural, all this flickering and vanishing of images; but that there lies beneath it a machine which seems to pursue it, frantically screaming.[22]

The machine becomes like a Schopenhauerian life-Will, subtending and informing all "this flickering and vanishing of images": this phenomenal world that has been cut to pieces and reassembled in a furious haste.[23] My reference to Arthur Schopenhauer is not incidental—and not only because the machine operates in the manner of the Will as a force at once productive and constructive, a condition of possibility and a condition of death; an undercurrent of the world of ideas, in Schopenhauer's terminology, objectified in perceivable forms and, indeed, our very own bodies. It is not just the aimless movement of this Will that Gubbio's machine resonates with, but its very inevitability: We cannot escape it, since we cannot but feel the movements within our bodies reminding us of our own "superfluity": our own, fateful, capacity for reflection that, for Gubbio, renders us chronically dissatisfied. *Shoot!* could thus be said to recast Schopenhauer's unconscious Will as a mechanical force impregnating all aspects of modern life.

The machine feeds, but also itself feeds on, life: This double bind epitomizes the paradox foregrounded in *Shoot!* How precisely does Pirandello thus move beyond a binary opposition between the human and the machine in *Shoot!*? And how, in turn, does this condition the idea of the "cinematographic" in the novel?

The complexity of the relations between human and machinic worlds in *Shoot!* is reflected in the degree to which reality and fiction here inform and produce each other, rather than being separate categories. Thus, on one level, there is the repeated reference to a drive of "making it real" in the film industry with props and decors ("Scene painters, stagehands, actors all give themselves the air of deceiving the machine, which will give an appearance of reality to all their fictions")—and the intrusion of a living prop, a tiger to be shot in actual fact, in the film Gubbio is shooting: *The Lady and the Tiger*: "India will be a sham, the jungle will be a sham, the travels will be a sham, with a sham Miss and sham admirers: only the death of this poor beast will not be a sham."[24] Life is sacrificed to the demands of machinic mimesis, and in this sacrifice displays its slippery demarcations as a material reality: that materiality is equally fictitious in, what will become, a snuff movie. In the movie's final scene a plurality of stories behind and before the camera fatefully intertwine: the tragedy of Duccella and Giorgio Mirelli, who lost their respective lovers to these lovers, and Nutti, who lost the Nestoroff to Carlo Ferro afterward. While Nutti is supposed to shoot the tiger, he shoots the Nestoroff and himself; Carlo Ferro will be devoured by the tiger, and the tiger will be shot. Thus, the genre of the melodrama inhabits different ontological planes that are always already intertwined: Narrative patterns of love and death format actual love affairs, while the consequences of these affairs are played out in the film as melodrama.

During the execution of these patterns, Gubbio continues to "turn the handle," and in this continuation a position is revealed that is at once "human and inhuman." As noted earlier, Gubbio has adapted himself to the camera in such a way as to have become its extension. As a character and a narrating voice, he is first of all a "hand" ("my soul does not serve me. My hand serves me, that is to say, serves the machine"), an operator whose vision is mediated by the camera. In turn, the characters, impressions, and events he narrates are specifically framed as passing projections in a flux: "on nothing, nothing at all ought we fix our attention. Take in, rather, moment by moment, this passage of aspects and events, and so on, until we reach the point when for each of us the buzz shall cease."[25] Gubbio *sees* cinematographically. This not only means that his perceptions mimic camera positions and movements, or that his visualizations foreground a "cameratic" play with light and colors in virtual close-ups:[26] "a wonderful sight was the play, on [the Nestoroff's] face, of the purple shadows, straying and shot with threads of golden sunlight, which lightened up now one of her nostrils of her upper lip, now the lobe of her ear and a patch of her throat."[27] Rather, the intensity with which Gubbio perceives the "external aspects of things" renders his vision cinematographic—it is a perception that is as distracted as it is dedicated to fleeting appearances; a perception that, as such, remains as impassive, detached as the camera-machine.

Detachment is a key concept in *Shoot!* It is present as much in the operator Gubbio as the faces and figures he projects on screen. In a famous passage that Benjamin used for his *Work of Art*, Gubbio relates how film actors are exiled from the public as much as from their voices and their bodies: "it is *their image* alone, caught in a moment, in a gesture, an expression, that flickers and disappears."[28] Here, already, one can see the apparition of the posthuman: a body transported on screen, a spectral presence projected primarily as a grimacing face, which extends and substitutes the Nestoroff as a material presence.[29] The difference between such a spectrality and materiality is, however, not a difference in kind but a difference in degree: already in real life, as we have seen, the Nestoroff is interpellated as a melodramatic subject, mediated by the scripts she performs onscreen (and vice versa). Insofar as the posthuman involves a technological contamination, this contamination becomes originary here: the Nestoroff is "in essence" an aftereffect of the imaginary.

Likewise, Gubbio's detachment as a cameraman/narrator is never simply a machinic alienation: In his detachment there is, as Allesandro Vettori has argued convincingly, a display of humanness in terms of an almost mystic disinterestedness.[30] Thus, it seems as if Gubbio's humanness is only preserved in his writing and corrupted by his work as a cameraman, as it is through his writing that Gubbio revenges himself on a world of automatized perception: "I satisfy, by writing, a need to let off steam which is overpowering. I get rid of my professional impassivity, and avenge myself as well."[31] Yet precisely through the camera Gubbio attains a selflessness that approaches the kind of disinterestedness which has been celebrated since the eighteenth century as a sign of cultivation, of human distinction: the art of willing desire away in the face of objects of sense; the art of no longer willing such objects to satisfy one's own needs and wants—of becoming purely, "objectively" cameratic.

Interestingly, therefore, in *Shoot!* the camera can be seen not only as a metaphor of the modern machine age, an age of alienation, but also as an escape route from this very same alienation through an alienation of a different kind: through the aesthetic gaze that, as a gaze subjecting experience to the mould of a synthesis in Kant's third critique, is constitutive of a shared sensible world that is here at once projected as the a priori or prestructuring power of the machine. This "double dealing" of alienation allows the "human" and "inhuman" to collapse into each other in *Shoot!*: The reduction of the one to the other at once becomes its own inverse.[32] Indeed, Gubbio's passivity becomes the perfect antidote against the human superfluity that is a constant impediment to human happiness—and a motor of the machine age.

Seen in this light, the "cinematographic" in *Shoot!* incorporates a beyond of the human that is imagined as a synthesis: the synthetic gaze of the machine and a synthesis of the senses that regulates reality as a scopic regime. On one hand, this synthesis involves the camera and editing techniques of early film, and the modes of automatized perception framed by it,[33] insofar as film represents a vision machine. On the other hand, transmediated (transmediation being the transference and transformation of one mode of mediation into another) techniques of early film in *Shoot!* as a print-based text blur distinctions between writing and this vision machine, that is, between a medium familiarly associated with "humanness" in the modern age and one perceived—in the earlier twentieth century—as a medium of the future (see Filippo Marinetti) and beyond of the human: as speed, projection. Yet precisely *as* a regime of visibility, "cinematographic" in *Shoot!* invokes a whole network of associations with selflessness, disinterested contemplation, and silence (what Gavriel Moses has called the film medium's "central metonymy," in the end inversed as Gubbio's very "physical reality"): in short, a strangely aesthetic-existential dimension that is both self and other to a voracious machine.[34] (And yet we may wonder whether Gubbio's indifference is not, in effect, an indifferentism that, as Jacques Rancière has noted, is potentially fatefully aligned with indistinction). Thus, "cinematographic" in *Shoot!* is never simply a given, a stable category outside of the text, but is rather made manifest *as an effect of* that text—after the fact—as a multifaceted dimension of the visual (perception) and (appropriate to the period) of the silent (impassive).

GRAVITY'S RAINBOW AND "THE PHANTOM OF THE MOVIE PALACE": PRERECORDINGS AND REASSEMBLAGES

The case of *Shoot!* already suggests that we had better use the concept of the "cinematographic" in literary studies not as a fixed or general but a singular concept, that is, always within the framework of a specific text using specific techniques, offering different meanings and concepts of cinema. There is, after all, a huge difference between "cinematographic" techniques in texts by H.G. Wells, Luigi Pirandello, John Dos Passos, James Joyce, or Alain Robbe-Grillet—as a concept it emerges anew, opening a field with every cultural and literary negotiation. Literature, too, shapes and affects the cinematographic.

At the same time, the instability of the cinematographic as a concept is obviously due to developments in the medium of film in Europe and the United States. Thus, in the postmodern age "cinematographic" has connotations different from Bergson's idea of the intellect carving up the flux of reality, or Eisenstein's notion of montage as a montage of attractions. Indeed, Stanley Solomon has argued that "cinematographic" in a postmodern sense bears most significantly on surface play or "texture," and an absence of classical narrative structures:

> Plot is being replaced by texture. By texture I mean incident or event or conversation—as distinct from structured action that has beginning, middle, and end. An incident is not sustaining in itself, but many incidents and many conversations strung together may resemble something like a traditional narrative. Texture includes tone and spectacle, and if it is constantly applied it is another principle of organizing narrative art.[35]

Cinematography has become special effects since, roughly speaking, the late 1970s, insofar as it revolves around visual texture in major Hollywood productions ranging from *Star Wars* (1977–2005) to *Titanic* (1997), *The Mummy* (1999), and *The Core* (2003), which mostly build a narrative with the mere purpose of fitting it in between scenes of special effects and violence.

This paradigm shift, if one may call it thus, is also felt at one remove. Thus, in novels like Robert Coover's *Gerald's Party* (1986), the plot revolves around the murder of the character Ros and a detective's attempt to solve it. The novel can be perceived as texture of numerous (in)consistent conversations that interrupt one another or occur simultaneously with violent events and dead bodies piling up as the evening wears off, parodying detective fiction and mimicking spectacle movies. This emphasis on spectacle inevitably invokes Guy Debord's idea of the society of the spectacle, where social relations are mediated by images, and the spectacle becomes a manufacturer of alienation.[36] We have already seen this process at work in Gubbio's camera perspective—though alienation here always has the double connotation of becoming machine and becoming transcendent at once—yet even in Debord's evocation as a Situationist the spectacle is not necessarily triumphant: there is still a place from which to combat the spectacle, just as Gubbio inhabits and instrumentalizes this space by using the camera as a means of surrender to and escape from the machine. As we know, the finality of the spectacle only becomes pressing in the perspective of postmodernist philosophers like Jean Baudrillard, where opposition to the spectacle is impossible as the spectacle reinforces itself with every repetition of itself as flashy mass-mediation.[37] It is this total surrender to the spectacle that is enacted but also problematized in postmodernist novels like Thomas Pynchon's *Gravity's Rainbow*.

Much has been said about cinematographic references and techniques in *Gravity's Rainbow*. Indeed, Charles Clerc has noted that *Gravity's Rainbow* "brings to bear the imprint of cinema on modern life. It demonstrates the pervasive influence of movies in all facets of our culture, down to indelible effects upon individual sensibilities."[38] Even in the 2000s cinema as a cultural influence is still present in novels like Danielewski's *Only Revolutions* and Hall's *The Raw Shark Texts*, with fragments of film patterning the texts: Cinema continues to be a powerful cultural metaphor in American and European literature. The "cinematographic" texture of *Gravity's Rainbow* may consist of references to films and of mimicking their mode of presentation, but it is given full force in the novel as a discourse that has co-shaped modern consciousness and storytelling: the images that cinema provides are the archetypical images once provided by myth. Scott Simmon observed long ago that "the complexity of *Gravity's Rainbow's* film-form comes from Pynchon's awareness that our whole way of approaching narrative itself has been altered by film."[39] Or most tellingly, the complexity of *Gravity's Rainbow* comes from Pynchon's characters, whose minds function "cinematographically" in the old Freudian sense of cinema as a dream sequence, fading in and out as ghosts on screen. Likewise, the plot is framed cinematographically, as if derived from screen, which gives the novel the semblance of being a *novelization* at its core: it presents itself as a transcription, "always already," just as *House of Leaves* had done over a decade earlier.

Copy and origin, technology and fantasy: they have become codependent and indistinguishable in this novel opening with a dream and ending in a movie theater. Like other modern technologies, cinema controls minds in *Gravity's Rainbow* and gives rise to reality effects of a very special kind, such as the imaginary Schwarzkommando in Gerhard von Göll's ("der Springer") fake documentary, which turns out to be a real African rocket unit serving under Germany, and Springer's belief that his film has brought these men into being (as German cinema in *Gravity's Rainbow* is accused of bringing certain realities into being). Cinematographic control does not exclude the reader, who in the end is caught as a viewer in the act of reading in front of a big, empty screen. As in *Shoot!*, where writing and recording become conflated, so in *Gravity's Rainbow* reading is repositioned within the frames of the imaginary. We cannot *but* be looking at a screen.

This inescapability of cinema as a "paranoiac" medium, shaping reality, and absorbing culture, epitomizes *Gravity's Rainbow*.

The cinematographic space-time frequently merges with the System-and Zone-realities of the characters respectively, at times drastically changing their lives. One example is the figure of Ilse—a child put into a concentration camp to blackmail her father, Franz Pökler—who was conceived after the screening of Pökler's film *Alpdrücken*: "how many shadow-children would be fathered on Erdmann that night?"[40] The star of the same movie, Margherita Erdmann, became pregnant during the shooting of the film, presumably due to a gang rape. Franz wonders if the "movie-child" whom the Nazi archvillain Lieutenant Weissmann sends him is, in fact, his daughter: "*Isn't that what they made of my child, a film?*"[41] Thus, the birth of Ilse and Bianca (Margherita's daughter) coincides with an act of filmic mediation. Bianca dies horribly on the ship *Anubis*, and Ilse's presence then assumes an episodic character:

> So it has gone for the six years since. A daughter a year, each one about a year older, each time taking up nearly from scratch. The only continuity has been her name, and Zwölfkinder, and Pökler's love—love something like the persistence of vision, for They have used it to create for him the moving image of a daughter, flashing him only these summertime frames of her, leaving him to build the illusion of a single child … what would the time scale matter, a 24th of a second or a year.[42]

Pökler's "24th of a second" here refers to Jean-Luc Godard's dictum that a film speed of twenty-four frames per second is ideal for accommodating "persistence of vision." Thus, in the novel, what connects Ilse and her father in "reality" has become a replica of the scenes from *Alpdrücken*—an effect of automatized perception related to "cinematography" as a freezer and reassembler of the flux of the real. As in numerous other scenes, cinema here conditions perception and apparitions of reality "itself" (see Von Göll's subsequent determination to "sow in the Zone seeds of reality" with images of his phony Schwarz-kommando footage).[43] Thus, the "cinematographic" in *Gravity's Rainbow* emerges as a prerecording of the real: formative and inevitable.

CINEMATOGRAPHIC AND TELEVISUAL MODES OF PERCEPTION

As a "cinematographic" text, *Gravity's Rainbow* still participates in a modernist discourse of automatized perception, while at once radicalizing that discourse: It further destabilizes ontological differences between "real" and "mediated" worlds—these worlds interact with, and collapse into each other. While *Shoot!* already stages such interactions, and thus likewise problematizes distinctions between filmed worlds and worlds captured by an I/eye that is nevertheless also a camera I/

eye, the cinematographic in *Gravity's Rainbow* regulates a regime of visibility that *becomes* the real. Indeed, it is the very possibility of a cinematographic regulation of the real as an illusionist and uncontrollable regulation that connects *Shoot!* to *Gravity's Rainbow*. The emphasis on calculated effect plays a central role in this, not only in *Shoot!*, where "real life" starts to adapt itself to the melodramatic formats of silent film, but also in *Gravity's Rainbow*, where films in a way animate life.

What is more, both novels critique the effects of the cultural colonization of cinema as a "mainstream" machine while at the same time drawing on the more experimental techniques of avant-garde cinema (as the numerous references to German expressionist film in *Gravity's Rainbow* attest to) to *materialize* that criticism in literary writing. This critique should be read, we feel, in the context of the precariousness of the literary with respect to cinema in the twentieth century—a similar precariousness as has been observed for literature in the digital age. While the transmedial adaptations of film in twentieth-century literature were frequent and fertile, film also threatened to suppress older media such as the theater and literature as dominant cultural media.

As for literature, the threat to its marginalization at once entailed a threat to literacy—and this threat moved far beyond the realm of the aesthetic into that of the social-political: democracy and the vote. Thus in 1940, George Duhamel's *In Defense of Letters* (1940), anticipating Sven Birkerts's *The Gutenberg Elegies* (1995), points to the centrality of print in Western culture, the vitality of literacy to democracy, and its possible erosion due to the perceived, imperialist expansion of film and radio in the twentieth century. In nineteenth-century Western Europe and the United States, as Robert Morss Lovett paraphrases Duhamel in a contemporary review, "an immense reading public was called into being [in direct relation to the liberal struggle for the extension of suffrage], and to this public literature became a religion."[44] In the twentieth century, for Duhamel, it is not so much the threat of illiteracy as the threat of new media (which carries for him another, repeated threat of illiteracy) that undermine the scope and depth of this reading public. According to him, print has been degraded into "popular" forms, while the mass mediations of film and radio undermine a culture of solitude that would lie at the foundation of the culture of reading since the Renaissance—a culture fostering autonomous thought and individual, reflecting minds. Even today, apocalyptic critics like Birkerts uphold this view, arguing that the electronic media have corroded humanist developments of print and after, and that privacy and autonomy, are now "values" of the past—as films such as *The Truman Show* and *Eternal Sunshine of the Spotless Mind* and novels such as Steven Hall's *The Raw Shark Texts* and Paul Auster's *Travels in the Scriptorium* might illustrate.

In different ways, *Shoot!* and *Gravity's Rainbow* perform this tense opposition between solitude (literature, literacy) and mediated minds (film, radio) and mourn the "lost" humanist values this opposition favors implicitly: Solitude in these novels never again is an unproblematic, nor even an attainable, state. Though in *Shoot!* the undecidability of "alienation" in terms of machinic isolation on one hand and aesthetic indifference on the other undermines a stable opposition between the automaton and human values, this is less ambivalent in *Gravity's Rainbow*. *Gravity's Rainbow* still offers an escape from the System, yet it is but a marginal escape from what Tony Tanner has called a "world of non-being, an operative kingdom of death, covering the organic world with a world of paper and plastic" ran by anonymous forces.[45] In the Zone, all meaning collapses, all becomes disconnected—an alienation of the drifting sort that is a far cry from the autonomous solitude of humanism. Conversely, in the System individual minds are framed and formatted by official meanings and narratives, thus likewise undermining the possibility of a freely thinking, individual mind that is at the core of the humanist tradition.

Is this how literature, or at least a certain literature, announces its "defeat," and the "defeat" of print literacy, in the twentieth century? By tapping into a discourse network of automatized perception that it presents as omnipresent, as an enemy to be fought in a cultural war? Kathleen Fitzpatrick has noted in this respect that what she calls late-twentieth-century "novels of obsolescence," novels announcing, in one way or another, the "end" of literature in an age of mass mediation, are implicated in an ideology of their own. Counting among its practitioners authors such as Pynchon and Don DeLillo, Fitzpatrick argues that the anxiety of literary obsolescence focuses typically on dehumanization, propaganda, and (once more) loss of individuality. While her analyses are framed not so much by the "cinematographic" as by the televisual, not so much in a specific as in a broad sense of multimodal, networked mass mediation, she also finds that anxieties over the imminent death of literature interact with other anxieties: those of white males who have been losing their privileged position within the domain of literature to female authors and those of other ethnicities. Thus, "the threat that television poses to the [white male] novelist functions as an acceptable cultural scapegoat for that much stickier social issue: the perceived dominance of the contemporary literary scene of fiction by women and racial and ethnic minorities."[46] What poses as the threat of new media only hides, for Fitzpatrick, the threat of the Other.

In Pynchon's *Vineland*, published one year before the first Gulf War, this threat of the televisual is, indeed, emphatically (one might almost say: predictably) rendered. Set in 1984, and revolving around California-based old hippie Zoyd Wheeler, his daughter, Prairie, and her vanished mother Frenesi (and—like *Shoot!*—around a snuff movie), *Vineland* displays and reflects a world modeled by TV programs, a world where television shapes the protagonists' desires, expectations, and behavior. There is a narcotics agent, Hector Zuniga, who tries to behave like cops he sees on TV, while at the same time persuading Zoyd that the model's representation is nowhere near the real undercover cop's life. Conversely, there is Frenesi, who encounters a "real" policeman after having masturbated in front of her favorite cop show, seeing him *through the screen of the door*, which functions in the geography of private spaces as an "outlook" on the world. This outlook is thoroughly mediated, since TV controls her response to the world outside: The cop show conditions her emotional state and submissive stance toward the policeman.

Everybody in the novel is shaped by the Tube—indeed, as Brian McHale has pointed out, the world in *Vineland* is divided into different TV genres, to which different characters and their worlds correspond (Zoyd and sitcoms, Prairie and soaps).[47] Switching from one world to the other is like switching channels—which situates the novel typically outside the linear domain of traditional narrative. Pynchon grotesquely depicts this TV-based culture through Thanatoids, a community of neither fully alive nor fully dead people, due to karmic imbalances: "like death only different," moving but motionless (like Benny and the Crew from Pynchon's earlier novel *V*), who watch TV all the time. Indeed, due to its (much-problematized) dimension of simultaneity or liveness, TV in *Vineland* acts as a household presence that people relate to, chat with, and masturbate with.[48] Culture in *Vineland* is a culture of reruns: an endless repetition of scopic regimes, constituting a virtual death-in-life, and hence a virtual timelessness, encapsulated in an eternal return. Seen in this light, it is not only the tube, but also technologies of video recording that recast the texture of reality in *Vineland* into tape materiality of endless replay.

And yet, if film and the even more menacing, domestic presence of TV here act out the perceived threats of a culturally diversified literary field, and if white male authors of the 1980s and 1990s—knowingly or unknowingly—use film and TV as a screen on which to project their anxieties of "best manhood" (in Kathleen Fitzpatrick's phrase), the very nature of TV mediation at once deconstructs this very projection. Let us, to this end, and near the end, go back to the beginning: to Henri Bergson's observations on the intellect and cinematographic mediation. For Bergson, as we have seen, the intellect makes snapshots of the flux of reality, rather than participating in that flux, which is the province of intuition. If film thus cannot cater intuition in Bergson's perspective, we may make a possible exception for TV. After all, if we elaborate on Raymond Williams's famous dictum in *Television: Technology and Cultural Form*, the experience of watching TV has been associated with flux or flow. While in literary and theater culture, the reading and viewing audience was accustomed to "discrete" entities such as books or pieces, TV offered an experiential flow that was to change cultural perception—and the cultural conception of sequence.[49] Fixed endings and intervals, such as the intervals in cinema, virtually disappeared in this technology.

Watching TV can thus be compared to stepping into a river—always *in medias res*—even though it is a rigidly scheduled river, and the river is in the plural.[50] Though the flow may in fact be a segmentation without end, Cecilia Tichi has emphasized print novels of the later 1980s and 1990s, absorbing the medium of TV, typically mimic this open continuity: "Readers are made to feel that, instead of a beginning, there is a point of entry. We are joining a program in progress, i.e., in process. We move into a sequence of events which are to be represented in a continuous flow."[51] Tichi refers to fictions by Ann Beattie, Brett Easton Ellis, or David Leavitt as "enacting the traits of broadcast television in the very form of their fiction"—offering narratives with no clear entry and exit points, a pervasive sense of the present, and moveable contexts or settings of focalization. Precisely for this reason, texts such as Bret Easton Ellis's *Less than Zero* have been typically downplayed as "shallow," but it is a shallowness attesting to a significant transmedial transfer: Framed by a dominant, televisual medium paradigm, the protagonist in such televisual fictions is "constructed as a figure in transit, and the reader also. Both are mobile figures, true to the cognitive experience of television.… The mobility of televisual "flow" is the fundament of fictional form."[52] If this is indeed the case, then the discontinuous continuity of cinematographic perception—revolving around the constant freezing, cutting, and reassembling of the real—has in the televisual era been replaced by a continuous discontinuity: a flow of infinite parts, beams. It is this continuous discontinuity that reapproaches Bergson's mode of intuition, if in a deeply synthetic way, at once "doing" and "undoing" the forms of automatized perception. The "end" of the novel, in this paradigm, is nowhere in sight: it has adapted itself to, and creatively absorbed the latter in a discourse of fluidity, impermanency, and simultaneity.

CONCLUSION

In this chapter, we have seen how the concept of the cinematographic works as a literary concept in modernist and postmodernist fictions. In *Shoot!* the cinematographic becomes the framework for rethinking the relations between humans and machines: to think a beyond of the human that is imagined as a synthesis—the synthetic gaze of the machine and a synthesis of the senses that regulates reality as a scopic regime. Yet if we think that cinema represents a disembodied, machinic perception here, while literary writing is attached to some kind of lost humanity and individuality, and the kind of solitude and privacy attached to this humanity, the very transmediation of the cinema in *literary writing itself* blurs binary oppositions between the two. Such blurring defines our reading experience of *Shoot!*, as the literary and the cinematographic here affect and contaminate each other.

Likewise, in *Gravity's Rainbow* the cinematographic and the novelistic—and all the values attached to both—spill over into each other. As we have seen, the novel still participates in a modernist discourse of automatized perception, but it also radicalizes that discourse: *Gravity's Rainbow* further destabilizes ontological differences between "real" and "mediated" worlds, as these worlds interact with, and collapse into each other. Here, daily life does not just adapt itself to cinematographic life—here, the cinematographic formats the real itself.

Is this, we have wondered, how literature, or at least a certain literature, announces its "defeat," and the "defeat" of print literacy, in the late twentieth century? By tapping into a modernist discourse network of automatized perception that it presents as omnipresent, as an enemy to be fought in a cultural war? With reference to Fitzpatrick, we have observed that there might be another enemy at work in these novels of obsolescence: the Other writing back to the center—the Other presented in the guise of new media that move "beyond" humanism. Cinema and, even more menacing, the domestic presence of TV may here be acting out the perceived threats of a culturally diversified literary field: White male authors of the 1980s and 1990s—knowingly or unknowingly—use film and TV as a screen on which to project their anxieties of "beset manhood." Yet if TV is used as such a screen, its particular mode of mediation may take us back to the very patterns of intuition that, in Henri Bergson's writing, film would not be able to cater: patterns of flow, of a continuity that mimics "becoming." *These* patterns, we have suggested, have helped to reinvigorate the form of the novel in the 1990s and 2000s.

ENDNOTES

1. For Eisenstein, montage epitomized the art of cinema. See for this Sergei M. Eisenstein, *Film Form: Essays in Film Theory*, ed. and trans. Jay Leyda (London: Dobson, 1951).
2. Ibid., 204–205; quoted in Laura Marcus, *The Tenth Muse: Writing about Cinema in the Modernist Period* (Oxford: Oxford University Press, 2007), 425. For more on Dickens and film—and on nineteenth-century literature projecting an epoch to come—see Graham Smith, *Dickens and the Dream of Cinema* (Manchester: Manchester University Press, 2003).
3. Alan Spiegel, *Fiction and the Camera Eye: Visual Consciousness in Film and the Modern Novel* (Charlottesville: University Press of Virginia, 1976).
4. Robert Stam, *Literature Through Film: Realism, Magic, and the Art of Adaptation* (Oxford: Blackwell, 2005), 148–154.
5. Eisenstein, *Film Form*, 12. For a more detailed analysis, see Alan Spiegel, "Flaubert to Joyce: Evolution of a Cinematographic Form," *Novel: A Forum on Fiction* 3 (1979): 229–243; and Scarlett Baron, "Flaubert, Joyce:

Vision, Photography, Cinema," *Modern Fiction Studies* 54 (2008): 689–714. In the scene from *Madame Bovary*, montage boils down to a simulated simultaneity as the prefect's voice at the fair continues to sound as Rodolphe and Emma speak, and vice versa—and the contrast between the former's talk of duty, the force of the law, or devotion to the rural countryside on the one hand, and the imminent transgression of Emma and Rodolphe, as well as their "urban" romantic pursuit of happiness on the other, somehow ridicules both sides.

6. Spiegel, "Flaubert to Joyce," 231.

7. P. Adams Sitney, *Modernist Montage: The Obscurity of Vision in Cinema and Literature* (New York: Columbia University Press, 1990), 17–19; Irina Rajewski, *Intermediales Erzä hlen in der italienischen Literatur der Postmoderne: Von den Giovani Scrittori der 80er zum Pulp der 90er Jahre* (Tübingen: Gunter Narr, 2003).

8. Marcus here also points to Winifred Holby, who already studied the inscription of the new medium of film in texts by Virginia Woolf, and cast her experimental technique as a specifically "cinematographic technique." See Marcus, *The Tenth Muse*, 129–130.

9. Julian Murphet and Lydia Rainford, eds., *Literature and Visual Technologies: Writing after Cinema* (New York: Macmillan, 2003).

10. David Trotter, "T. S. Eliot and Cinema," *Modernism/Modernity* 13, no. 2 (2006): 240.

11. Garrett Stewart, *Between Film and Screen: Modernism's Photo Synthesis* (Chicago: University of Chicago Press, 1999).

12. As Trotter indicates, in this instance Stewart "draws productively on Frederic Jameson's description of the "confluence," in a passage from E. M. Forster's *Howards End* (1910), "of movie technology on the one hand, and of a certain type of modernist or protomodernist language on the other," both of which seem to offer some space, some "third term," between the subject and the object of perception. For Jameson, Stewart observes, that third term is in effect the (literary/photographic) apparatus, the "disembodiment of perception by technique; automatism, in short." Trotter, "T. S. Eliot and Cinema," 240.

13. Garrett Stewart, "Cinecriture: Modernism's Flicker Effect," *New Literary History* 4 (1998): 727–768.

14. "Cinematographic" is, of course, a very broad term. As Steven Kellman has noted, it could mean anything from "Hollywood-plot-like" to "avantgardist montage novel." Here: "cinematographic" is not used as a stable concept, but rather as emerging from the texts discussed. What these texts have in common is the *critical* foregrounding of a "cinematographic" perception, rather than its utopian embrace (as in the Italian futurists). Steven Kellman, "The Cinematic Novel: Tracking a Concept," *Modern Fiction Studies* 3 (1987): 467–475.

15. Henri Bergson, *Creative Evolution*, trans. A. Mitchell (New York: Henry Holt, 1911), 306.

16. As Bergson puts it in his *Introduction to Metaphysics*, the difference between intuition and intellect amounts to a difference between synthesis and analysis, between imagining or virtually participating in an object and taking that object apart: "By Intuition is meant the kind of *intellectual sympathy* by which one places oneself within an object in order to coincide with what is unique in it and consequently inexpressible. Analysis is the operation which reduces the object to elements already known, that is, to elements common to it and other objects. To analyse, therefore, is to express a thing as a function of something other than itself. All analysis is thus a translation, a development into symbols, a representation taken from successive points of view from which we note as many resemblances as possible between the new object which we are studying and others which we believe we know already. In its eternally unsatisfied desire to embrace the object around which it is compelled to turn, analysis multiplies without end the number of its points of view in order to complete its always incomplete representation, and ceaselessly varies its symbols that it may perfect the always imperfect translation. It goes on therefore to infinity. But Intuition, if Intuition be possible, is a simple act. It is an act directly opposed to analysis, for it is a viewing in totality, as an absolute; it is a synthesis, not an analysis, not an intellectual act, for it is an immediate, emotional synthesis." Elsewhere, Bergson repeatedly states that he does not privilege intuition at the expense of intellect—but rather only claims a space for the former. Henri Bergson, *Introduction to Metaphysics*, trans. T. E. Hulme (London: Macmillan, 1913), 7.

17. This assumption is, of course, problematic. Yet it is an assumption that is dominant in earlier twentieth-century conceptions of film and (infinite) mechanic reproduction.

18. Gavriel Moses, "Gubbio in Gabbia: Pirandello's Cameraman and the Entrapments of Film Vision," *Modern Language Notes* 94 (1979): 36.

19. Luigi Pirandello, *Shoot! The Notebooks of Serafino Gubbio, Cinematograph Operator*, trans. C. K. Scott Moncrieff (Chicago: University of Chicago Press, 2005).

20. See Frank Nulf, "Luigi Pirandello and the Cinema," *Film Quarterly* 2 (1970–71): 40–48.

21. Pirandello, *Shoot!*, 7.

22. Ibid., 8–9.

23. In Arthur Schopenhauer's philosophy, the Will is a noumenal dimension that manifests itself as object, as phenomenon, in the bodies, gestures, and shapes of the world: the world, human beings, animals, vegetation, etc. are all objectifications of a blind, irrational, ungraspable Will—an collective, unconscious drive. Friedrich Nietzsche further develops this philosophy of the Will as life-Will, craving and feeding on life, in *Die Geburt der Tragödie*. See for this Arthur Schopenhauer, *Die Welt als Wille und Vorstellung* (Frankfurt: Suhrkamp, 1986); Friedrich Nietzsche, *Die Geburt der Tragödie aus dem Geiste der Musik* (Frankfurt: Insel, 1987).

24. Pirandello, *Shoot!*, 57, 59.

25. Ibid., 9.

26. See Gavriel Moses's extensive analyses of film-mimetic schemes in "Gubbio in Gabbia," 39–41.

27. Pirandello, *Shoot!*, 83.

28. Ibid., 68.

29. Following Katherine Hayles's analysis, posthuman subjectivities are here understood as (openly) mediated subjectivities—whether they be culturally or technologically "extended": subjectivities that are not "naturally" but "artificially" informed. For more on the posthuman, see Chapter 4. See also Katherine Hayles, *How We Became Posthuman: Virtual Bodies in Cybernetics, Literature, and Informatics* (Chicago: University of Chicago Press, 1999).

30. Alessandro Vettori, "Serafino Gubbio's Candid Camera," *MLN* 113 (1998): 79–107.

31. Pirandello, *Shoot!*, 7.

32. As Alessandro Vettori observes, "[the negative passivity] has eliminated all encumbering worldly burdens from his life, purifying his personality to the mode of mysticism, if only a secular version of mysticism." Ibid., 100.

33. These involve, as we have seen, close-ups, but also montage: Insofar as film captures Bergson's cinematographic mode of selecting or freezing and reassembling, this is rehearsed in, for instance, Gubbio's evocation of the modern city in chapters 1–2 of book 1—an evocation that typically goes hand in hand with allusions to film and cinematographic techniques in novels such as Alfred Döblin's *Berlin, Alexanderplatz* (1929) or John Dos Passos's *Manhattan Transfer* (1925) and the literary mimicry of "the external, that is to say, the mechanical framework of the life which keeps us clamorously and dizzily occupied and gives us no rest" (4)—or, as Gavriel Moses points out, the "tendency to build up a context through the accumulation of metonymic details"; that is, the "sectioned anatomy of facial and bodily features"; the "technique of placing a [virtual] camera on a moving object and photographing the resulting alteration in one's view of the world" (cf. the scene in the film studio laboratories), or the ways in which *Shoot!* approaches the status of a film script. Moses, "Gubbio in Gabbia," 40–42.

34. Moses, "Gubbio in Gabbia," 46.

35. Stanley Solomon, "Aristotle in Twilight: American Film Narrative in the 1980s," in *The Cinematic Text*, ed. R. Barton Palmer (New York: AMS, 1989), 76.

36. Robert Coover, *Gerald's Party* (New York: Grove Press, 1985); *La société du spectacle* (Paris: Gallimard, 1996). There is also a film adaptation of the book, made in 1973.

37. Jean Baudrillard, *Simulations*, trans. Paul Foss, Paul Patton, and Philip Beitchman (New York: Semiotext(e), 1983).

38. Charles Clerc, "Film in *Gravity's Rainbow*," in *Approaches to Gravity's Rainbow*, ed. Charles Clerc (Columbus: Ohio State University Press, 1983), 104.

39. Scott Simmon, "Beyond the Theater of War: Gravity's Rainbow as Film," in *Critical Essays on Thomas Pynchon*, ed. Richard Pearce (Boston: G. K. Hall, 1981), 127.

40. Thomas Pynchon, *Gravity's Rainbow* (New York: Penguin, 1991), 397.

41. Ibid., 398.

42. Ibid., 422.

43. Ibid., 388.

44. Robert Morss Lovett, "Literature and Its Rivals," *The Kenyon Review* 1 (1940): 97.

45. Tony Tanner, *Thomas Pynchon* (London: Methuen, 1982), 79.

46. Kathleen Fitzpatrick, *The Anxiety of Obsolescence: The American Novel in the Age of Television* (Nashville, Tenn.: Vanderbilt University Press, 2006).

47. Brian McHale, *Constructing Postmodernism* (New York: Routledge, 1992), 127.

48. Stanley Cavell, "The Fact of Television," in *Themes out of School* (San Francisco: North Point Press, 1984), 235–268. For a different perspective, see Samuel Weber, *Mass Mediauras: Form, Technics, Media*, ed. Alan Cholodenko (Stanford: Stanford University Press, 1996), and Jacques Derrida and Bernard Stiegler, *Echographies of Television* (Cambridge: Polity, 2002).

49. Raymond Williams, *Television, Technology, and Cultural Form* (Lon-don: Routledge, 2003).

50. John Ellis, *Seeing Things: Television in the Age of Uncertainty* (London: I. B. Tauris, 2000). See also Ellis's classic *Visible Fictions: Cinema, Television, Video* (London: Routledge, 1992).

51. Cecilia Tichi, "Television and Recent American Fiction," *American Literary History* 1 (Spring 1989): 121–125.

52. Ibid.

1. How is mise-en-scène defined in the discipline of film? What are the components of mise-en-scène?

2. According to the author Robert Spadoni, what is the meaning of *profilmic* space in terms of filmmaking? How is that term significant?

3. According to author John Mateer, what new on-set film role was created with the advent of digital filmmaking? How is this role significant?

4. In John Mateer's article *Digital Cinematography: Evolution of Craft or Revolution in Production*, what is meant by the article's last line: "Cinematography has not essentially changed in 100 years and it's not going to change. It is the process of artistry that will evolve.'?"

5. In what way would traditional filmmakers argue that film "looks" better than a digital format?

6. How do filmmakers Chen Guofu and Cai Mingliang manipulate mise-en-scène to highlight their protagonist's emotional state?

7. In Hsiu-Chuang Deppman's essay, *Cinema of Disillusionment*, what does Chen Guofu say about the relationship between Hollywood and "Third Cinema?

8. According to Grmusa and Wurth's essay *Cinematography as a Literary Concept in the (Post)Modern Age*, how is authoring a film considered the same as authoring a book?

Amidst the deluge of critical editing theory, stands Todd Berliner and Dale Cohen's boldly fascinating oeuvre *The Illusion of Continuity: Active Perception and the Classical Editing System*, which suggests the very act of assembling the moving image exploits the limitations—or rather accommodates—the extant cognitive process by which viewers ingest visual stimuli. Alan William's *Historical and Theoretical Issues in the Coming of Recorded Sound to the Cinema* is a notable survey

THE WAY WE DECIDE

of the early history of film sound and presents the student with a rich context of commercial cinema by which to understand the extrinsic motivations for putting sound to film in the first place. K.J. Donnelly's wickedly fascinating analysis challenges the very definitions of film music and film sound in the context of horror films.

TODD BERLINER AND DALE J. COHEN

THE ILLUSION OF CONTINUITY: ACTIVE PERCEPTION AND THE CLASSICAL EDITING SYSTEM

INTRODUCTION

In the movie *The Matrix* (1999), characters experience a completely virtual world- created by sending electrical signals directly to their spinal cord and brain—that contains the sensations of the "real" world but without a corresponding physical environment. The psychology behind this scenario is essentially accurate. Our experience of the physical world exists in our brains, and a controlled stimulus can cue our brains to experience a world that is virtually physical.

Virtual realities can exist because the brain does not experience the physical environment directly. Information in the environment exists in the form of physical energy. Cells in the brain, however, communicate through the release of neurochemicals. Each of our five senses contains "receptor cells" that translate the information in the environment into the neurochemical language that the brain can understand.[1] For example, specialized cells on the retina, called photoreceptors, respond to the physical energy of light by releasing neurochemicals, thereby converting the physical energy into the language of the brain. Creating a virtual world involves artificially stimulating the cells that lead to the brain in the same way that receptor cells would.

The *Matrix* scenario is an emblem of the cinematic experience. The sights and sounds presented in the cinema have the potential to stimulate the visual and auditory receptor cells in ways that are similar enough to those experienced in the physical world that, under specified circumstances, many of our perceptual processes[2] do not distinguish between stimuli generated by the cinema and those generated by physical environments. When organized according to the principles of classical continuity editing,[3] the cinema stimulates a series of cognitive processes[4] that construct a coherent model of on-screen space. Indeed, the cognitive processes that generate spatial coherence for classical cinema spectators are, this article shall demonstrate, the very same cognitive processes that generate coherence for spectators in the physical world.

This article proposes a new model of how the human perceptual system extracts coherence from discontinuous cinematic images edited according to classical continuity principles. Based on the current understanding of real-world perception, our *model of spatial continuity* lays out the cognitive basis of classical editing conventions. Drawing on research from both film studies and perceptual psychology, this article explains how classical editing devices exploit and accommodate the cognitive processes people use to perceive the physical world.

The field of film studies has seen a variety of approaches to explaining the predominance of the classical editing system, including psychoanalytic (Mulvey, Silverman, Oudart, Dayan), semiotic and structuralist (Metz, John Carroll), auteurist (Bazin), and ideological approaches (Baudry, Heath, Zavarzadeh), and many theorists combine several different approaches. But none of this research answers the following straightforward question: if you are watching *The Philadelphia Story* (1940), and you see a shot of C. K. Dexter Haven (Cary Grant) at the front of a house, followed by a shot of a front door opening (see Figures 10 and 11), what are the cognitive processes that lead you to perceive the two depicted spaces as connected? Film textbooks, in explaining the continuity system, will note eyeline matches and other narrative and stylistic devices, but identifying continuity devices does not explain how and why the spectator perceives continuity. Our model does. It addresses a key concern of the classical continuity system that no previous scholars have addressed comprehensively: how the fundamental conventions of classical editing accommodate our perceptual and cognitive processes and stimulate the perception of continuity.

The principles of Irvin Rock's inferential theory of perception, often termed "constructive perception," supply the foundation of our approach (*Indirect, Logic*). Simplified, constructive perception holds that perception is essentially a problem-solving process. Here, the perceptual system builds models of the world by proposing and testing hypotheses based on sensory input. Film scholar David Bordwell employs the same principles in his research on space perception in the cinema, particularly in his *Narration in the Fiction Film* (99–146), and perceptual psychologists Daniel Levin and Daniel Simons ("Perceiving Stability") similarly discuss the role of constructive perception in their research on spatial continuity. Psychologists Julian Hochberg and Virginia Brooks ("Perception") collected empirical evidence establishing the validity of the constructivist theory of film perception.[5] All of this research shares a common idea: that classical cinema practices developed in the ways they did because the human brain developed in the way *it* did.

Although each of these researchers has provided key insights into the perception of film space, no one has offered a holistic understanding of how spectators perceive continuity when watching the fragmented imagery presented by classically edited cinema. This article attempts to better define the field of the cognition of film by presenting a broad model of film perception from sensation to interpretation, rooted in the current understanding of the human perceptual and cognitive systems. The article synthesizes the available research in psychology and film studies in order to provide a comprehensive explanation of the perception of cinema continuity. Researchers, moreover, can use the proposed model to make predictions about continuity perception and can therefore test the model empirically.

The article focuses on the relation between Hollywood's classical editing system and what cognitive psychology calls active perception, which enables the human perceptual system to interact with the environment rather than passively observe it. For the purposes of this article, the "classical editing system" refers to a conglomerate of stable principles that enable movies to create spatial coherence among shots:

- *Continuity editing:* a system of editing devices that establish a continuous presentation of space and time. For instance, in a classically edited movie, a character moving from left to right in one shot will, for purposes of continuity, likely be shown moving left to right in an immediately subsequent shot.
- *Point-of-view (POV) editing:* a system for communicating story information by depicting the visual field observed by characters. An eyeline match—in which one shot depicts a character looking at something and the subsequent shot shows what she sees—is the definitive point-of-view editing device.
- *Analytical editing:* the practice of organizing shots in accordance with narrative information, so that spectators infer logical relationships among shots. A shot in which someone admits to murdering someone, followed by a flashback in which we see her commit the murder, relies on spectators' inference of a logical relation between the two shots.[6]

The foregoing principles have resulted in a set of standard practices (including matching techniques, establishing shots, camera movement practices, sound overlaps, the 180-degree rule, the 30-degree rule, cheat cuts, and shot/reverse-shot), many of which this article addresses. It cannot address each practice thoroughly, which would require a series of articles, nor can it address all classical editing devices, which are too numerous to tackle effectively here, but we propose that our model accounts for all of them. In short, the model explains "how well," as Brooks puts it, "the moving picture works as a substitute stimulus, a surrogate that provides essentially the same pattern of light as would some real event in the real world" (107). Our perceptual and cognitive abilities have limits, and the cinema, like all optical illusions, sneaks into our brain through its limitations. Without these limitations, the perception of cinema continuity would be impossible.

We begin with an abstract description of our model and follow it with a more detailed discussion of the model's stages and evidence for their validity.

MODEL OF SPATIAL CONTINUITY

Continuity, in both real-world perception and cinema perception, is an illusion, enabled by our brain's ability to conjoin fragmented images when such images follow certain patterns and logical principles. We propose that the series of images produced through classical editing are similar to those experienced in everyday life in that both types are noncontinuous (images come upon our senses in a fragmented way), both follow similar patterning (classical movie images follow patterns that people regularly perceive in their everyday experience), and both obey the same logic (the progression of images in both situations adhere to many of the same principles). Because of these similarities, the same perceptual systems that create the illusion of continuity in the real world also create the illusion of continuity in classical cinema space.

Figure 11.1 presents a graphical depiction of the model, which has two broad stages: a sensory input and encoding stage and a mental transformation stage. The phenomenological result of these two stages is the perception of continuous space. During the first stage, the brain selects and encodes the stimuli that enter the system. We propose that, unlike other editing systems—such as Sergei Eisenstein's "Intellectual Montage" (45–63) or Yasujiro Ozu's "360-Degree System" (Bordwell, *Ozu* 89–102)—the classical editing system selects inputs similar to those selected by active perception. "Active perception" refers to the cognitive and perceptual processes for selecting and encoding stimuli in the physical world. Governed by the interests and intentions of the perceiver, active perception is a volitional process for searching the environment for information. People do not gaze randomly around their field of vision but rather direct their gazes with intention, looking for answers to spatial questions. For instance, a glimpse of someone on the street may spur the viewer to direct his or her gaze at the person's face in order to determine who the person is. The classical editing system takes on some of the volitional burden for the perceiver by preselecting stimuli, thus limiting the range of viewer activity. Classical editing works as a

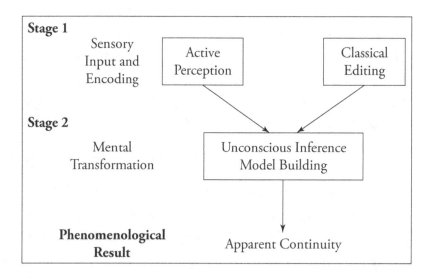

Figure 11.1. Diagram of the Model of Spatial Continuity

surrogate for active perception, posing spatial questions and answering them, specifying spatial information that perceivers in the real world are accustomed to specifying for themselves.

In stage two, that of mental transformation, cognitive systems process the information selected and encoded by active perception and classical editing. During this stage, the information is manipulated and augmented by cognitive processes—known in cognitive psychology as unconscious inference and model building—that evolved to compensate for information lost in the encoding process. "Unconscious inference" refers to the brain's tendency to automatically resolve ambiguities in stimuli presented to the visual system (this article explains unconscious inference more fully in the later, more detailed discussion of stage two). "Model building," here, refers to the process of creating a mental representation of space. The mental transformation stage is the engine that derives continuity from the discontinuous input provided by active perception and classical cinema. Classical editing produces "similar enough" images to those produced by active perception so that the brain's mental transformation processes do not distinguish between the two.

The phenomenological result of the model-building process is the experience of continuity. This experience results from our perceptual system's assumption of spatial coherence and its insensitivity to the discontinuities of the stimulus.

The rest of this article explains, investigates, and presents evidence for our model. By necessity, the model simplifies the explanation of perception, which encompasses a large range of cognitive processes. The article focuses on explaining those processes integral to the perception of spatial continuity in cinema and real-world perception.

Stage 1. Sensory Input and Encoding: Active Perception and Classical Editing

Classical editing leads to easily understood and perceptually coherent spaces because it preselects visual information similar to that selected by the individual during active perception. The two selection processes produce images so similar, in fact, that the brain encodes the visual information presented by classical editing *as if* it were selected by the spectator. By mimicking the kind of visual information the brain selects and encodes regularly, classical editing tends to create images that fall within the range of stimuli that the perceptual system can accommodate automatically.[7]

Abundant scientific data demonstrate that perception relies on both automatic and controlled cognitive systems (Neisser; Schneider and Shiffrin). Automatic systems process information effortlessly and efficiently. Such systems, largely unconscious, do not require our attention. By contrast, controlled systems require both conscious control and focused attention. Figure 11.2 provides demonstrations of automatic and controlled processing. We effortlessly spot the "T in

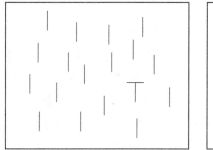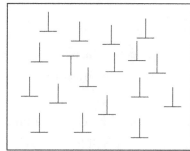

Figure 11.2. A demonstration of automatic versus controlled processing. The "T" in the left square "pops out" automatically, whereas viewers must scan for the "T" in the right square.

the square on the left because the "T" "pops out." This "pop out" effect is a signature of automatic processing. By contrast, we must consciously search for the "T" in the square on the right. Such effortful, sequential activity characterizes controlled processing. Comparatively slow and inefficient, controlled systems cannot effectively process the massive amount of information in the typical field of vision. Because automatic systems process large amounts of information simultaneously while leaving controlled systems unaffected, automatic systems perform most of the processing of visual information. Automaticity, for instance, allows us to drive a car while focusing attention on a conversation with a passenger. When an unexpected obstacle appears in our view, however, we must stop conversation in order to divert attention to the task of avoiding the obstacle.

Our automatic perceptual systems evolved to process the kind of information that human beings typically encounter in the world (three-dimensional spaces, continuously moving objects, etc.). Researchers have shown that automatic systems will also process visual information that is suboptimal (degraded, rotated, simplified, etc.), as long as it is similar to the information such systems evolved to process (Beiderman; Fei-Fei, VanRullen, Koch, and Perona). The visual system's ability to accommodate a range of suboptimal stimuli also allows us to process moving pictures. The same systems that process the continuous-motion information in the physical world will also process a series of still images as "apparent motion" when the images are presented within a specified range (for example, at 24 frames per second). Indeed, researchers have demonstrated that perceivers cannot distinguish between real motion and apparent motion (e.g., Hildreth and Koch). No matter how keen our perception, we cannot see motion pictures for what they really are—a series of still images. As long as the information falls within a range that our perceptual systems can accommodate—termed here the "accommodation range"—then the systems will process that information, regardless of our will. Each space-perception system (for perceiving motion, continuity, depth, etc.) will have separate accommodation ranges for the information processed by that system.

Classical editing tends to produce information within the accommodation ranges of the systems that cause us to see spatial continuity. Indeed, whether or not they realize it, filmmakers regularly make use of such ranges when combining film images. When filmmakers present space as continuous (such as in the space of a single scene), they present images within the accommodation ranges required for perceiving continuity (for instance, by using matching techniques). When they distinguish spaces (such as during crosscutting or scene transitions), they present images outside the accommodation ranges (e.g., with a fade-out and fade-in). Indeed, filmmakers intending to distinguish separate spaces *must* present information outside the accommodation ranges or else risk an inadvertent perception of spatial continuity.

By studying the similarities between stimuli produced by classical editing and stimuli produced by active perception, one can begin to define the accommodation ranges for perceiving continuity. Defining the parameters of such ranges would go a long way toward both explaining film perception and enabling filmmakers to predict whether spectators will perceive continuity when viewing a given series of shots.

This article makes an initial effort by defining three key parameters of the accommodation ranges for perceiving continuity: both classical editing and active perception produce fragmentary images, follow similar patterns, and employ the same logic.

First, *classical editing and active perception both tend to create a succession of noncontinuous images that the perceiver then combines into a spatial whole.* Perhaps the most surprising common feature of active perception and classical editing is that both supply the perceiver with a series of fragmentary images. Common sense says that because the physical world is continuous, whereas cinema edits together image fragments (or shots), our perception of cinema must differ greatly from our perception of the physical environment. Common sense is wrong. When we look at our environment, our eyes do not see continuity; they see fragments. Psychologists have long known that the brain cannot process the totality of the environment. Consequently, we sample the environment with our eyes, instead of perceiving everything at once, and then reconstruct the total environment in our brains (Niemeier, Crawford, and Tweed). The eye's limited focusing ability, for instance, causes perceivers to scan the environment for information rather than take it all in simultaneously. Indeed, at a given moment, very little of our environment is in focus because only the fovea (the central part of the retina) registers visual detail. We see only about one-ninetieth of our total field of vision in focus at any moment (Brooks 108).

To understand how little of your environment you see in focus, perform the following simple experiment. Hold out your left index finger in front of you as far from your eye as possible, pointing at the ceiling. Focus your eyes on your left fingernail and at the same time hold your right index finger out to your right side, so that your two arms form a right angle; point your right index finger at the ceiling too. Notice that you can't even see your right index finger. While continuing to stare at your left finger, with your arms extended, slowly bring your right index finger closer to your left. You will soon see your right index finger in your peripheral vision, but the finger will not come into focus until it touches your left finger because the range of the fovea is only about the size of a thumbnail held at arm's length. Because we see only a tiny portion of our field of vision in focus at any moment, we actively scan our surroundings through "saccadic" eye movements, in which we dart our eyes in different directions. During "saccades" (the darting movements of the eyes), people see only blur. Between saccades, people's retinas register fragmentary images, each one displaying only a tiny portion of the physical space.

Although panning or tracking might intuitively seem more consistent with our perception of the continuous environment, in fact edited images more closely resemble our common perceptual experience during visual transitions than do continuous camera movements. A typical eye movement performs more like a whip-pan than a pan and more like a cut than any other cinema device. Note the difficulty of moving your eyes continuously from one corner of a room to another: You cannot help but stop on an object of interest and quickly saccade to another one. But let's change the conditions: Now follow a *moving* object, such as your finger, from one corner of your visual field to another. You can easily move your eyes in a continuous motion now because during pursuit movement, the object's image remains fixed on the retina. Generally, Hollywood films move the camera when spectators can fixate on an object, such as during the opening credit sequence of *The Graduate* (1967), in which the camera tracks Ben Braddock (Dustin Hoffman) as he stands on a moving walkway at the airport. The image poses no special perceptual difficulties because the main focus of our attention remains relatively fixed in our field of vision, and only the background moves across the retina. Most camera movements in Hollywood films involve simple reframing, in which the camera shifts slightly to pursue character movement. Hollywood cinema offers examples of moving shots that do not pursue moving objects, such as the 360-degree panning shot that begins the cattle drive in *Red River* (1948), but we predict that, during such shots, the eyes saccade from object to object in the frame, rather than follow the moving focal point of the shot. Except during pursuit movement, images that involve continuous spatial transitions violate our common perception of space more than edited images do.

In summary, classical editing and active perception are analogous in that they tend to create discontinuous images that the perceiver later integrates into a continuous space. "We accept a disrupted flow [of images] quite naturally," writes perceptual psychologist James Cutting; "it is a part of our everyday visual world" (19). Hence, film editor Walter Murch is wrong when he writes that, unlike edited film, our day-to-day experience presents us with "a continuous stream" of images (5–6). On the contrary, cuts produce discontinuous fragments similar to those the brain processes all day long.

Second, to produce stimuli that fall within the accommodation ranges for perceptual continuity, *classical editing tends to follow the patterns of active perception.* Images in the physical world and classical cinema do not come upon the perceiver randomly; rather, they follow patterns based on some of the same probabilities. For instance, in both active perception and classical editing, perception of a new space likely begins with a wide, undetailed view followed by closer and more discrete images of areas of interest. Perceptual researchers Sanocki, Michelet, Sellers, and Reynolds have demonstrated that viewers understand a space better if they are first "primed" with a wide view. The details required to distinguish between similar objects, researchers have shown, are generally acquired later through the slow, effortful process of focused attention (Fei-Fei, Iyer, Koch, and Perona). Classical editors' intuitions about scene construction accord with this psychology research. Editors tend to begin a new scene with an establishing shot, which delineates the overall space of the scene and the relative positions of characters and objects. Afterward, editors typically offer closer views of some of the space's component parts.[8] Other editing devices also follow the typical patterns of active perception. Bordwell has shown that shot/reverse-shot follows the pattern of turn-taking in conversation and simulates the "change of glance" an observer of such a scene would perform ("Convention" 88–89). Even though shot/reverse-shot, which favors three-quarter views over profiles, does not provide the optical POV of someone watching a conversation, it structures visual information in a familiarly patterned way. Similarly, the 180-degree rule, matching devices, and many sound-editing practices rely on audiovisual stimuli that follow probable patterns of real-world experience.

Third, *classical editing follows the same logic as active perception,* organizing visual information in ways that mimic the cognitive processes for perceiving real-world spaces. Film scholars call this type of organization "analytical editing"—the practice of combining shots so that they progress logically from one to the next. In both analytical editing and active perception, one image poses a spatial question that is then answered by a second image, which poses another question, answered by another image, and so on. Almost every scene in every classical movie employs analytical editing; three shots from *Stagecoach* (1939) illustrate the device. In shot 1 (Figure 11.3), we see two men looking off-screen. The shot prompts spectators to wonder, what do they see? Shot 2a (Figure 11.4) answers the question: they see the prostitute, Dallas (Claire Trevor), stepping onto the stagecoach. Shot 2b (Figure 11.5) then shows Dallas glancing back at the men, which prompts another question: what does she see? The film cuts just after her backward glance, and shot 3 (Figure 11.6) answers the question. The scene progresses from shot to shot, prompted by spatial questions posed by the information in each image, playing on spectators' curiosity about what information they will find in another portion of the diegetic space.

Active perception works according to the same logical principles: with active perception, our eyes dart to different areas of the environment, collecting visual information, prompted by our curiosity about what we will see (Brooks). Indeed, the manner in which filmmakers and film scholars often describe analytical editing almost replicates the manner in which cognitive psychologists describe active perception. Bordwell, Staiger, and Thompson, for instance, note that classical Hollywood editing uses a "backing-and-filling movement, opening a spatial gap and then plugging it," so that "shot two makes sense as an answer to its predecessor" (59). Similarly, perceptual psychologist Julian Hochberg describes active perception as follows: "The content of each glance is always, in a sense, an answer to a question about what will be seen if some specific part of the peripherally viewed scene is brought to the fovea" (65). The brain readily processes analytically edited images because analytical editing is a controlled version of what we do freely in everyday environments. According to Hochberg and Brooks, "good, rapidly comprehended cuts are those that provide the viewer with the answer to the visual question that he or she would normally be free to answer" ("Perception" 277). Classical films present stimuli that have already been sampled for the spectator in accordance with the spatial questions the filmmakers predict spectators will have.

Stage 1 of our model explains the ways in which the brain encodes information presented by the classical editing system, which acts as an analog for active perception. Stage 2 explains the ways in which the brain processes the information it encodes, stitching together the fragmentary images generated by active perception and classical editing to create a mental model of continuous space.

Stage 2. Mental Transformation: Unconscious Inference and Model Building

Let's return to our example from *The Philadelphia Story*. In one shot, Haven (Grant), Elizabeth Imbrie (Ruth Hussey), and Macaulay Connor (James Stewart) are standing at the front of a

Shot 1

Shot 2a

Shot 2b

Shot 3

Figures 11.3. Three shots from *Stagecoach* (1939) that follow a question-and-answer logic.

house (Figure 10), and the subsequent shot shows a man opening a door (Figure 11). With no spatial overlaps between the two shots, why do spectators understand that the depicted spaces are connected? Unconscious inference and model building answer this puzzling question.

Active perception and classical editing provide the raw data of perception, but the brain must still process the data in order to make it intelligible. That process requires transforming incomplete information into a mental model of space. Whether the raw data comes from active perception or classical editing, the transformation process is the same.

To understand the transformation process, one must understand what a model is, what it is for, and how the brain constructs one. Models are representations used to make predictions. Although imperfect representations, models can still have predictive value. A road map, for example, shares none of the visual information of the geographical location it represents save one crucial piece:

The locations of the lines representing roads on the map correspond to the relative locations of the roads in physical space. That single correspondence makes the representation useful when predicting the location of roads in relation to one another. Similar to the road map, the visual system constructs an imperfect model of the physical world, far more imperfect than most people recognize. Nevertheless, the visual system's model contains enough information to accomplish the limited goals of vision. Vision does not require mapping the environment in detail but merely requires, as Marr states, the accurate encoding of shape, space, and spatial arrangement (36).

All visual information about the world passes through one's retinas, but the retina has inherent limitations: the retina is two-dimensional, whereas the physical world has three dimensions; the clarity of the image on the retina is maximal only on the fovea and decreases dramatically toward the periphery; and the retina cannot see the entirety of a space at once. Consequently, the retina degrades significant information from the physical world. Information loss poses a problem for model construction: the brain must construct a coherent three-dimensional model of the world based on insufficient information passing through the retina.[9] Because the visual information cannot unequivocally specify a model, the same information can potentially lead to different perceptions. Take, for example, the Necker Cube (Figure 11.7), which is perceived either from slightly above and to the left (panel A is the front of the cube) or from slightly below and to the right (panel B is the front of the cube). You can toggle at will between the two available three-dimensional perceptions of the Necker Cube, but you can see only one at a time. In the real world, at any one time, the visual information processed by the brain is consistent with an infinite number of three-dimensional structures (Bordwell, *Narration* 101–04). Now the question is, how does the brain settle on a single, accurate-enough three-dimensional model of the physical world based on incomplete visual information?

Because survival likely hinges on an accurate-enough perception of the physical world to enable safe navigation, the brain has evolved automatic cognitive processes—termed "unconscious inferences" because perceivers perform them automatically and un-aware—that (according to Rock and legions of cognitive researchers after him) attempt to resolve spatial ambiguities inductively (Rock, *Logic*). These cognitive processes use the visual information as evidence from which they come to a conclusion concerning the physical source that likely gave rise to the visual data. The conclusion must be parsimonious

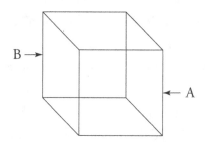

Figure 11.4. The Necker Cube leads to the perception of two different three-dimensional structures.

(the simplest conclusion is best) and unambiguous (only one conclusion at a time). Once the cognitive processes reach a satisfactory conclusion, they fill in missing information to construct a spatial model that explains the initial visual data. For instance, notice that you perceive the Necker Cube (Figure 11.7) as three-dimensional, although the lines on the paper are two-dimensional. The brain inserts the three-dimensional features, looking for a conclusion consistent with the three-dimensional world. Without your awareness or consent, your brain interprets the visual data, automatically filling in missing information. Your retinas see the two-dimensional lines (visual data), your brain builds a three-dimensional cube that explains the lines (mental model), and then you perceive your own model.[10]

This perplexing concept does not make intuitive sense, so let's consider an illustrative analogy. Suppose that you were shown incomplete and partially distorted pieces of a puzzle. Further suppose that your brain automatically inferred what the complete puzzle looked like and unconsciously filled in the missing information. Because your brain completes the puzzle unconsciously, you perceive only the mentally reconstructed puzzle, not the distorted, incomplete pieces. Your perceptual system performs that quick, unconscious mental gymnastic all day long, encoding distorted and fragmentary spatial information, drawing a conclusion as to the source that gave rise to the information, and perceiving its own conclusion and not the distorted fragments. Hence, perceivers experience a mentally *reconstructed* world, not the physical world itself.

Spatial continuity in the cinema is possible because the right kind of stimulus can, by exploiting the reconstruction process, trick the perceiver into seeing continuity. As noted earlier, active perception and classical editing both produce noncontinuous images (separated by saccades in active perception or cuts in classical editing), follow patterns based on similar probabilities (e.g., wide views tend to precede closer views, turn-taking in conversation), and obey the same logic (employing a question-and-answer format). Because of these similarities, classically edited images tend to come within the accommodation ranges for constructing coherent spatial models. After the perceptual system encodes the visual data, the brain employs identical model-building processes for both real-world and cinema space. With active perception, we sample the environment, and then our brains automatically reconstruct a model of space around us. With classically edited images, our brains automatically reconstruct a model of on-screen space after encoding the images presampled by the editing system. The only difference is that with real-world perception, the reconstructed space typically exists.

The example from *The Philadelphia Story* can help us understand how, in practice, unconscious inference and classical editing combine to cue spectators to form coherent spatial models. A conventionally shot scene from the film begins with an establishing extreme long shot of the Lord home (Figure 11.8), a repeated setup, familiar since the first diegetic shot of the movie, that tells us roughly where the scene takes place. The shot includes a convertible coming up the driveway. Shot 2a shows, in long shot, the car pulling up to the front of the house (Figure 11.9) and Grant, Hussey, and Stewart stepping out of the car and up to the house (Figure 11.10). The new setup in shot 2 contains many discontinuities with shot 1 because the cut has changed both the angle on the action (we now see the car from the point of view of the front of the house, a change of about 100 degrees) and the distance of framing (from extreme long shot to long shot). Hence, the image has changed significantly during the cut between the two shots.

Despite the discontinuities in the stimulus, unconscious inference processes identify visual and auditory cues and attempt to create a parsimonious and unambiguous model of on-screen space. First, a match-on-action (in which movement begun in one shot continues in the next shot) of the moving car cues the spectator to conclude that the depicted areas are conjoined. Movement is highly salient in our perceptual process and distracts us from spatial changes that occur with a cut, such as changes in camera angle and distance.[11] Indeed, although it is extremely hard to see the car in Figure 11.8 (the car is between the tree and the house), its presence is pronounced when the car is shown moving. The cars in shots 1 and 2 look similar and move at what looks to be the same rate. Such movement not only cues the perceiver to conjoin the moving objects in the separate shots; it also ensures that viewers train their attention on a powerful continuity cue, so that viewers look at the car instead of gazing at a portion of the frame that might afford a graphic discontinuity during the cut.

Other perceptual evidence buttresses the brain's conclusion that the spaces in the two shots are continuous. Repeated objects in the setting (pillars, bushes, lawn, etc.) reappear in roughly the position one would predict if one were looking at the setting from the new angle. And the tonality of the images (contrast, exposure, and lighting on the objects) in the two shots remains consistent. Finally, the soundtrack bolsters the perception of continuity because sounds of a car engine and tires continue across the cut. In short, the brain encodes the perceptual cues (a match-on-action, graphic and tonal similarities between shots, and sound overlaps), unconsciously infers an explanation for a single source that could give rise to the cues, and creates a model of one space.

Why, though, does unconscious inference come to the conclusion that the spaces depicted in the two shots are the same? Why doesn't the brain infer, for instance, that the pillars in shot 1 (Figure 11.8) are different from the pillars in shot 2 (Figures 11.9 and 11.10) or that at least they *might be* different? Remember that, for the sake of survival, unconscious model building is

Shot 1

Shot 2a

Shot 2b

Shot 3

Figures 11.5. Three shots from *The Philadelphia Story* (1940) that rely on classical editing and mental model building to create spatial continuity.

parsimonious and unambiguous. Accordingly, as Rock and others have demonstrated, the inferential process assumes that no piece of perceptual evidence arises by chance; unconscious inference discounts coincidence (Rock, *Logic* 134–64). Hence, parsimony ensures that the pillars in two shots look similar not by chance but because they are in fact the same pillars. By assuming a reason behind low-probability events, the unconscious inference process eliminates an infinite number of interpretations of the perceptual data so that the brain can settle on a single, unambiguous model of space.

Shot 3 (figure 11.11), a medium shot of a butler opening the door for the characters, contains no spatial overlaps with the previous shots, providing a view of a space we have not yet observed in this scene. Given the spatial differences between this shot and the two previous shots, how do spectators incorporate shot 3 into their spatial model? Unconscious inference and classical editing afford us an answer. In fact, spectators' models likely included the space depicted in shot 3 *before* the shot appeared. Recall that the perceptual system unconsciously fills in gaps during model formation. When spectators built a model of the cinematic space during shots 1 and 2, their model likely contained a door at the top of the stairs because spectators know that the fronts of houses normally have doors and, furthermore, that people entering a house first walk up to its door exactly as Grant did. Spectators' spatial models have Grant standing in front of a door—a door as real to spectators as Grant- even though they have not yet seen it. Hence, although shot 3 contains no spatial overlaps with shot 2, it likely overlaps with the spectator's spatial model.

Analytical and POV editing reinforce the model-building process enabled by unconscious inference. Several narrative cues establish a logical relation between shots 2 and 3 that encourages spectators to infer a single space. Before the butler answers the door in shot 3, for instance, shot 2 shows Grant push his finger against the wall (like someone ringing a doorbell) and, just before the cut, glancing in a direction slightly to the right of the camera (Figure 10). The glance prompts spectators to wonder, "What does he see?" and the eyeline match of the butler opening the door answers the spatial question (cf. Noël Carroll 127–29). The shot of the butler opening the door provides roughly Grant's field of vision, establishing the spatial arrangement of the characters. Moreover, our knowledge that the characters are standing at the front of a home and the logical connection between the act of ringing a doorbell and a door opening combine with the eyeline match to cue viewers to incorporate the shot of the door into their model of the depicted space.

These three shots from *The Philadelphia Story* demonstrate how classical filmmakers rely on unconscious inferences and classical editing to cue spectators to build spatial models. One can see from this conventional example the number and variety of redundant cues—far more than are necessary—for model building typically employed by classical filmmakers in even the most ordinary and spatially simple instances.

However, we do not fully understand how spectator models result in the perception of continuity. Given the fragmented nature of the raw data supplied by cinema and active perception, why is our perception of space not equally fragmented? An assumption of coherence, we propose, constrains the spatial-model-building processes. This constraint explains why real- world and cinema spectators see spatial continuity when their retinas see discontinuity.

THE ASSUMPTION OF COHERENCE

Spatial coherence indicates physical connectedness. Because the physical world appears spatially coherent, perceivers believe that the visual information received from the world must also be coherent. In fact, the perceived coherence of space is an illusion. Some compelling empirical evidence suggests that the unconscious inference process *assumes* spatial coherence, even in the absence of true physical connectedness. Such an assumption would result in an automatic perception of spatial continuity unless sufficient perceptual evidence demonstrated discontinuity to the perceiver.

Human beings evolved in a continuous physical world, whereas, as we have seen, the perceptual system encodes discontinuous fragments—a sampling of the world—on the retina. However, if the perceptual system assumes continuity in the world by default, then it would tend to build spatial models consistent with the physical world, rather than models as fragmented as the retinal data. Hence, a bias toward continuity in the perceptual system would have significant survival advantages, affording the perceiver a more accurate perception of the world than a system without any bias at all.

The assumption of coherence also explains some compelling and counterintuitive research data on perceived continuity. An abundance of research indicates that perceivers do not identify *many* discontinuities in perceptual raw data. Cognitive psychologists have termed the phenomenon whereby people do not encode information in their field of vision *inattentional blindness* and termed the failure to notice changes to the field of vision *change blindness.* Levin and Simons conducted a series of experiments that dramatically demonstrate our blindness to visual discontinuities. In one experiment—following a technique employed by surrealist filmmaker Luis Buñuel in *That Obscure Object of Desire* (1977)—they created a short movie in which they replace one actor with another actor in a subsequent shot. Few subjects watching the movie noticed the change, even though the actors wore different clothing ("Perceiving Stability" 370–75). (You can view the movie at http://viscog.beckman.illinois.edu/grafs/demos/23.html) In another experiment, the researchers made a movie of two people talking, shot in a conventional shot/reverse-shot pattern, with nine intentional continuity violations (involving changes in clothing, blocking, and props) across cuts (http://viscog.beckman.illinois.edu/flash- movie/n.php). Even when subjects were cued to look for the violations on a second viewing of the scene, most noticed fewer than two of the nine (Levin and Simons, "Failure").

Levin and Simons have demonstrated that people often fail to register visual changes that would seem obvious, not just when watching cinema but also in the real world. In one wily study, an experimenter incognito asks directions from random adult subjects on the street. In the middle of the conversation, through a clever trick, the experimenter is switched in an instant, without subjects' knowledge, and subjects find themselves continuing the conversation with a different person (Figures 11.12–11.14). Here, subjects' primary focus of attention is the person they are talking to, yet many of them do not recognize that they have suddenly found themselves talking to someone else. Across several experiments, Levin and Simons found that "30–50% of pedestrians are oblivious to the change, continue the conversation as if nothing had happened, and are quite surprised to learn of the switch" ("Perceiving Stability" 374). They conclude that blindness to changes in the environment is not so much a failure but rather "a natural and even necessary prerequisite for sensing continuity" because people's sense of continuity might be disrupted if they did not ignore unexpected changes (377). Indeed, if we noted all of the changes in the environment around us, as we scanned our eyes this way and that, our cognitive processes would likely become overwhelmed.[12]

The Levin and Simons experiments—which demonstrate a striking inattentiveness to discontinuities in the visual field—can be explained by a bias in the perceptual system toward continuity: if the system assumes continuity by default, then perceivers would, as demonstrated in Levin and Simons's experiments, regularly register continuity when presented with discontinuous visual information. By contrast, no available research indicates that perceivers regularly register discontinuity in the face of continuous visual information. These findings argue strongly for the conclusion that space perception relies on an assumption of continuity in the perceptual system and on perceivers' insensitivity to gaps in the continuity of space.

Given these findings, it should come as no surprise that changes in movie images across cuts do not much disrupt our experience of spatial coherence, because the perceptual system tends to ignore discontinuities and infer spatial coherence even where coherence does not exist. Indeed, filmmakers need not create flawless continuity between shots, and movies get away with a lot of unperceived continuity disruptions, many of which are intentional. Classical filmmakers, for instance, sometimes violate the 180-degree rule when circumstances (such as the need for sunlight or the strategic placement of the camera) make it artistically beneficial to do so. Filmmakers might replay a part of an action in successive shots in order to ensure that spectators see it, or they might alter characters' positions in two shots in order to ensure frontality (the practice of facing actors at a three-quarter angle toward the camera).

During "cheat cuts"—a regular practice in which filmmakers intentionally mismatch mise en scène elements in two shots—filmmakers rely on the fact that perceivers often ignore visual discontinuities. In *Raging Bull* (1980), a shot of Jake La Motta (Robert De Niro) holding up two photographs of a girl precedes a close-up of the two photographs (Figures 11.15 and 11.16). The graphic similarities between the photographs represented in the two shots (both are rectangular photographs with white borders) and salient story information (the characters discuss the two photographs) distract viewers from manifest discontinuities between the shots: in the first shot (Figure 11.15), De Niro pinches one photograph in front of the other between his thumb and forefinger, whereas in the second shot (Figure 11.16) the two photographs are perfectly aligned side by side; the actor's fingers do not appear in the second shot; and the photographs in the second shot rest against a black backdrop absent in the first shot.

The inattentional and change blindness studies and the prevalence of cheat cuts and other continuity violations in Hollywood movies (evidenced by the nonprofit cottage industry that has emerged on the Internet Movie Database, in which scrupulously attentive film spectators report untold errors in film continuity that spectators fail to notice on regular viewings) support our hypothesis that space perception contains a bias toward continuity.

CONCLUSION

Classical editing conventions developed not arbitrarily but deliberately to exploit and accommodate the processes and limitations of our perceptual

Figures 11.6. A subject in a Levin and Simons experiment talks to two different people, who wear different colored clothes and hats, but does not notice the switch.

system. The spaces presented by classical cinema are imperfect, disjointed, and filled with gaps and discontinuities. However, the brain perceives spatial coherence when observing classically edited cinema because the perceptual system evolved to accept imperfect and disjointed visual information, to reconstruct the fragmented information into a model of the physical world,

Figures 11.7. Consecutive shots from *Raging Bull* (1980) that contain gross discontinuities.

and to ignore gaps and discontinuities. Given classical cinema's common goal to create utmost spatial clarity, some technical devices for depicting space are more probable than others because they obey the format, patterns, and logic of active perception. The more probable devices became the standard practices of the classical editing system because they fell within the accommodation ranges of the cognitive and perceptual processes required for perceptual continuity and therefore have been handed down through apprenticeship, film schools, production handbooks, and film studies textbooks.

Our model explains the perception of continuity in cinema and, more broadly, the perception of cinema space in general. It explains, for instance, how cinema spectators perceive continuity when viewing cinema's fragmentary images, how the brain unites the images, and how classical editing devices facilitate the perception of continuity. It accounts for the fact that filmmakers regularly create spaces in movies without specifying them with shots or sounds because spectators' models fill in implied areas. Doors, ceilings, doorbells, characters, or any space or object at all, will, given the right conditions, exist in spectators' spatial models, despite their absence in the film stimulus.

Even manifest spatial discontinuities between shots do not inevitably violate the coherence of spatial model building. If spectators perceive film space as coherent by default, then filmmakers can assume that spectators will connect spaces unless spatial information falls outside the accommodation ranges of the processes required for perceptual continuity. Indeed, because the brain regularly ignores spatial discontinuities, cheat cuts and other relatively minor violations of continuity are likely in classical cinema. More salient visual discontinuities within the depiction of a single space are less likely, but one would expect more of them when filmmakers use other cues (such as matching techniques) to distract viewers from the discontinuities, encourage coherent spatial model building, or make spatial relations redundantly clear. Hence, the so-called rules of continuity editing are, for purposes of perception, merely guidelines, and filmmakers can abandon them when other conditions are met. Indeed, evidence suggests that filmmakers can at times forgo even technical imperatives, such as the 180-degree rule or the physical similarity between stars and their body doubles, whenever other visual, auditory, or narrative cues make spectators' spatial models robust. Devices that lead to salient discontinuities *within* the space of a scene (such as freeze frames and jump cuts) are permissible within a classical filmmaking system but highly unlikely in comparison to devices that facilitate the perception of continuity (such as matches, analytical editing, and the 180-degree rule). When films present viewers with discontinuities that the perceptual system will not ignore (e.g., a fade-out and fade-in or a sharp change in image tonality) because the stimuli fall outside of the accommodation ranges for perceptual continuity, then spatial coherence breaks down.

Of course, plenty of non-classical filmmakers disregard the practices of matches (Stan Brakhage, for instance, in *Window Water Baby Moving* [1962]), analytical editing (John Cassavetes), and the 180-degree rule (Yasujiro Ozu); and Jean-Luc Godard intersperses jump cuts throughout *Breathless* (1959). Such violations of classical convention indicate that cognition can accommodate non-classical film stimuli. Their work also helps define the parameters of cognition, given that many of their films challenge spectators' ability to form coherent spatial models. But a jump cut in *Breathless,* say, does not demonstrate that classical cinema heeds continuity conventions that might have developed in other ways. On the contrary, non-classical filmmakers such as Godard pursue aesthetic effects that the classical editing system discourages or forbids, including making spectators less complacent about the coherence of film space. Because *Breathless*'s jump cuts result in an automatic perception of jarring motion, the film demonstrates the imperative of obeying convention if a filmmaker wants to maintain fluid continuity. There is evidence—from the films of Ozu and even classical filmmakers, such as John Ford, both of whom violate classical editing practices—that Hollywood depends on some practices (such as the 180-degree rule) too staunchly; however, the standard practices nonetheless serve to facilitate coherent model building, and willy-nilly violations of them threaten spectators' perception of continuity. Ozu created a viable alternative to the 180-degree system, and John Ford violated continuity when narrative information and object cues in the frame made spatial relations clear or irrelevant. Theirs were not wanton violations. Classical continuity employs time-tested filming and editing conventions that exploit and accommodate the brain's automatic model-building process.

Continuity conventions have remained relatively stable for about ninety years. The primary reason for their stability is not, as some scholars think, Hollywood's marketing dominance or other externalities but rather that the early filmmakers who first developed the conventions were guided by their intuitive understanding of space perception and the reactions of cinema spectators.

Just as expert pool players learn—not through direct study but intuitively, through trial and error—the principles of Newtonian physics that govern pool playing, as well as matter and energy generally, the filmmakers in the early twentieth century who first developed the conventions of the classical editing system, without directly studying psychology, discovered the structure of human perception.

ENDNOTES

1. The process of converting a physical stimulus into a neurochemical response is termed "transduction."
2. A perceptual process is a system in the brain that encodes and decodes the sensory information in the physical world. Examples of perceptual processes are the transduction of light into a neural response, identifying boundaries between objects, and so on.
3. By "classical," we mean that the editing system emphasizes certain formal properties (including harmony and control), has a stable and influential history, and respects artistic norms and standard practices. See Bordwell, Staiger, and Thompson (4).
4. A cognitive process is a system in the brain that manipulates or transforms information with or without conscious awareness. Examples of cognitive processes are thinking, reasoning, and unconscious pattern recognition.
5. Other researchers, such as Joseph Anderson and James Cutting, rely on Direct Perception Theory, which, following the tradition of perceptual psychologist J. J. Gibson, posits that the human perceptual system offers us direct, unmediated awareness of the external world.
6. For explanations of continuity editing and point-of-view editing, see Bordwell and Thompson (231–40). For a discussion of analytical editing practices, see Bordwell, Staiger, and Thompson (198–203).
7. For anthropological evidence that suggests that editing conventions rely on universal perceptual processes, see Hobbs, Frost, Davis, and Stauffer. Prince discusses some of the ramifications of this study on film theory in "Discourse of Pictures."
8. The practice of beginning scenes with establishing shots and then cutting up the depicted space into more detailed views has been well documented in the film studies literature and is described in most introductory film textbooks, including Prince (*Movies and Meaning* 58–59), Bordwell and Thompson (235), Giannetti (131), and Barsam (252).
9. Scientists term this situation an "inverse problem," which exists when a set of data is insufficient to fully specify a model.
10. The perceiver's model must be consistent with the sensory data; one cannot see whatever one chooses. The Necker Cube has only two parsimonious conclusions consistent with the sensory data: the viewer will not perceive an elephant, for instance, when viewing the Necker Cube.
11. The salience of movement in the visual field has been well established. For instance, Smith and Henderson have demonstrated, using eye-tracking technology, that dynamic scenes (scenes with at least one moving object) create greater attentional synchrony among perceivers than static scenes.
12. Beck and Levin write, "Recent research suggests that our visual system is not able to monitor every detail in our visual field. In particular, subjects fail to notice large changes to the location, properties, and identity of objects" (458).

Anderson, Joseph. "A Cognitive Approach to Continuity." *Post Script* 13.1 (1993): 61–66. Print.

_____. *The Reality of Illusion: An Ecological Approach to Cognitive Film Theory.* Carbondale: Southern Illinois UP, 1996. Print.

Barsam, Richard. *Looking at Movies: An Introduction to Film.* 2nd ed. New York: Norton, 2007. Print.

Baudry, Jean-Louis. "Ideological Effects of the Basic Cinematographic Apparatus" and "The Apparatus: Metapsychological Approaches to the Impression of Reality in the Cinema." *Narrative, Apparatus, Ideology.* Ed. Philip Rosen. New York: Columbia UP, 1986. 286–318. Print.

Bazin, André. "The Evolution of the Language of Cinema." *What Is Cinema?* Vol. 1. Ed. and trans. Hugh Gray. Berkeley: U of California P, 1967. 23–40. Print.

Beck, Melissa R., and Daniel T. Levin. "The Role of Representational Volatility in Recognizing Pre- and Postchange Objects." *Perception & Psychophysics* 65. 3 (2003): 458–68. Print.

Beiderman, Irving. "Recognition-By-Components: A Theory of Human Image Understanding." *Psychological Review* 94.2 (1987): 115–47. Print.

Bordwell, David. "Convention, Construction, and Cinematic Vision." *Post Theory: Reconstructing Film Studies.* Ed. David Bordwell and Noël Carroll. Madison: U of Wisconsin P, 1996. 87–107. Print.

_____. *Narration in the Fiction Film.* Madison: U of Wisconsin P, 1985. Print.

_____. *Ozu and the Poetics of Cinema.* Princeton: *Princeton UP, 1994. Print.*

Bordwell, David, Janet Staiger, and Kristin Thompson. *The Classical Hollywood Cinema: Film Style & Mode of Production to i960.* New York: Routledge, 1988. Print.

Bordwell, David, and Kristin Thompson. *Film Art: An Introduction.* 8th ed. New York: McGraw-Hill, 2008. Print.

Brooks, Virginia. "Film, Perception and Cognitive Psychology." *Millennium Film Journal* 14–15 (1984–85): 105–26. Print.

Carroll, John M. *Toward a Structural Psychology of Cinema.* New York: Mouton, 1980. Print.

Carroll, Noël. *Theorizing the Moving Image.* Cambridge: Cambridge UP, 1996. Print.

Cutting, James. "Perceiving Scenes in Film and the World." *Moving Image Theory: Ecological Considerations.* Ed. Joseph. D. Anderson and Barbara Fisher Anderson. Carbondale: Southern Illinois UP, 2005. 9–27. Print.

Dayan, Daniel. "TheTutor-Code of Classical Cinema." *Film Quarterly* 28.1 (Fall 1974): 22–31. Print.

Eisenstein, Sergei. *Film Form: Essays in Film Theory.* Ed. and trans. Jay Leyda. New York: Harcourt, Brace & World, 1949. Print.

Fei-Fei, Li, Asha Iyer, Christof Koch, and Pietro Perona. "What Do We Perceive in a Glance of a Real-World Scen*e?' Journal of Vision* 7.1 (2007): 1–29. Print.

Fei-Fei, Li, Rufin VanRullen, Christof Koch, Pietro Perona. "Why Does Natural Scene Categorization Require Little Attention? Exploring Attentional Requirements for Natural and Synthetic Stimuli." *Visual Cognition* 12.6 (2005): 893–924. Print.

Giannetti, Louis. *Understanding Movies.* 7th ed. Upper Saddle River, N): Prentice Hall, 1996. Print.

Heath, Stephen. "Narrative Space." *Narrative, Apparatus, Ideology.* Ed. Philip Rosen. New York: Columbia UP, 1986. 379–420. Print.

_____. *Questions of Cinema.* New York: Macmillan, 1981. Print.

Hildreth, Ellen C., and Christof Koch. "The Analysis of Visual Motion: From Computational Theory to Neuronal Mechanisms."*Annual Review of Neuroscience* 10.1 (1987): 477–533. Print.

Hobbs, Renee, Richard Frost, Arthur Davis, and John Stauffer. "How First-Time Viewers Comprehend Editing Conventions." *Journal of Communication* 38.4 (1988): 50–60. Print.

Hochberg, Julian. "The Representation of Things and People." Art, *Perception, and Reality.* Ed. E. H. Gombrich, J. Hochberg, and M. Black. Baltimore: Hopkins UP, 1973. 47–94. Print.

Hochberg, Julian, and Virginia Brooks. "The Perception of Motion Pictures." *Cognitive Ecology: Handbook of Perception and Cognition.* Ed. M. P. Friedman and E. C. Carterette. 2nd ed. New York: Academic P, 1996. Print.

_____. "Movies in the Mind's Eye." *Post Theory: Reconstructing Film Studies.* Ed. David Bordwell and Noël Carroll. Madison: U of Wisconsin P, 1996. 368–87. Print.

Levin, Daniel T., and D. J. Simons. "Failure to Detect Changes to Attended Objects in Motion Pictures." *Psychonomic Bulletin and Review* 4.4 (1997): 501–06. Print.

_____. "Perceiving Stability in a Changing World: Combining Shots and Integrating Views in Motion Pictures and the Real World." *Media Psychology 2* (2000): 357–80. Print.

Marr, David. *Vision.* San Francisco: W. H. Freeman, 1982. Print.

Metz, Christian. *Film Language: A Semiotics of the Cinema.* Chicago: U of Chicago P, 1990. Print.

Mulvey, Laura. *Visual and Other Pleasures: Theories of Representation and Difference.* Bloomington: Indiana UP, 1989. Print.

Murch, Walter. *In the Blink of an Eye: A Perspective on Film Editing.* 2nd ed. Los Angeles: Silman-James, 2001. Print.

Neisser, Ulric. *Cognitive Psychology.* New York: Appleton-Century-Crofts, 1966. Print.

Niemeier, M., J. D. Crawford, and D. B. Tweed. "Optimal Transsaccadic Integration Explains Distorted Spatial Perception." *Nature* 422 (6 Mar. 2003): 76–80. Print.

Oudart, Jean-Pierre. "Cinema and Suture." *Screen* 18.4 (Winter 1977/1978): 35–47. Print.

Prince, Stephen. "The Discourse of Pictures: Iconicity and Film Studies." *Film Quarterly* 47.1 (Fall 1993): 16–28. Print.

_____. *Movies and Meaning: An Introduction to Film.* Needham Heights, MA: Allyn & Bacon, 2001. Print.

Rock, Irvin. *Indirect Perception.* Cambridge, MA: MIT P, 1997. Print.

_____. *The Logic of Perception.* Cambridge, MA: MIT P, 1983. Print.

Sanocki, Thomas, Kimberly Michelet, Eric Sellers, and Joseph Reynolds. "Representations of Scene Layout Can Consist of Independent, Functional Pieces." *Perception & Psychophysics* 68.3 (2006): 415–27. Print.

Schneider, W., and R. M. Shiffrin. "Controlled and Automatic Human Information Processing: I. Detection, Search, and Attention." *Psychological Review* 84.1 (1977): 1–66. Print.

Silverman, Kaja. *The Acoustic Mirror: The Female Voice in Psychoanalysis and Cinema.* Bloomington: Indiana UP, 1988. Print.

Smith, T., and J. Henderson. "Attentional Synchrony in Static and Dynamic Scenes" [abstract]. *Journal of Vision* 8.6 (10 May 2008): 773, 773a. Web. 28 Jan. 2010.

Zavarzadeh, Mas'ud. *Seeing Films Politically.* Albany: State U of New York P, 1991. Print.

ALAN WILLIAMS

HISTORICAL AND THEORETICAL ISSUES IN THE COMING OF RECORDED SOUND TO THE CINEMA

The period of the transition to sound film offers a splendid example of historical overdetermination. Separating out the various cultural, economic, and technological determinants involved is a complicated and delicate task. This essay will examine several problems related to the adoption of synchronous sound technology. In some of them, issues of historiography and film theory intertwine, and only tentative answers can be suggested for complex questions. One takes the transition to sound so much for granted: things happened the way they did, therefore they *must*, it seems, have happened the way they did. There is no ready way of conceptualizing the role of historical contingency in the process, nor of thinking precisely about the extent to which it may indeed be true that recorded sound came to the commercial cinema because it was, in fact, inevitable.

TELEOLOGIES

To consider the latter question is somewhat unfashionable because it invokes the idea of teleology. From the point of view of many film scholars, it would be idealism pure and simple to argue that there is something intrinsic to the cinema that calls for the addition of recorded sound to the recorded images which first defined the medium. Here, however, one must make the distinction between cinema as technology and as institution. However much we must avoid teleological thinking about the former, the latter often seems to call for it. In this area, as in so much else, contemporary thinking reacts against the legacy of André Bazin, who once described the transition to sound cinema using a religious metaphor. So-called "silent" cinema—it was almost never truly silent—is the "Old Testament" of the art form; by implication, sound filmmaking is the New Testament, and sound technology the Savior (Bazin 1967, 23). Bazin viewed cinema history as characterized by an ever-increasing drive toward realism; the advent of the talkies fits so well into his thinking that he simply takes it for granted in his essays on film history.

In the post-Bazinian era, this schema has been denounced without being replaced by anything significantly more satisfactory.[1] Broadly speaking, the "realism" of narrative cinema, both "silent" and sound, is held to be an illusory construct created through conventions, the multiply-determined product of a need for unity and transparence on the part of the viewing subject. The logical consequence of this view, however, is a new teleology based on the cinema's elaboration of an increasingly convincing simulacrum of the real, the desire for which is grounded in human psychology in the same general way as is Bazin's idea of a fundamental need for realism.

The problem for any such view of film history is that sound cinema seems to have had little appeal for spectators—beyond its curiosity value—for more than twenty-five years after it became technologically practical. The first successful public presentations of synchronized sound processes were made at the Paris Exposition Internationale in 1900. The modern reconstructions of several of the films presented there seem crude enough in terms of sound quality and image manipulation (there is no editing), but one does understand the words, and certain sound effects (dancing feet on a stage, for example) have real impact. No one seems to have complained, in any event, that these early sound films were fundamentally unsatisfactory from the point of view of realism. Nor were there such complaints about the Pathé Frères and Gaumont processes test marketed in the decade that followed. Public reaction to them, however, was so tepid that the French producers gave up their pioneering efforts entirely, only to become victims of German and American patent holders in the late 1920s.

Until Vitaphone, in fact, the history of sound filmmaking is the history of repeated failure, not of technology but of marketing. Even Thomas Alva Edison, with his great resources and flair for publicity, failed miserably at it. Edison's technology, it is true, was surprisingly primitive. The electrical recording and amplification systems which came later almost certainly produced better quality sound, but if there were an innate vocation of the cinema to be an art of the real, or of spectators to demand an aural complement to cinematic duplication of the Lacanian mirror-stage, surely these cannot have been terribly strong—at least not before 1927. It is often argued that the problem of attracting audiences was mainly technical, due to inadequate amplification and synchronization. But the early Gaumont sound films were presented to audiences of 5000 (!) patrons at the Gaumont Palace in Paris, using an amplification system based on compressed air. And Lee DeForest's Phonophone process, virtually immune to synchronization problems, was extensively test marketed in the early 1920s. One journalist titled his review of this direct ancestor of modern sound-on-film processes: "New Talking Picture Is Shown—But What of It?" (Geduld 1975, 98).

If there was an evolutionary pressure at work in cinema history which eventually culminated in the general adoption of synchronized recorded sound, this trend arguably has little to do with demand, the sphere of consumption, and much to do with the logic of industrial production. For what the triumph of Warner Bros.' Vitaphone finally accomplished was to complete a process begun long before: the progressive mechanization of the cinematographic spectacle. Years before the 1895 debut of the Lumière Cinématographe, Emile Reynaud's Optical Theatre projected moving images (painted, not photographed) onto a screen. The Lumière apparatus did not immediately drive this competition out of business but did exert considerable economic pressure, because Reynaud's spectacle was *incompletely mechanized.* Not only were his images painted rather than photographed (thus taking much time and skill to produce), but each projection was in the fullest sense a performance, in which sequences of images were run forwards and backwards, at varying rates (and hence required a well-trained, adept operator).

Emile Reynaud had, as did the Lumières, a musical accompaniment played on a piano. The intervening years before Vitaphone had further mechanized the film show in virtually every respect except for that. For example, most films had some form of color. At first, as in Reynaud's spectacle, color was hand-painted by brush onto individual copies, but soon stencil processes such as Pathécolor and the cheaper methods of tinting and toning became widely adopted. There remained great variability—even among individual copies of the "same" film—until the general adoption of "natural" (completely mechanized) color processes.[2] The coming of synchronized recorded sound to world cinema essentially completes the mechanization of the medium. And with full mechanization comes the most pervasive, general change brought about by the conversion to sound: increased standardization. Silent film presentations had been notoriously variable. Works could be projected at different speeds, with operators advised in some manuals of their trade to vary the rhythm of projection within a given film. A single work could exist in different versions: black and white, or colored by one of several methods; long, short, or medium length; accompanied by large orchestra using carefully planned cue sheets, or by a single drunken pianist. Between individual films, there were enormous variations, perhaps most notably in running time. Acting styles, set design, and other elements of film style also varied widely—far more than they would with the arrival of the talkies.

This tendency toward mechanization and standardization outlines a teleology considerably less mystical than the Bazinian one or its possible successors.[3] It also helps explain why pressure for the adoption of recorded sound came persistently from the production sector of the industry, and not from exhibition. The new technology engendered a radical rebalancing of power relations within the industry: whereas before the talkies the luxury and particular style of a cinema theatre and the popularity of its musical performers were often more important (and directly controllable by the exhibitor) to total revenues than the films themselves, after the transition to recorded sound the films, and almost only the films, counted. Warner Bros, owned few cinemas, which largely explains why it, of all studios, was the pioneering force in the drive to mechanize cinema sound. But exhibitors did in fact make windfall profits from the talkies when they finally arrived. And this is one of the great mysteries of this part of film history. Why, with no previous indications of dissatisfaction, did audiences suddenly embrace the talkies, acting as if they had been dissatisfied with "silent" cinema for a long time?

We can only speculate on the answer to this question, but such speculation is not necessarily fruitless. It is worth remembering that the partisans of the "art of silence" denounced the coming of the talkies as cutting down in its prime a "mature" art form. This may have been, precisely, the point. If mass culture works as a kind of corrupt, speeded-up parody of traditional, elite culture, then one would expect change precisely at a point of "maturity," where novel effects within an established system of conventions become increasingly difficult. What is surprising about the demise of the "silent" feature is how *soon* it occurred, and not *that* it occurred. And this problem introduces the other major mystery of the history of sound cinema: why did momentum for change grow irresistible in the wake of one specific film, a work which is widely considered so clumsy and unconvincing as to be unwatchable today?

WHY *THE JAZZ* SINGER?

If *The Jazz Singer* had not existed, culturally inclined historians would be tempted to invent it. Few films crystallize the contending forces in a given historical moment as clearly as this one does, and few have had more direct impact on what happened to the medium after them. It had, perhaps most crucially, the distinction of combining two film forms that until then had been kept distinct. These corresponded to the two uses that Warner Bros, envisioned for Vitaphone: canned musical (and other) stage performances, filmed with synchronous sound; and "silent" narrative films accompanied not by a live orchestra but by a recorded one (with, as in standard live accompaniments, selected sound effects). These were, perhaps not coincidentally, the two formats through which Lee DeForest had exhibited the Phonophone, and while Warners stuck with them as separate entities it had only somewhat more success in marketing its process than had the inventor. In *The Jazz Singer*, the barriers come down and the two genres contaminate one another, with cataclysmic results. Many modern viewers experience the transition from the musical numbers to the silent narrative as almost physically painful, and from the latter to the former as liberating, like a chance to breathe anew. Did contemporary audiences feel the same way? Almost certainly not, but it seems likely that the film's curious structure invited its viewers to participate in a kind of do-it-yourself test or referendum on the uses of the new medium. The crucial difference between *The Jazz Singer* and all previous attempts to market recorded sound was this co-presence of two kinds of discourse *within a single work.*

But there is another, somewhat less obvious aspect of the film's persistent duality. As Robert L. Carringer has astutely argued, if one removes the sequences about Jackie Rabinowitz's relations with his family, "what we are left with—the drive to success, the relentless pace of the chorus line in rehearsal, the show-must-go-on motif, the miraculous last-minute leap over film and circumstances, the resounding triumph at the end—are the main plot elements of one of the most successful genres in the studio's history, the backstage musical of the thirties" (Carringer

1979, 27). In this way the film looks forward in cinema history; but in another way it offers the beginnings of a farewell to another kind of cinema, and another sensibility. The other parts of the film form an equally recognizable, if abbreviated version of a major film genre: family melodrama, written and executed in the hyperbolic, ultra-sentimental style that characterized the melodrama in cinema before the talkies.

Jackie's feeling for his mother, for example, is evoked on the sound track by a full-blast rendition of the love theme from Tchaikovsky's *Romeo and Juliet*. In these parts of the film Jolson's gestures, such as clasping both hands together over his heart, could have been taken from an old stage melodrama handbook for actors—not from a handbook written for players in the late twenties, however: by the time of the film, this kind of playing and subject matter was considered horribly outdated by most opinion leaders in the theatrical communities of major cities. As many reviewers and later commentators have pointed out, the film coarsens and all but caricatures its already not terribly subtle source, the Broadway hit by Samson Rafelson (Carringer 1979, 20–28). But it does this primarily in its domestic melodrama sequences. This sort of story, and performance style, had been a staple of Hollywood since well before World War I, but by the late twenties it was on the wane.

What is important about this is that the sync sound performances are persistently associated with the backstage musical strand of the film. Even the two performances (out of eight in the film) by Jackie's father are made major turning points of the stage musical plot, and in other ways recuperated by it. The first, "Kol Nidre," is later sung by Jackie as his farewell to his heritage just before (in film, though not fictional time) he goes on the Broadway stage to sing "Mammy." The second is a performance by Cantor Rabinowitz which Jackie attends unbeknownst to his father—not at all by coincidence the "Yahrzeit," a secular work sung in commemoration of a death (the son's symbolic death in the eyes of his father). (For further details on these and other religious and ethnic aspects of the film, see Carringer, 1979, *passim*.)

And if the father's performances are made to function as aspects of the son's tale, Cantor Rabinowitz attempts, at one highly charged moment, to have his own say about his son's singing. It is often said that the only dialogue in *The Jazz Singer* got there virtually by accident (Jolson's supposedly irrepressible urge to improvise), but there is ample reason to doubt this. Jackie's father's reaction to his rendition of "Blue Skies," in any event, is not written on a title card: aghast at the desecration of his house by "jazz," he cries "STOP!" It seems one of the most momentous spoken words in all of sound cinema, wrenching the film out of its most developed music-with-speech sequence and back into the traditional discourse of "silent" cinema. It is as if the older man is also saying stop to the sound recording machines, and they obey. In this way and in others as well, the film persistently associates the old cinema with the Rabinowitz family, and the new one with Jack Robin, as Jackie is called in the other parts of the film. If one identifies with the leading character's desire to succeed, to please audiences, to find freedom outside of what is presented as a quaint but stifling immigrant tradition, as the film throughout invites one to do, then one is led also to prefer the medium by which "Jack" finds fulfillment: the talking picture.

THE IMPACT OF THE TALKIES

People involved with film production everywhere felt their world shake with the sustained popular success of *The Jazz Singer*. Frances (Mrs. Sam) Goldwyn reportedly called the film's Los Angeles premiere "the most important event in cultural history since Martin Luther nailed his theses on the church door" (Berg, 89, 173). The standard textbook account is of massive disruption: producers panicked; careers were ruined; no one knew how to use the new technology, and so sound recordists became *de facto* directors; the art of the film took a giant, if temporary, step backwards, particularly in editing and camera movement. Some specific points in this account are clearly in need of revision. The power of the sound engineers, for example, seems to have varied from company to company and even project to project, and a strong-willed producer, director, or cinematographer could often obtain spectacular movement out of the primitive early sound cameras. However, most scholars accept the basic story of panic and drift.

In this context, the account given in Bordwell, Thompson, and Staiger's *The Classical Hollywood Cinema* is refreshingly counterintuitive. In a (significantly) brief chapter of that massive work, David Bordwell argues that recorded synchronous sound produced only certain "adjustments in film style.... Sound cinema was not a radical alternative to silent filmmaking; sound as sound, as a material and as a set of technical procedures, was inserted into the already constituted system of the classical Hollywood style" (Bordwell *et al* 1985, 298, 301). Although certain qualifications of *The Classical Hollywood Cinema*'s account of the transition will be suggested here, the usefulness and significance of the book for an understanding of the period is great. Bordwell's central thesis seems unassailable (though its terms are limited to a relatively narrow definition of visual style). But how is one to reconcile his vision of industry calculation and stylistic continuity with the more popular image of near-revolution (or reformation)? On the most important level, there is really no problem at all: Bordwell is working with relatively large temporal units, as many modern historians do, and from his perspective continuity and calculated adjustment emerge against a background of temporary "noise" (the two years or so of the heart of the transition).[4]

Even more important, *The Classical Hollywood Cinema* does not construct its model of "silent" cinema using the films most film scholars know from the period.[5] The accepted canon of "silent" masterpieces has inevitably tended to center on works *not* like the talkies, presumably to give audiences habituated to sound some reason to want to see something else. But films like Howard Hawks' *A Girl in Every Port* (1928), or—to give a European example—Henri Fescourt's *Les Grands* (1924), really are stylistically very much like talkies without the sound—more so than many better-known "silent" features. They do not, for example, have the dissolves within continuous scenes accepted by audiences and filmmakers before recorded sound but virtually prohibited afterwards. But this small example raises an interesting point: the possibility of confusion about what the "real" silent cinema was like suggests that there may well have been greater heterogeneity, more stylistic options within the classical system before the talkies came. If sync sound did not fundamentally *change* the textuality of Hollywood films, it did arguably make the system stronger and more normative.

Why would this have occurred? An extremely useful avenue of approach to the question was indicated by Sergei Eisenstein in his "Statement on the Sound-Film": "every ADHESION of sound to a visual montage piece [shot] increases its inertia as a montage piece and will increase the independence of its meaning." He worried that this greater inertia and semantic independence of shots with synchronous sound would be "to the detriment of montage," and indeed montage as he knew it largely died with the coming of the talkies (Eisenstein 1928, 258). Whether these characteristics of the sound film were the *only* reasons for the decline of Eisenstein's and other alternative approaches to cinema is a complex historiographical issue, as we will briefly see in the next section. But inertia (phenomenologically, the sense of weight and "presentness" of the image) and semantic independence not only work against montage in the strong, Eisensteinian sense; they also pose problems for continuity editing, making it more difficult to end shots unobtrusively and connect them "transparently" to other shots. Furthermore, "silent" cinema had a fundamental source of continuity which was largely absent from sound film, except at points of narrative discontinuity (for example, scene changes or temporal ellipses) or heightened emotion: the musical accompaniment, which appears to have acted like a secondary narrator for the spectator. With the talkies, musical continuity all but disappeared at the same time that the individual shots acquired greater inertia and semantic independence. And so it is no wonder that the "rules" of the continuity system which is the fundamental basis of classical Hollywood style suddenly seem to be in force with greater vigor in the early days of the talkies.

The narrowing and increasing codification of visual style does not, however, entirely account for the widespread intuitive sense of an enormous break with the coming of sound to the American cinema. But the purely technological transition to sound cinema, and the stylistic adjustments to it, are by no means the only factors at work in film history between 1927 and the early 1930s. The adoption of sound recording causes other historical currents to surface, or to intensify. Although Hollywood film (visual) *style* may have changed relatively little, film content is another matter entirely. Pressures for change that had been building over the years seem to have been released with the coming of recorded sound, and American filmmaking quite strikingly all but abandoned an *ethos* which had been a major component in its definition in earlier years.

For the coming of the talkies coincides with the decline of traditional stage melodrama in mainstream commercial cinema, virtually the last place where it still thrived. This is the melodrama of D. W. Griffith, of pure maidens tied to railroad tracks, of spectacular confrontations between good and evil. Melodrama in this historically specific sense was born in the aftermath of the French Revolution and shared for most of its history the Revolutionary ideal of *sensibilité*. Characters poured out their feelings to one another and to the audience, baring their souls in moments of moral transparency. Contrary to modern, dismissive stereotypes of the genre, good did not always triumph over evil; it was the battle that mattered most, and the lessons that could be learned from it.

Nothing intrinsic to the new machinery obliged filmmakers to reject this kind of story and manner of storytelling—particularly the expressive gestures and eye-catching, non-naturalistic settings—when the industry converted to sound. Nothing, that is, unless one assumes that pressure inevitably existed to employ extensively the most obvious kind of synchronous sound, human speech. Assuming this pressure existed, then the melodramatic tradition was almost automatically imperiled. There was little talk, and a great deal of music and sound effects, in traditional melodrama, which is what made it an ideal match for "silent" cinema. One is tempted to argue that it is precisely melodrama, and the melodramatic esthetic which characterizes so much of pre-talkie world cinema, that kept the silent film viable as an entertainment form. From this point of view, when the former ceased to appeal to audiences, the latter was doomed, and all it took was the right sort of push to bring the edifice crashing to the ground. As it happened, that push was given by *The Jazz Singer*, but if it not been made, some other, similar work would probably have done the job as well.

Whether one wishes to make the decline of traditional melodrama a primary factor in the transition to sound or not, it remains a key element for the explanation of many aspects of the transition. For example, the decline in the careers of certain stars of silent cinema, such as John Gilbert or Ramon Novarro, is said to have occurred because their voices "recorded badly." This is at best an obscure notion, except in the cases of players such as Vilma Banky who had such thick accents that their lines were difficult to understand. Listening today to Gilbert or Novarro, one is struck by how *well* their voices recorded. And even foreign accents were not an insurmountable barrier to success in the talkies, as Garbo's case demonstrates. Leaving aside the truly vocally impaired—probably only a handful of players at most—the "bad voices" of the most notorious Hollywood stars were probably in part a product of their association with melodramatic *sensibilité*.

It was, most notably, certain of the men who suffered, those whose acting was expressive, whose screen personas were somehow feminized, in the terms of the new film culture. For them, perhaps, *no* voice would have "recorded well." It is, for example, around the time of the transition to sound that male characters begin to cry far less frequently—and that crying begins to signify, not admirable sensitivity, but hysteria and sexual ambiguity. Perhaps the most striking symptom of the decline of the melodramatic sensibility in American cinema is this change in male gender definition, but it is not the only sign of transformation. Women characters, too, underwent a similar but less complete sea change. Wise-cracking, irony, and self-control characterized many of the new female roles and star images, but some of the older sensibility survived in the generic ghetto of the "woman's picture" and in the larger category of family melodrama. Is the decline of traditional melodrama causally linked in some way to the transition to sound cinema? The new, post-melodramatic males and females would have seemed strange indeed and difficult to comprehend before the talkies, their behaviors grounded in a denial of what made the "silent" film tick: bodily expressiveness. The liberation of speech brings with it the repression of the body; whether this is technologically and psychologically inevitable or, on the other hand, historically contingent (the expression of the transition from one sort of social structure to another) deserves to be the subject of debate and further research.

HOLLYWOOD AND THE WORLD

It is too rarely remarked that the shape of the transition to sound in the rest of the world seems to have been rather different from what happened in the United States. In Europe, the coming of sound brought relative stylistic uniformity to a diverse set of textual strategies produced by a remarkable variety of art movements, tendencies, and stubborn individualists. In France, for example, this period coincides with the death of the "Impressionist" film art movement, as well as the near-total decline of the extra-industrial avant-garde or experimental cinema that had proliferated during the years between 1924 and 1929. In Germany, only a few Expressionist works were made with the new technology.[6] And in the U.S.S.R., the first sound feature—Ekk's *The Road to Life*—is also the first manifestation of Soviet Socialist Realism (or classical Hollywood style in the service of the Party).

As the last case should suggest, here we encounter the crucial historiographic problem that the transition to recorded sound occurred at a moment of great social and political change throughout the world. There is no immediate, local connection between the final stage of the basic mechanization of the cinema and the consolidation of Stalin's power in the Soviet Union, which finds expression (among many other places) in the adoption of Socialist Realism as the only sanctioned method of filmmaking. Or rather, there is no connection except that the new medium offered a powerful pretext for imposing uniform adherence to a new "line," and that it makes film production more capital-intensive and thus a more pressing target for administrative centralization. What the Soviet example shares with the more typical disruptions linked to the market economy is a demonstration of what we might call the "earthquake theory" of film history: upheavals such as the coming of recorded sound intensify and help direct the progress of trends already in place. In continental Europe, for example, these included the weakening and fragmentation of the post war avant-garde movements.

Everywhere, the coming of sound appears to have reduced diversity and acted against those who would oppose the classical Hollywood cinema with an alternative of their own. Was this uniquely the result of something intrinsic to sound recording technology? This seems unlikely. But it seems defensible to attribute the worldwide imposition of classical Hollywood style in at least some measure to the peculiarities of the development of sound technology and of spectator psychology. With early equipment, maximum intelligibility was obtained only with direct recording of dialogue; "dubbing" was not a satisfactory option for roughly a decade. Those films which succeeded best at the box office were the ones which continued (and perhaps also marked the consolidation of) the classical Hollywood style. And yet Hollywood itself was suddenly in a position of competitive international inferiority in the production of precisely this kind of product, because of the linguistic specificity of its films. American producers experimented with producing multiple, foreign language versions of their films, but these proved unprofitable in most markets and were almost completely abandoned by 1932.

Why the multi-language system of production was so spectacularly unsuccessful is a matter of no small interest to students of film sound. It cannot be exclusively the fault of the American studios' desire to make such projects very cheaply; the German mega-studio UFA made a similar effort (mainly directed at the French market) with much greater financial and artistic resources, only to fail more slowly and less dramatically at it than American studios such as Paramount and MGM. One reasonable hypothesis might be that recorded speech, as opposed to written titles, fatally introduced an element of cultural and social specificity into narrative film that simply hadn't been there before. Spectators reading title cards to themselves provided their own voices for them. Suddenly, with the talkies, there were *other* voices, having clearly identifiable social origins. Once this happened, the cultural and social sensitivities of different audiences would have become vastly more easily to disturb, since film stories with spoken dialogue took place in a world more solidly grounded in the experience of everyday life—as opposed to fantasies about it. Postsynchronization—which even in the most proficient hands reintroduces an element of the abstract, "neutral" voices of silent spectatorship—would later emerge as a kind of perfect compromise between the painful cultural specificity of recorded speech and the abstract, spectator-generated "voices" of silent titles. By the late 1930s, dubbed films would help Hollywood regain its world hegemony. The exact role of sound technology in this is, evidently, a potentially fruitful ground for historical and theoretical reflection. (For a related commentary in this area, see Williams 1981.)

Thus, for a while at least, sound cinema brought a measure of protection to the formerly all too porous non-American market. Having created a great public demand for a certain type of product, the talkies also (temporarily) weakened the most efficient producer of that product in most of the world. No wonder that new production companies throughout the world rushed to supply the works that the U.S. could now provide only in English. Ambitious European producers no longer were obliged to remain in the "art cinema" niche of their own markets, and production capital migrated to where rates of return were the highest. This, perhaps acting in tandem with the greater "inertia" and semantic independence of images with synchronous sound, would have all but doomed both the radical avant-garde and the commercially oriented "art cinema" in Europe—though the exact relationship between these two determinants remains to be specified. All of which is to suggest that if *The Classical Hollywood Cinema* is right, and sound recording in and of itself changed Hollywood filmmaking relatively little, it nonetheless helped change the rest of world cinema in a quite fundamental way.

K. J. DONNELLY

SAW HEARD: MUSICAL SOUND DESIGN IN CONTEMPORARY CINEMA

Film sound has seen some radical developments in both technological and aesthetic terms over the last thirty years or so. The traditional basic speaker system in cinemas in many cases has been replaced in many by a multi-speaker system which involves a significant spatialization of film sound allied to a remarkable improvement in sound definition. These changes augur an altered psychology at the heart of much new cinema, instilled by sound's increased importance for films.

> The sound of noises, for a long time relegated to the background like a troublesome relative in the attic, has therefore benefited from the recent improvements in definition brought by Dolby. Noises are reintroducing an acute feeling of the materiality of things and beings, and they herald a sensory cinema that rejoins a basic tendency of … the silent cinema.
>
> The paradox is only apparent. With the new place that noises occupy, speech is no longer central to films. (Chion 155)

Michel Chion points to technological developments in cinema that have had a notable impact on film aesthetics. Any movement from a speech-centred cinema to one that allows more prominence to "noise," is potentially a move from a cinema dominated by synchronized dialogue to one with significant amounts of asynchrony and sound as an effect in itself, be that through loud music or featured sounds.

The series of *Saw* I–IV (2004–7) demonstrates a situation where film music has an intimately close relationship with the film's overall sound design: where there is a convergence of sound effects, ambient sound and music. On the one hand, this might be attributed to the development of digital surround film sound and the corresponding importance of sound design in mainstream films. On the other, though, it might be accounted for by social and cultural aspects: there has been a gradual but exponential increase in the degree of ambient sound and ambient music over the past couple of decades. Sound effects are often less used to bolster a sense of verisimilitude than they are as an aesthetic effect, as, to all intents and purposes, music. Sound design in these films might be understood as essentially musical in nature, following a musical logic rather than any other.

The first film in the series, *Saw*, has a highly distinctive soundscape, which I will be discussing in this chapter. There is no solid demarcation between incidental music and sound design: consequently, sound effects can sound synthetic and music can sound like sound effects. The film has a very intimate relationship of sonic elements that makes it unconventional, although many recent films do not follow the dominant conventions of music-sound effects-dialogue atomization. The film's music was written and performed by first-time film music composer Charlie Clouser. Up to this point, he was known for his remixes of existing songs, adapting and rebuilding sonic material rather than "creating" as such. Hence, it might be possible to approach Clouser's work in the *Saw* films as an adaptation, a partial remix, of the sound world as a whole rather merely than the music alone. Clouser's music in the films is often unmelodic, unmemorable and anempathetic but focusing instead on texture and timbre and plays upon a confusion between what might be termed "film music" and "sound effects." The films wield sound often either explosively or in a disconcerting and semi-dislocated manner. Furthermore, *Saw* illustrates the assimilation of new technologies and new techniques and concomitantly different assumptions about cinema's diegetic world and the place of sound in this.

TRANSFORMATION

In certain recent films there has been a notable fusing of elements of the soundtrack, much as classical musicals fused music with dialogue (or more accurately we should use the term "voices"), some recent films have fused music with sound effects, creating a sonic continuum. Music in film has a significant interaction with other elements of the soundtrack as well as with the images, and one might even argue that its interaction with dialogue outweighs its interaction with images. In recent years, the development of converging digital sound technology has allowed sound designers to use musical software to enhance sound effects in films and allowed music composers to produce their own music incorporating elements of sound effects. Such developments, in line with technological convergence, aesthetic convergence and harmonizing platforms and industries has meant that music is no longer simply a "bolt-on" to films but integrated almost genetically on a conceptual level: instigating film titles and narratives, perhaps even having films as spin-offs from existing music, while continuing to inspire and articulate the most emotional and exciting moments of the overwhelming majority of films and other audiovisual media.

Technology has played an important part in recent developments in film sound and music, and technological determinism is always an attractive if too-easy answer. The availability of relatively cheap and easily programmed keyboard synthesizers at the turn of the 1980s led to an explosion of popular music and musicians premised upon the use of these instruments. This had a notable impact on films. In the 1970s, John Carpenter's scores for his own films sounded unique in their use of simple textures with monophonic synthesizers, but by the next decade they were sounding more like some of the contemporary pop music they had partly inspired. Greek keyboard player Vangelis came to some prominence for his scores for *Chariots of Fire* (1981) and *Blade Runner* (1982), and while rock keyboard players like Rick Wakeman and Keith Emerson had dipped their toes into film scoring, by the mid-1980s pop groups using drum machines and synthesizers were producing scores, such as Wang Chung's for *To Live and Die in L.A.* (1985). The revolutionary development from analogue to digital sound has had a notable impact on many aspects of cinema (Sergi 30), and on music and sound perhaps more than most other areas, allowing minute alteration and precise manipulation of all aural aspects. By the turn of the millennium, it was possible for musical scores to be constructed and fitted to a film on a computer screen at home, using AVID (or similar) and digital audio workstation (DAW) technology. Consequently, film makers like Robert Rodriguez are easily able to construct the scores for their films themselves, making film less of a collaborative medium, and making music less collaborative perhaps than ever. The elevation of the DAW has revolutionized music production, allowing easy construction of relatively high quality music on a home computer, although most of the top Hollywood film composers only use them for "mock ups" until the final recording with an expensive orchestra. However, the development of sequencing software has had a direct influence on the styles of music being produced in the popular music arena. Examples of the dominant types of software sequencer include Steinberg Cubase, Sony Logic, Ableton Live and Propellerheads Reason. One of the central tenets of such computer technology is that music can be reduced to recorded components that are then processed, through audio enhancement/distortion and through the process of looping, where a passage of music is repeated verbatim. This latter aspect has been responsible for the proliferation of dance music in the 1990s that was developed in home studios, with an emphasis on the manipulation of sound samples, pre-recorded passages of music, which could be adapted, treated and woven together into a new musical composition. Such music technology instils an awareness of sound and ability to manipulate electronically. This encourages a "sound for sound's sake" approach focusing on the manipulation of sound on a basic level (e.g., reverb, filters, placing in stereo mix, etc.) more than the traditional virtues of composition enshrined in so-called "classical training" (harmony, counterpoint, orchestration, etc). This can lead to a confusion about what might constitute "music" and what might constitute "non-musical sound," and at the very least has challenged the limited concepts of music that were in wide circulation. Such technology is not only used by "musical" people but also by sound designers and editors, who use digital technology and techniques to "manipulate" sound effects the same way that composers use the same procedures to "compose" music. While on the one hand, composers are more aware of sound as an absolute than perhaps ever before, film sound people are approaching soundtracks in a manner that might be termed "musical," or at the very least betrays a musical awareness of the interaction of elements and their particular individual sonic qualities.

[...]

Film incidental music's effects includes eliciting and affirming emotion, clarification or provision of information (such as mood and setting), providing a sound bath that immerses the audience in the film world, as well as the more traditional functional aspects that include attempting to provide continuity across edits and joins between shots and time-spaces. As such, the score can also furnish a sense of, or emphasize filmic movement while also functioning to clarify and articulate a formal structure for the film (through punctuation, cadence and closure). Related structural functions might also include anticipating subsequent action in the film, and commenting on screen activities or providing a further symbolic dimension not evident in other aspects of the film. In separate writings, Noël Carroll (139), Jeff Smith (6) and Roy Prendergast (213–22) all quote a newspaper article where in the 1940s respected concert hall composer Aaron Copland posited five categories of film incidental music function. These functions are: "creating atmosphere, highlighting the psychological states of characters; providing neutral background filler, building a sense of continuity; sustaining tension and then rounding it off with a sense of closure" (28). Music has many material functions. It regularly has an enormous influence on the pacing of events and "emphasizing the dramatic line" (Burt 79). David Raksin notes that it was common to enter before the required emphasis, with what was called "neutral" music in the trade (in Burt 80), before being more emphatic with the music or making a specific musical effect. Such neutral music has given rise to pejorative descriptions of film music as "wallpaper" or "window dressing" which, perhaps in some cases, is justified. Music regularly performs an instructive role, creating meaning through representing ideas, objects and emotions. Indeed, it performs a primary role in eliciting emotional responses in the audience, and in providing consent for the audience's emotional responses.

Without assuming an unassailable cinematic ideal of sound and image in harmony, it should be admitted that in mainstream films sound overwhelmingly is functional. It works to elide itself as contract more than perhaps any other element of film. Some theorize that we perceive the diegetic world on screen as an unproblematic reality (on some level) (Kracauer 33–4), and sound is one of the principal elements that convince us that the space on screen is "real." After all, one might argue that most sounds in films exist essentially to bolster or "make real" the images we see on screen and the surrounding world we imagine. Consequently, when we see faces on screen talking we expect to hear what they are saying, when a car drives past we expect to hear those sounds corresponding. The fact that we hear a representation of those sounds, a convention allowing crisply-heard voices and unobtrusive car engine sounds rising then falling in pitch and volume, but not intruding on the important conversation, underlines just how conventional film sound is. Certainly, this is apparent if it is compared to the sounds recorded from an integrated microphone mounted on a home video camera.

However, having stated this, film sound still retains a principal function that is to guarantee the illusionistic world on screen. Random sound effects used in avant garde films might serve as an obtrusive reminder of the fabricated nature of film sound (and indeed synchronized cinema more generally), and point to our expectation of film sound to be merely a vehicle for the illusions on screen. Now this is a very different traditional function from that of music in films. Perhaps such a unity of sound effects and music might be approached as just moments of aesthetic effect, where sound effects are precisely sonic *effects*, such as the disconcerting noise from the attic early in *The Exorcist* (1973). This instance is not simply a sound—it is an emotional effect, more like an emanation from the Id, a manifestation of primary psychology. Such opportunities are opened by the recession of sound's representational function, which frees it to fulfil more in the way of direct emotional and aesthetic roles, in short, making film sound more like, or perhaps even a part of, the musical dimension of films. Consequently, great care can be taken with qualitative aspects of certain sounds—as the sounds have value in themselves rather merely than being conventionally representative of sounds from a small repertoire of stereotypical sounds (as remains the case in much television production).

Michel Chion discusses the new sonic space offered by directional multi-speaker surround sound as a "superfield," "which changes the perception of space and thereby the rules of [audio-visual] scene construction" (150). Although it retains much of tradition of monaural film, he insists that it is an extension of off-screen space and qualitatively different from previous sonic space, while similarly Philip Brophy uses the term "acousmonium" to articulate the new tactile and multidirectional space (38). Chion continues with his description:

> I call superfield the space created, in multitrack films, by ambient natural sounds, city noises, music, and all sorts of rustlings that surround the visual space and can issue from loudspeakers outside the physical boundaries of the screen. By virtue of its acoustical precision and relative stability this ensemble of sounds has taken on a kind of quasi-autonomous existence with relation to the visual field, in that it does not depend moment by moment on what we see onscreen. (150)

This new field is not simply one of dialogue and sound effects, but one where their interaction with music can be the key to its organization. This development has inspired a new aesthetics. According to Chion, Dolby multitrack favours passive offscreen sound, which works to establish a general space and permits more free movement for shots (and more of which are close ups) within that space, without any spatial disorientation of the viewer-auditor (85), although there is a corresponding tendency to keep speaking characters on screen as spatial anchors.

A further part of this process, evident in some films, is the convergence of music and sound effects, with a concomitant collapse of the strict demarcation between the two that reigned earlier. Of course, to a degree, it has always been impossible to fully and clinically separate musical score from sound effect. Music regularly has mimicked, emphasized or suggested certain sounds in the diegesis. Similarly, sound effects in films are regularly more than simply an emanation from the illusory diegetic world constructed by the film. They often have symbolic or emotional effects that outweigh their representational status. Indeed, it might be argued that much time and energy have been spent in attempting to approximate, or at least take inspiration from, the natural world, from birdsong to the rhythmic sounds of machinery. So, talking in terms of a solid distinction between the diegetic sound effect and musical accompaniment becomes difficult upon closer scrutiny and deeper thought. However, in terms of film production, there has been a relatively solid divide: musicians and composers produce music for film, and foley artists and sound editors are responsible for constructing a conventional series of sound effects to accompany on-screen action. The advent of digital sound technology and the relative accessibility of complex sound-treating equipment have had a notable impact on the production process. An early example of this was the development of special sound for *Evil Dead 2* (1987), where the sound of a rocking chair creaking was merged with sound recordings of a scream, using digital synthesizers to fuse the sounds on a genetic level. A more recent example of the process is *Resident Evil* (2002). The film begins with a voice-over narration accompanied by metallic and booming "non-musical" sounds, leading into a loop of one of the electronic themes Marilyn Manson wrote for the film as the action follows the events of a laboratory accident. Shortly afterwards, when protagonist Alice studies what appears to be her wedding photograph, we hear music that sounds like it was composed from various "non-musical" sound samples, in other words, re-organized and repeated shards of sound effects. Her contemplation is halted abruptly by a nearby door opening. Sonically, this involves a very loud and percussive sound matched to the image of an automatic door. Yet the consistency of the sound is certainly not at odds with the preceding music, firmly supplying the impression of a continuum of organized sound that is able to be more rhythmic and more melodic while retaining a foot in diegetic sound effects and ambiences.

Such a unified field of music and sound effects is evident in a good number of recent films, although this marginal tradition might be traced back to an origin in silent cinema, where the live music performed to accompany the film in many cases "did" the sound effects. This tradition is probably more evident in the film scoring tradition where music will mimic or suggest certain diegetic sound effects, even through they may well be present on the soundtrack anyway. There was a minor tradition of certain sound films having a sonic continuum that fully merged music and sound effects. Probably the best example is *Forbidden Planet* (1956), which had a soundtrack of "electronic tonalities" by Louis and Bebe Barron. For the purposes of film production this could not be credited as "music," and indeed, its origins in recordings of "cybernetic sound organisms" that were then collaged to fit the film evinces a process far removed from the dominant traditions of Hollywood film scoring. There a direct confusion of origins of sounds. Some of the electronic sounds appear to be functioning like incidental music, some clearly are synchronized with images on screen (such as the monster, for example). Others appear to be environmental, marking the ambience of the unfamiliar alien planet, and adding to the sense of the exotic and uncharted that the film represents. In his study of the sound and music for *Forbidden Planet*, James Wierzbicki notes that this was not an isolated case, and through traversing the membrane of conventional sound functions pointed to a new psychology:

> In contrast [with traditional orchestral scores of the time], electronic sounds in scores for many 1950s science-fiction films were strikingly non-traditional, and thus they tended to blur the long-standing boundary between non-diegetic underscore and diegetic sound effect. Electronic sounds did not simply accompany "foreign" narrative objectives; in many cases, they seemed to emanate directly *from* them. (26–7)

Similarly, Hitchcock's *The Birds* (1963) has a soundtrack that mixes sound effects and music. It contained no underscore in the traditional sense. Instead it used electronic "sound design" (apparently Herrmann's idea), which was recorded in Munich with experimentalists Remi Gassmann and Oskar Sala. Hitchcock's regular composer at the time, Bernard Herrmann was "advisor" and the final product, while using synthetic bird noises, remains related to the *musique concrete* produced by experimenters such as Pierre Schaeffer and Pierre Henry in the 1940s and 1950s. *The Birds'* sound design approached music as merely another element of the soundtrack and replaced a musical underscore with "sound effects," that nevertheless are fairly musical in their inspiration.

While the soundtrack appears to represent bird sounds that match the action on screen, they are in fact produced electronically and only vaguely synchronized with the birds on screen. It might be more apt to characterize the soundtrack to *The Birds* as a continuum of ambient bird sounds most clearly in the sequences of bird attacks.

Another film that has a soundtrack that goes beyond simple sound effects and music is David Lynch's *Eraserhead* (1977), which makes particularly harrowing use of ambient sound in the background through the film. The sound design for the film, by Alan Splet, collaged industrial sounds, metallic noises, rumbles and wind into a disturbing and continuous sonic backdrop for the film's action. It is not unchanging and moves to the foreground at times. Arguably, it takes something from the general function of film scores, which provide a sonic backdrop and a vague mood for the action. The fact that these sounds were not easily classified as non-diegetic music meant that they were more satisfactorily accounted for as acousmatic sound effects: seemingly the sounds emanating from some dreadful but indistinct industrial machines somewhere in the distance. Indeed, Alan Splet's sound work was far more than merely recording and compiling sounds for use in films. An available 3-disc set, *Sounds From a Different Realm*, showcases Splet's work along with his collaborator Ann Kroeber. Some of the pieces are called "Unusual Presences" and illustrate the construction of nearly autonomous sound environments, some of which were used in David Lynch's films. Despite the collection nominally being a sound effects set, they manifest more a sustained, "canned atmosphere" rather than being simply "recorded sound effects" ready for general use.

FILM SOUND AS MUSIC (AND FILM MUSIC AS SOUND)

The effect of a unified field of sound and music is the destruction of conventional use of sound in films, with a concomitant questioning of the relationship of sound to image. Certain contemporary films evince a unified sound design that conceives of the film's sound in holistic terms rather than as the traditionally separate music, dialogue and sound effects. Miguel Mera and David Burnand note:

> Modernism is inherent in the technologically enabled means of audio production in filmmaking that encourages the alliance of music and sound design as a recorded and edited form, and thus is at odds with the rehashed nineteenth-century orchestral scores typical of classic cinema, flown into the virtual orchestra pit of the movie theatre. (5)

Such films with a unified sound field deal with it in highly sophisticated terms. Sound effects are not simply about matching what the screen requires to verify its activities. Instead, sound effects can take on more of the functions traditionally associated with music, such emotional ambiences, provision of tone to a sequence or suggestions of vague connections. In short, film sound as a unified field has taken a high degree of its logic from music, and more specifically from music in films in the form of non-diegetic or incidental music. Films such as *Se7en* (1997) or *Ju-On: The Grudge* (2003) have notable sequences where sound could be construed as music or as sound effects. In both cases, the ambiguity is doubtless part of the general effect of the film. In *Donnie Darko* (2001), a voice (belonging to "Frank") appears in the night, telling Donnie to wake up. This is accompanied by deep ambiguous rumbles and what might be construed as supernatural sounds. It certainly is not easily recognizable as film score, but equally fails to identify itself as sound effects for anything in the diegetic world. There is a seemingly organic mixture of diegetic sound and music evident in the London underground-set *Creep* (2004). At the start of the film one of a pair of sewage workers disappears down a tunnel and as the other searches for him the soundtrack embraces deep sub-bass rumbles that are ambiguous as to whether they are diegetic or not. As his desperation grows, the music grows in volume, featuring metallic sounds and developing from the deep rumbles into a more clearly organized pattern, and thus more clearly becomes "music."[1] Like much of the film, this sequence exploits the dramatic and psychological possibilities of an extended range of bass tones available to 5.1 Dolby sound.

[...]

As an aural counterpart to the rare "non-diegetic insert,"[4] we might wonder if recent cinema is wielding the "non-diegetic sound effect," which likely has the same ambiguity of acousmatic sound, although it sounds like it could emanate from the world on screen yet *cannot* be retrospectively understood and placed in the surrounding (diegetic) world. It indeed has lost its synchronization absolutely, in that there is no possibility of its matching the screen world and thus manifests an extreme of mental confusion and potential threat. The horror genre often has been premised upon the drama of off-screen space concealing the unknown, such as in films like Hitchcock's *Psycho* (1960). However, in *Saw*, these sounds not only are "offscreen," they are "off world."

They are sounds "from nowhere," occupying the same space as the film's non-diegetic music, which also emanates from an obscure space somewhere that is not existentially connected to the world represented on screen. Now, non-diegetic music is purely conventional, and as such does not invite direct questions about its origins. However, sound effects are anchored to screen representations. They provide the spatial and conformational aspects of activities on screen or nearby still in the diegetic world. From time to time, however, sound effects appear to come from outside the diegetic world, most notably in surreal or horror films. For example, in the remake of *The Fog* (2005), as DJ Stevie Wayne (played by Selma Blair) sits in her car, there are deep threatening sounds. Their status is ambiguous—they might be part of Graeme Revell's non-diegetic music, or they could be diegetic sounds of the mysterious fog itself. However, in all likelihood, they are non-diegetic sound effects.[5] This appears literally to be an occult aesthetic, yet such general "ambiences" function to immerse the audience in the film more effectively in sonic terms than might be available as a visual effect. There are highly-effective low-volume continuums, such as Freddy Kruger's basement in the *Nightmare on Elm Street* films, or in space ships such as the Starship Enterprise in the *Star Trek* films and television series. Rick Altman, McGraw Jones and Sonia Tatroe note that some Hollywood films in the 1930s had continuous low-volume "atmosphere sound," which had a function of "enveloping" the audience in a film's sonic space (352). Such "enveloping" is an effect of the extension of sonic space, which is a characteristic of surround-sound but also an effect of the degree of reverberation (or "reverb") evident on any recorded sound. In audio terms, reverb expresses "space" as the equivalent of showing open space visually. Furthermore, the use of electronic reverb, adding a sense of space around a recorded sound, might be seen as a prime signifier of sound as aesthetic in films rather than following any vague attempt to reflect the space represented visually on screen. Philip Brophy notes that, "psychoacoustically, reverb grants us an out-of-body experience: we can aurally separate what we hear from the space in which it occurs" (108). This inconsistency of sound space represented on the soundtrack and the expected sound ambience that would have emanated from the space represented on screen. This is not only evident in *Forbidden Planet* but also in films such as *Saw*. It illustrates a degree of mental separation emanating from the evident mismatch in *Saw* of expansive, reverb-drenched music and sounds, with an enclosed and circumscribed visual space. We might go further, and approach electronic reverb and echo as a manifestation of a state of mind more than it is a representation of anything. After all, it does not signify diegetic space but something beyond, an emotional and unconscious enveloping of sound. In his discussion of *Forbidden Planet*, Philip Brophy continues,

> Reverb is heavily applied to *Forbidden Planet*'s synthetic sound effects firstly to invoke the expansive opening of interplanetary frontiers, and secondly to invoke an imposing sense of size and space. At least fifteen centuries of European church architecture used reverb to conjure up thundering scale and omnipotent power; sci-fi movies followed suit with their own brand of technological mysticism and God-fearing morality. (108)

So, it is nothing to do with representing the world on screen and more to do with providing an effect and an emotional tone. Annabel Cohen notes that:

> The affective quality [of music] is consistent [with the diegesis]; the acoustical aspects of the music are not. Although the affective associations produced by the music seem to belong to the corresponding images, the sounds that produced those associations do not. Somehow, the brain attends to this affective meaning, while ignoring or attenuating its acoustical source. (373–4)

As registered earlier, the unification of sound effects and music conjoins the distinct psychologies of music and sound effects. The use of electronic echo and reverb marks a *musical* appropriation of sound space, unifying diegetic and non-diegetic sound as a psychological effect more than as a representational counterpart of the images on screen (and diegesis of recorded voices). Sound theorist David Toop points to the "... attraction to the synthetic mimicry of resonance, the structural potential of delays and the physicality of sound waves in enclosed space has evolved into a wider exploration of time, space and sound ..." (64). This quotation may have been aimed at a certain tendency in music, but is equally applicable to the use of sound in some films, films that are interested, one way or another, in exploring mental and psychological space. In other words, these films are *about* mental space, enabled by the sonic dimension of the film that is beyond representational functions.

CONCLUSION

Of course, music and sound effects have always been mixed despite efforts to keep them separate. Film scores have regularly imitated diegetic sounds (as indeed has music habitually imitated the sounds of nature). However, in recent years there has been more in the way of radical confusion of score and sound effects. These two aspects of film sound, distinct since the coming of synchronized sound cinema, have converged and cross what once was a fairly impermeable membrane between these two sonic aspects. The personnel involved in their production often remain as distinct as they had in the heyday of the Hollywood studio system, but techniques and hardware have encouraged a convergence. Developments such as this need acknowledgement from those studying film. The increased depth of aestheticization evident in many recent film soundtracks renders many analyses that ignore their nuances little more than naïve descriptions of "what happens" in those films. Narratological concerns should allow for the fact that sound-dominated films are essentially sensual experiences.

Now, on one level, some of this discussion might seem naïve. Austere music might well sound like "sound effects" to the uninitiated. I am aware of this—but there is a tradition of sound effects in film (and television, and video/computer games), and these recent scores/soundtracks engage those traditions more than they come from outside (from art music, for example). However, a number of recent films offer very rich sonic landscapes that work on their own independently of their film. This could be traced to the tradition of programmatic music, illustrating vistas and places through sound, a tradition reinvigorated by certain ambient music and new age music. There might also be an influence from sound art, which has been a burgeoning area of the art world over the past couple of decades. As a concrete instance, one artist relevant for discussion and who has crossed a number of boundaries is Brian Williams (usually known artistically as Lustmord). Starting in left-field rock music, some of his early recordings were of specific spaces (such as the Dunster Abattoir in Bangor and Chartres Cathedral on *Paradise Disowned* [1984]). He worked with experimental rock group SPK when they were using "found" metal percussion and he went on to produce regular recordings that sounded like they were inspired by horror film soundtracks. His 1990 album *Heresy* is seen as inaugurating the "dark ambient" (sub)genre, while albums such as *The Monstrous Soul* make copious use of horror film samples in their nightmarish soundscapes. Over the past decade or so, Williams has worked in Hollywood as a "musical sound designer," usually in collaboration with composer Graeme Revell (with whom he collaborated in SPK in the 1980s). Williams's role in films like *The Crow* (1994) was to provide certain sounds and ambiences that can be used in the film or in Revell's score. This suggests a unified sound design that is "musical" in its origin, as testified to by Williams's screen credit.

It is incontrovertible that the category of music has expanded to include much other sound. For instance, CDs of natural sounds, not just of singing whales, but recordings of natural landscapes, such as the Global Journey CD *Nature Recordings: Thunderstorm*,[6] not to mention the recorded soundscapes of sonic artists such as Hildegard Westerkamp. Such "soundscaping" is perhaps less to do with any attempt to objectively record a sound environment than it is to configure sound "psychogeographically" as personal and emotional landscapes. To a degree, this process might also be identified in some films, which aim to produce a mental and psychological aural landscape, as is the case in *Saw*.

Freed from a functional role, freed from the diegesis, and freely mixing with music, film sound is able to manifest a direct emotion, and a primary psychology. The tradition of sound mixing and construction developed by classical Hollywood and influential the world over was premised upon a solid demarcation of sound effects, dialogue and music, and with a concomitant clarity of purpose for each and the system as a whole. This appears to reflect a sense of clarity of purpose and solid understanding of the relationships between things in the world that mark protean American cinema of the time. By the same token, the collapse of consensus of sonic clarity might reflect social and political developments—perhaps the cultural confusion is a reflection of, or simply emanates from a social and political confusion. We can speculate about such "reflection," but what is beyond doubt is that there is a remarkable collapse of the *space* between diegetic sound and non-diegetic music. This manifests a collapse of mental space, between the film's "conscious" and its "unconscious," and perhaps not only between rational and irrational elements in such horror films but also in wider cinema.

ENDNOTES

1. When protagonist Kate runs along the deserted underground train, the music consists of a rhythmic loop of treated metallic sounds that are more "sound effects" than "musical" in origin. This piece has notable similarities with some of Charlie Clouser's kinetic music in the *Saw* films.
2. Such as in other celebrated "sonically based" films like *The Conversation* (1974) or *Blow Out* (1981).
3. Clouser worked in television music with Australian composer Cameron Allen in the late 1980s before working with Nine Inch Nails and as a remixer. He worked on shows including *The Equalizer* and *Kojak*, and more recently on *Fastlane* and *Las Vegas*.
4. These are the proverbial shots of trains going into tunnels that allegedly implied sex scenes in silent films. They are likely apocryphal stories and the fodder of comedy. Probably the most famous non-diegetic insert is the intrusion of a shot of a bull being slaughtered at the violent riot concluding Eisenstein's *Strike* (1926).
5. A philosophical problem is posed by the notion of the non-diegetic sound effect. The concept of diegetic is itself highly questionable, being dependent on an assumption about the illusory world on-screen, made by an idealized audience member.
6. On Global Journey records, GJ3638, 2001.

REFERENCES

Altman, Rick. *The American Film Musical*. London: British Film Institute, 1987.

Altman, Rick, McGraw Jones and Sonia Tatroe. "Inventing the Cinema Soundtrack: Hollywood's Multiplane Sound System." *Music and Cinema*. Eds James Buhler, Caryl Flinn and David Neumeyer. Hanover: Wesleyan University Press, 2000.

Brophy, Philip. *100 Modern Soundtracks*. London: British Film Institute, 2004.

Burt, George. *The Art of Film Music*. Boston: Northeastern University Press, 1994.

Carroll, Noël. *Theorizing the Moving Image*. Cambridge: Cambridge University Press, 1996.

Chion, Michel. *Audio-Vision: Sound on Screen*. Edited and translated by Claudia Gorbman. New York: Columbia University Press, 1994.

Clouser, Charlie. "Interview" at *ign.com*. http://music.ign.com/articles/562/562509p1.html (accessed 03/12/2004).

Cohen, Annabel J. "Film Music: Perspectives from Cognitive Psychology." *Music and Cinema*. Eds James Buhler, Caryl Flinn and David Neumeyer. Hanover:Wesleyan University Press, 2000.

Copland, Aaron. "Tip to the Moviegoers: Take Off Those Ear-Muffs." *The New York Times*, 6 November 1949, section six.

Kracauer, Siegfried. *Theory of Film: The Redemption of Physical Reality*. New York: Oxford University Press, 1960.

Mera, Miguel and David Burnand. "Introduction." *European Film Music*. Eds Miguel Mera and David Burnand. London: Ashgate, 2006.

Prendergast, Roy M. *Film Music: A Neglected Art*. New York: Norton, 1992.

Sacks, Rob. "Charlie Clouser's Scary Soundtrack for *Saw*" (interview with Charlie Clouser) in *NPR*'s "Day to Day," Friday 9 October 2004. http://www.nrp.org/templates/story/story.php?storyId=4132853 (accessed 15/11/2006).

Sergi, Gianluca. *The Dolby Era: Film Sound in Contemporary Hollywood*. Manchester: Manchester University Press, 2004.

Smith, Jeff. *The Sounds of Commerce: Marketing Popular Film Music*. New York: Columbia University Press, 1998.

Toop, David. *Haunted Weather: Music, Silence and Memory*. London: Serpent's Tail, 2004.

Weis, Elisabeth. "Sync Tanks: The Art and Technique of Postproduction Sound." *Cineaste*. 21.1–2 (1995): 42–48.

Wierzbicki, James. *Louis and Bebe Barron's* Forbidden Planet: *A Score Guide*. London: Scarecrow, 2005.

1. According to Todd Berliner and Dale Cohen's article *The Illusion of Continuity*, what evidence is given that suggests that classical editing conventions leave room for experimentation, such as disjointed editing and other non-classical film stimuli?

2. Define and contrast *continuity editing, point-of-view editing* and *analytical editing.*

3. According to K.J. Donnelly's *Saw Heard: Musical Sound Design in Contemporary Cinema*, what are the similarities between sound effects and music?

4. How is diagetic sound and non-diagetic sound defined?

5. According to Alan Williams' *Historical and Theoretical Issues in the Coming of Recorded Sound to the Cinema*, how did "talkies" revolutionize Hollywood cinema?

6. According to Alan Williams' *Historical and Theoretical Issues in the Coming of Recorded Sound to the Cinema*, why did the effort to make foreign language versions of films fail miserably after the advent of sound films?

ABOUT THE EDITOR

Linus Lau is a veteran professor of film studies at Long Beach City College where he was the recipient of the 2012 Sterling Award for his contributions to the Department of Visual and Media Arts.

A sought-after guest lecturer in the Los Angeles area, Linus has, in previous incarnations of his life, served as a projectionist, film festival judge, game conference panelist, and radio DJ.

Mentored by the great composer and conductor Lynn Shurtleff, Linus makes his academic observations on film through his unique lens on the industry as a movie composer. His film scores have been positively reviewed by Alt Film Guide and Fangoria Magazine; his music has had premieres at a wide variety of venues, including The San Francisco Conservatory of Music, Woodstock Film Festival, FrightFest London, and Tribeca Film Festival.

He has a particular passion for teaching and regularly runs courses in music video production and film scoring. He has lectured on the films of Věra Chytilová and Otto Preminger. In the spring of 2016, with the blessing of the director's family, he created an eight-week lecture series on the life and films of the great Samuel Fuller.

Having also served as the Program Chair of the Music Video, Film and Television Program at Musicians Institute, Mr. Lau holds an undergraduate degree in music from Santa Clara University and a master's degree in film from USC.

Prior to coming to his senses, he was an executive assistant to several A-list directors. He has sworn to secrecy.

CPSIA information can be obtained
at www.ICGtesting.com
Printed in the USA
FSHW011612140520
70244FS

9 781516 502394